THE ORPHANED SOLDIER

DARYL TE'NADII

Author: Daryl Te'Nadii

ABN: 25719012481

Website: www.The Orphaned Soldier.com.au

Email: daryltenadii11@gmail.com

Facebook: The Orphaned Soldier

ISBN: 978-0-6487812-3-3

In memory

Of my two brothers and sister—Brian Leslie Te'Nadii,
Dale Lee Te'Nadii, Teena Lynette Te'Nadii,
and my half brother - Darren Lewis

A tribute

To my beautiful wife, Janet Fiona Te'Nadii; loving children,
Damien Travis Te'Nadii,
Casie J. Te'Nadii and Baila Rae Te'Nadii.

Along with my nephews and nieces,

Heidi, Tammy, Tamika, Mathew and Robbie,
Adam, Lauren.
Also, Jarrod, Troy and Sarah.

"

*Nothing could have prepared
me for what was going to
become my life, or the loss of so
many loved ones.*

"

CONTENTS

Hodderville Boys Home

> *In Australia, they called it the **'Stolen Generation'**, the forced removal of indigenous children from their families.*
>
> *In New Zealand, we were known as the **'Lost and Unwanted'** Generation.*

We were orphans, unwanted by our families and left in the hands of The Salvation Army.

" *They would sexually assault us, beat us near to death, and take away any dignity we had left as humans, just to satisfy their sick and perverted ways.*

This was a normal day, and how I will always remember my life under their care as an orphaned boy at Hodderville Boys' home in New Zealand.

Daryl Te'Nadii

PROLOGUE

"The Unwanted Generation"

In Australia, they called it the "STOLEN GENERATION"—The forced removal of Indigenous children from their families. This is a reminder that the wound is deep, in every way, in the hearts of millions of people around the world. Accepting we were wrong is something that is recognised in Australian today. We respect those who suffered the indignity, shame, and loss of their children, when many indigenous children around Australia were forcibly removed from their families, between 1910 and 1970, because of a government policy.

Stolen Aboriginal children were often deprived of education and exploited. They lived in strictly controlled institutions. Scared, lost, lonely and grieving for their families, they suffered frequent bouts of harsh punishment and neglect—and were left wet, cold, hungry and in despair. Children were wrongly told that their parents had died or had abandoned them, and many never knew why they were taken, or why they were passed on to families they'd never met before.

Most children were forced to work as manual labourers and domestic servants for their adoptive families, and were often subjected to psychological, physical, and sexual abuse, while under their care. Efforts were made to make these stolen children reject their culture, which often made them feel ashamed of their Indigenous heritage.

Since then, medical experts have reported high incidences of depression, anxiety, post-traumatic stress, and suicide among the Stolen Generations.

Finally, investigations were undertaken, thanks to those who believed what they were told had taken place, and efforts were made to find and reunite families, where possible. This was a criminal act, for which Australia accepted responsibility, and compensation was offered. A national public apology was made to indigenous parents and children, around Australia, as well as the numerous indigenous community groups.

It was little comfort for the families whose lives had been destroyed.

In New Zealand, between 6000 and 8000 children had their own hell. For ten years, thousands of children in New Zealand, including me, suffered the same atrocities as our indigenous counterparts; not at the hands of our government but from one of the most trusted organisations in the Pacific; the Salvation Army. This occurred in the fifteen centres that they operated, between 1903 and 1993.

We were called "THE UNWANTED GENERATION".

As I read the many articles, which tried to understand how the Australian government had allowed such despicable acts to continue for so long among their indigenous people, and why it took over sixty years to acknowledge what took place, I found it was beyond my comprehension.

When you read my story, it may be hard for you to comprehend how a supposedly reputable organisation that was known and loved for its work, could inflict similar psychological, physical, and sexually abuse on children, as young as babies, while they were living in state care with the Salvation Army in New Zealand.

Both of these appalling historical events are not included in Australian or New Zealand history books—but they should be.

I hope my story will help to change that.

My two brothers, my older sister, and I are only four voices out of the thousands of children who suffered painful atrocities and torment while institutionalised as wards of the state, in various Salvation Army orphanages in New Zealand. The acts that occurred were so severe, so appalling that many died prematurely, cloaked in memories of horrors, which plagued them and from which they couldn't escape. I am the last living member of my family, from my biological father and mother's side; the sole survivor of my generation to share our story.

PREFACE

Reasons

This is my life story; all sixty-three years of it, the truth and pain of which I have carried every day for all those years.

Do I blame any *one* person? No. There are *many* who will never escape the responsibility I place upon them, for their part in forcing us into a life that we should never have had to live. I lay the blame for not being wanted, of being robbed of my innocence and of a child's growing up with his family without a valid reason, squarely at the feet of my biological "FATHER AND MOTHER".

For being abused, beaten, and having any remaining dignity taken from me as a child, right up to my teenage years, I blame the "SALVATION ARMY", along with my mother.

For carrying so much hurt and pain for so long without standing up to what was wrong, I blame "MYSELF"

For twelve years, I have painfully recalled moments I wish to God I couldn't, to complete this book. I have written them out and laid my life out on the blank pages until they were full. You may wonder why? I've asked myself that same question hundreds of times, as I wrote, feeling intense heartache, grief, pain and deep sadness as well as the light, happy, and joyful moments with which I tried to relieve the former. I wrote my story to answer my question, and maybe yours. I wrote in the hope that I can finally release some of the hurt that has weighted me down for the better part of sixty years. I wrote to be the voice for the thousands who never got the chance to tell their story, and to share my family's story for my children and those of my brothers and sister.

I've battled shame, guilt, and fear of judgment, to release this book. I know that by putting this book out there, I may be questioned by many, including friends and people I've met, but who don't know my story. It is my hope that those who abused me and the thousands of other orphans under the Salvation Army's care stand up—finally, and say "SORRY" to us—the "LOST GENERATION", and our families, just as has been done for the indigenous people of Australia.

Drowning was a word I seemed to use a lot when I was writing, and the truth is I drowned in life, more times than I would like to remember, after I was put into an orphanage in my birth year (1958), and for the many years that followed.

I drowned in constant lies, emotions, and the absence of love, which seemed to be never-ending. It was like walking down an endless road that had no exit, and no way to escape from all the hurt, pain, and suffering I endured.

These memories, and everything I encountered, seemed to pull me down into an abyss, which I later called the "abyss of living hell". I kept asking myself; do I really want to pick myself up? Or did I want to keep drowning in the destructive pattern that had been built around me by some of the cruellest men I had ever encountered in my life?

The truth is… I JUST WANTED TO DIE.

MY road in life seemed to consist of being pulled from pillar to post, up, down, and sideways, at a young age, and then being dumped onto the back streets, on foreign soil and in a country I knew nothing much about. It was this road that became one of the many reasons I wanted to give up on life, at such a young age . . . suicide seemed to make sense, and seemed the only way to escape a world of which that I was not supposed to be part.

If hate was a word, I hated everything about my life more than anyone can imagine. If I could have been free of it, by taking my own life, then I would have done that with pride and honour.

I WOULD BE SAVED!

There seemed to be so much missing, and so much more that I needed from life, which simply was not there. Soon, these questions in my mind, and the friends I built my life around, became a reason to live.

With many questions—I needed answers. I found myself continuously walking along that empty road, in my life, as an unknown and lost child, in an unknown immense world. It's hard for me to accept or explain to others why, after sixty years, I have decided to stand up and write our stories, but our voices need to be heard.

Wrongs need to be righted. It was tough writing this book, when I knew that the journey I was about to go on would bring me back, face-to-face, with every bit of pain, suffering and grief until I felt as if it was yesterday. However, I felt that in some ways, doing this might honour the ones who are no longer here, and might play a very important role in helping me understand my roots, as well as how, and why my life was so horribly shattered at such a young age.

After much searching, investigation, and letter writing, I found myself content with the answers I got, over the first few years after arriving in Australia. I got to a point where I felt the gravity and weight leave me, and many more doors were opened and I could finally walk tall through life. But, it also brought many more memories to the surface, ones I later wished I had never un-earthed.

Thinking back now, and being realistic, I also know there is much more about my life I will never understand, because those, who could have answered my questions, have passed away since, or could not be found.

Later in life, I learned that drugs, alcohol, mental depression, and suicide were among the biggest reasons many of the children, from my Hodderville Boys' home days, took their lives—in an effort to escape the pain. Like me, I guess much of what they faced as they grew up in the home from hell, or "Horrorville" as some of us called it, just got too much to live with.

The sad truth is that so many options are available on the streets that help mask the hurt and pain, and which give you a feeling of protection. I just got lucky and never went that way.

It is hard for me to accept their loss of life, knowing it could have been avoided, but the damage has been caused. Those kids, my friends, my non-blood brothers; the very people I woke up with, played with, went to school with, and cried with, had been scarred and the only way out for them was to leave this planet for good.

I have reduced or censored a lot of the information about my family, to protect them and to soften the harsh truths I know my brothers and sister's children will read and understand one day. I don't want to hurt them, or make them feel ashamed of their parents, but I do know they have a right to know how their parents were raised, abused, and left to live an abandoned life, both in the supposed care of the Salvation Army and their biological mother. Additionally, I just couldn't write about some things; one, because their unearthing would be just too excruciating for me and my family; and two, out of respect for those who are no longer here.

The hardest questions to face by far are those such as, "Why did you let it happen?" and "Was it that 'BAD'"? or "There must have been someone to talk to?" Writing this book also means I risk being asked them all over again and more; so I have omitted some things to preserve my sanity in any way that I can. The truth is I could not face it then, and I am 100% sure I couldn't face them today. I don't think anyone can ever fully understand the hell we experienced every day of our young lives, nor grasp the painful memories I have lived with and will take to my grave.

I have tried to justify writing this to myself, so many times over the years. Many questions fill my mind such as, "How do you sit and write about the abuse and tragedies that happened during your childhood, knowing others will read it?" "To what extent should I open up, and if I do finally admit all the disgusting things I witnessed, on paper, will I and the other orphaned boys and girls be judged by others in a way we don't deserve?" "Am I doing the right thing?" I guess that after so many years of uncertainties, and so many painful memories, I need to blank out my personal views and tell it as it was, and say how I feel about it today. I see this as the only true option, and the pathway to what has been the demon within me my entire life.

As the years have gone by, I have had cause to give thanks to many amazing people, who seemed to come into my life in the nick of time, to restore my reasons to live and to be here still, to tell this story sixty years on.

I was born Darryl Keith Te-Nadii. I am Daryl Keith Te'Nadii, *the sole survivor of my generation*, and this is my true story, along with that of my brothers and sister. I was a young boy, amongst thousands, who escaped from the hell of psychological and physical violence and abuse. It happened behind closed doors in the Hodderville Boys' home, under the care of the Salvation Army and endured until I escaped to the home of a mother, who I didn't even know until I was eleven years of age.

"Without Reason"

A powerful statement and one I don't use lightly!!!

Why were we subjected to these atrocities, without reason?

I will probably never get answers from the Salvation Army, as then, and now they seem(ed) to put the blame on others, to twist the truth, to ignore, reject, or pretend the complaints aren't real.

On the few occasions they have actually admitted the truth, in the face of ever-increasing allegations—they've hidden behind the following media statement…

"For all the complaints of hurt, the children were subjected to by a few officers we have received words of thanks and gratitude from many".

To the Salvation Army, this seems to completely outweigh and negate any complaints that were reported. This was their way to escape the outrage within many communities.

If this book shows others the Salvation Army for what it truthfully was, then I know this book will have put a right to the wrongs, in some way. I hope my readers will see the many lies the Salvation Army hid—and continue to hide—behind, each time a frightened little boy tried to tell the truth back then, or a now-grown and shattered, yet courageous man brings forward today. If this happens, I know my battle to write this book and to get the words out has not fallen on deaf ears–again.

Despite the many things I have learnt over time, and no matter how much time passes or the amount of writing I do, I will never forget what took place in that Salvation Army orphanage.

To forget would mean that I had forgotten about all the children who lost their souls, in the hell hole of Hodderville.

The Salvation Army

The Salvation Army operated fifteen Children's Homes in New Zealand.

Eleven of these homes have been investigated for child abuse including:

- "The Grange", Auckland. A girl's home where my sister Teena was placed.
- "The Nest", Hamilton. A home for male and female infants up to the age of five-years of age. My two older brothers, my sister and myself were there until we were five.
- "Hodderville Boys' home", Putaruru. My brothers, Brian and Dale, and I were placed here.
- "Whatman Home", Masterton. A boys and girl's home.
- "Florence Booth Girls Home", Wellington. A girls-only home.
- "Island Bay Boys' home", Wellington. A boys-only home.
- "Russell Boys' home", Russell. A boys-only home.
- "Wallaceville Boys' home", Upper Hutt. A boys-only home.
- "Bramwell Booth Home", Temuka. Initially a boy's home, and later it admitted girls as well.
- "Andersons Bay Girls Home", Dunedin. A girls-only home.
- "Mercy Jenkins Boys' home", Eltham. A boys-only home.

Out of these eleven Salvation Army Orphanages, the most abuse cases were reported from:

- Hodderville Boys' home
- Whatman House

- Bramwell Booth Home

- Florence Booth Home

- The Grange.

Salvation Army officers, Mr. John Gainsford and Mr. Raymond Vince were found guilty of both mental and physical abuse, which included sexual assaults on children. They were each convicted for their offences at the Bramwell Booth Home. Records showed the Salvation Army moved officers to other homes, each time there was an investigation or if a child complained to a schoolteacher.

At the time of publication of this book, I could find no other Salvation Army officer who had been brought to justice for their crimes against children.

Drifting – A poem in memory of my childhood friends

Written by Daryl Keith Te'Nadii

Finding a way to understand -
The meaning of rage and inflected pain.
Born in a world with little care -
I look around for what should be there.
My days were short – My love so lost.
They lost control - They took my soul.
As I walk through life, I live in shame -
My thoughts complete with disbelief.

Drifting – Drifting Away.
Drifting - The only way I can.
Is there any hope – Do they understand.
My soul, my life; beaten without escape.

Looking for ways to get back home - I shout I swear
And live in fear.
To many times I lost my way - It seemed so wrong, it seemed unfair.
Never belonging here or there - I sit in shame feeling every tear.
To take my life would they understand -
Their selfish ways turned me weak and frayed.
All I asked was to be a boy - A boy with hope and not despair.
Is there anyone out there to pick me up -
To hold me tight on those painful nights?

Drifting – Drifting Away
Drifting - The only way I can
Is there any hope – Do they understand
My soul my life, beaten without escape

My final walk as a shed a tear -
Walking away from who I loved so dear.
Such simple words and thoughts of hope -
A single word to help them cope.
Please leave us alone, please stop the hurt -
I cannot go on, I'm broken and torn.
You struck so deep with your hands of pain -
Forcing fear upon me in every way.
You speak your voice with lying words -
Saying sorry now, after all those years.

Drifting now – Drifting now as a man.
I hope and pray in many ways.
The world will listen to what I have to say.

PART 1

Eleven Years of Hell

CHAPTER 1

From One Nest to Another

I was one of those kids you see who have had such an horrific upbringing that when the truth comes out, it is splashed on every current affairs program on TV, read about in magazines, newspapers, or on the internet and spoken about in conversations for years to follow. I have been able to find the missing pieces of my life's puzzle—how I became an orphaned baby at birth—through searching, investigations and reading the many documents I found over the years in the New Zealand State of Care Archives as well as the few documents given to me by the Salvation Army. What follows is what I discovered.

I was born on June 11th, 1958, well at least that's what the majority of documents that I have say. There are some, which say I was born in 1959, but the one thing they all agree on was that I was born in the suburbs of Grayland, Auckland in New Zealand, the fourth child of Wally Lamona Lapatez Te'Nadii (Tomuri – Te Awa) and Mavis Joan Te'Nadii. My mother was of Scots descent. She was born Joan Mavis Wylie in 1935, but later switched her first and middle names as she favoured her middle name over her first. My father was born Walter Lamona Lapatez Te'Nadii (Tomuri – Te Awa) on a little-known French-governed island called Otorangi Nine Island, on October 18th, 1928.

Before my birth, my mother and father were already living through difficult times with their three children. My mother was said to have been a party girl and there are accounts of her, from family members, telling how she would stay out all night with strangers. My father gave up hope of ever taming her, and his anger often turned to rage and abuse as he hit the bottle to self-medicate and to numb the rejection he felt from my mother.

Years later, I was told that he ended up in jail for his abusive ways towards my mother. I searched for years to find evidence of this, or any truth in the story, but years passed before I Iearned that this wasn't the case. Some years ago, I discovered he had admitted to being held in the cells overnight, several times, but not because of his drinking or his aggression towards my mother. Rather it was for leaving his kids at home alone, while he was at work.

It was incredibly difficult to unravel fact from fiction, with a mother who lied to escape both we children and the responsibility—and maybe guilt—of abandoning her children. My father also told his fair share of lies, at that time, in order to begin a new life.

Truth is I will never really know the full truth and impact, because my father passed away months after I searched for and met him, and my mother now suffers from dementia (or so I have been told).

I was placed into a foster home on the day I was born because my mother had a mental breakdown. Shortly afterward, I was put back into her care for just a few short weeks, in which she continued to struggle to care for me and my brothers and sister. Ultimately I was sent off to another foster home, until I became a ward of the state at around five months of age. I then was passed into the care of the state and the Salvation Army, in 1958.

I have learned that my older brothers and sister were also placed into care at the same time as I was, and in the same orphanage. My first five years passed, and I grew up from birth, under the banner of the Salvation Army in a little place called "THE NEST", in Hamilton New Zealand. The name alone implies it was a place for the very young to grow and learn.

The Nest Children's Orphanage

Many friends still ask me today, "How can you remember so much about your life from such a young age?" I can go back to the age of four years, which is amazing, but I'm not sure why, considering it would have been a blessing to forget. Why was I blessed with such a great retention of memory? Who knows? I guess the many memories I have from The Nest are those I never wanted to let go of as they were all I had as I grew up.

I still recall every detail of a day when I was five, and we kindy kids had the chance to venture out and attend the royal visit of the Queen and Duke of Edinburgh! We boarded our bus, which had those old wooden seats and pull-up windows and snaked slowly along the white cage barricaded and police lined streets to a massive park that was filled with a heap of other buses. We were given a stern talk about behaviour, expectations and an overview of what was about to occur. Then we were paired off with another kid to hold hands and walk with. I remember I wasn't too impressed about being paired up with a girl!

Our group of 30 kids was accompanied by Salvation Army officers and a couple of policemen. We were shown an area where we had to stand behind the barricades. I was so small I had to peer between the bars. Even stretching up on tippy-toes, I had no hope of getting a look over them. I spotted a huge area of water off in the distance and was told it was the ocean. I'd never seen it before, but had had plenty of stories read to me about the ocean. It was mesmerizing and so beautiful with ships and boats all bobbing around on it. They were an incredibly charming sight, but I wondered how they sat on top of the water and didn't sink.

As time wore on, we could hear the noise building around us. Then, slowly and without notice, a beautifully dressed woman, with people all around her, walked slowly past us, a very tall man by her side. We had been given little flags to hold and wave, which all the kids did with one hand, while the other was to be kept held in the hand of our paired partner.

We didn't really have any concept of who the Queen or the Duke of Edinburgh were at the time; only that we were very lucky that this was a special day because they chose to walk through the crowd rather than drive through, so we were able to see them clearly and for longer.

Most children have parents, grandparents, uncles, and aunts and, as they grow, their parents and extended family become their book of life. Page by page, their memories, and achievements are documented and fondly told at many family gathering. They are shared several times, over the years, so the story isn't forgotten, and it is passed on through families and generations. Photos, birthday parties, holidays, and playtime are just a small part of learning and helping you to remember. When you forget something, your parents will remind you, and that's how life starts for most children. I had to do it alone, with no help, and no memories from parents; just moments—my moments.

I can't really say whether I was wanted or not. In later years, when I had contact with many members of my biological family, I was told that I was doomed to be an outcast, from birth, by my biological mother. In many ways, over the years to follow, she had no care for anyone but herself. Being the youngest child was always going to be my demise.

The Nest children's home cared for kids from broken, neglectful, or abusive homes, for seventy years. It also took in children with disabilities, and children whose parents were unable to take care of them because of illness or hardship. Some children stayed only a few weeks, whereas some stayed until they were old enough to move on to other homes, as was the case for my two older brothers, my sister and me.

The Nest welcomed its first child in October 1919, but the home did not officially open until December 1920. By the following year, The Nest was home to 42 children. In 1955, The Salvation Army purchased an adjacent three-quarter-acre section. The house on this new property was moved to the rear of the main buildings and, during the 1960s, plans were drawn up for a new and improved children's home, to replace the existing one.

In 1967, the Nest opened its new home, four years after my move to Hodderville Boys' home. In 1968, a decision was made to raise the age of the children staying at the Nest from five to seven years of age, after which they would be moved to other orphanages, such as Hodderville. It was also decided they would go to school in an attempt to help young families stay together. By 1970, it housed children up to seven years old and, by 1982, they took in children up to the age of fourteen years.

Many of the children came to the Nest from birth, just as I did. As all kids do in an orphanage, we played and enjoyed what we believed to be life; sharing and caring for each other. These young years at The Nest were filled with happy moments that masked the many uncertainties I had as a child. It could be expected that a growing child might forget the times in its life, reflecting on good times and little as possible on the bad times. I must have been very lucky, because all I can remember about the Nest were days of smiles, laughter and fun.

It really was an amazing place for a child. The staff seemed to have endless hours in a day, wanting to play with every child there. At times, I would look and wonder how any person could have so much energy and so much loving care for me, yet still find more to share with the other kids around me. This was how I started my life, and I thought it was a normal life.

We went for walks out into the streets and parks just for a change. I would see other children and think how lucky I was to have so many friends to play with, as many of the kids I saw had only one, or none. I never really understood, and I guess that was for the better.

I would run up to these strange kids and say hello, or ask them to play, but that soon got shut down, because their mother or father would scoop them up and walk away. I learnt why later in life why. . . Being an orphan has its downs.

It's funny how so many things come to mind when you're sitting at a desk filling in gaps that are representative of your life. Thinking about The Nest and my life there did this, and so much more. I remember being part of a small group, learning songs, and instruments and other happy memories I have brought them with me into my adulthood and they are as fresh today as they were over fifty years ago.

At four years of age, I thought I had it all—with over 100 brothers and sisters, there were always heaps of friends to play with every day—we were just one big happy family.

I did what kids do today, woke up, and got dressed, had breakfast, had playtime, read, played music and games, and learned strange and wonderful things. More food, more play and learning, and then it was dinner time. We had big group showers, a night-time story, and off to bed we'd go. That was the day-to-day life for a young orphan boy, and one I loved until I reached the age of five. But, how soon we grow, and how soon we can be taken from those who are so close.

Turning five, and still being an orphan, meant I was too old to stay at The Nest, which only took children up till five at that time. I would have to be moved to the bigger boys' orphanage.

At the time, and still being so young, I didn't understand, and I asked myself "Why am I being taken away from my home and all whom I love?" The Nest was all I knew. I was taken away from my carers, my friends, and the people I had spent all of my years with, so far.

It's like, "Here you go, enjoy this ice cream", only to have the dog next door snatch it from your hands . . . gone for good.

Prior to being relocated, I had spent around six months in the children's choir, singing in church on Sundays, and in music studies on Tuesday nights. It seems I had a good voice and, on my last day at The Nest, I was asked to sing a song.

Feeling sad and still confused as to why I was being removed, I reluctantly sang the one song I grew up with that seemed to have meaning in my life—Tutira Mai Nga Iwi. The meaning of this amazing passage of words is—Stand Together!

Tūtira mai ngā iwi

"MAORI" Version

Tūtira mai ngā iwi
Tātou e
Tūtira mai ngā iwi
Tātou e
Whai-a te marama-tanga
Me te aroha - e ngā iwi!
Ki-a ko tapa-tahi,
Ki-a kotahi rā.
Tātou e.

Sing it all a second time.
Then finish with...
Tā - tou, tā - tou E!!
Hi aue hei!!!

"ENGLISH" Translation

Line up together, people
All of us, all of us.
Stand in rows, people
All of us, all of us.
Seek after knowledge
And love of others - everybody!
Be virtuous
And stay united.
All of us, all of us.

Sing it all a second time.
All of us, all of us!!
Hi aue hei!!!

It was my first stage performance and one I will never forget. This song had so much relevance both then and throughout my life, that many years later, I taught it to my son, Damien.

The time had come, and with many tears and hugs, I said goodbye to the many kids I had spent the past five years with, growing up. The captain of the Salvation Army, who had come to collect me, could see my sadness as tears flowed down my cheeks. Five-year-old boys and girls were segregated—the boys went to Hodderville Boys' home in Putaruru, which was to become my new home, and the girls were sent to the Grange in Auckland.

I didn't know it then, but I would see many of those carefree, happy little boys again later, when they turned five too, and were sent to the hell hole of Hodderville. They also were sent to live an orphaned life, and became victims of the Salvation Army and its abusive officers. I say victims because that's what the reality of life soon became for many.

I will never forget my last day at The Nest. I was a happy-go-lucky little boy, nurtured, cared for, and surrounded by kind and caring people, with love and laughter. I felt safe.

It would be some forty years before I would feel that way again.

In 1989, The Nest children's home officially closed and a new family home, catering for up to eight children, opened in a different location. In 1990, The Nest children's home reopened as a Community and Family Service Centre. Both are currently operating today.

CHAPTER 2

Hodderville

Five years

Driving from Hamilton to Putaruru, in the winter of 1963, seemed to take forever, sitting in the front seat of a big car, trying to look over the dashboard. To my knowledge, I had never been in a car before; a bus, yes, but not a car, so the experience was new to me. As I tried to peer over the dashboard, the task soon became impossible. I would slide back and forth across the shiny and slippery leather seats with every turn along the windy road.

My personal belongings were all packed neatly into a small, brown leather case, not unlike the ones you see in the old 1960 movies, next to a family that's standing on the platform waiting for the next train. It had two straps wrapped around the case and two push down latches that closed into locks, next to the handle. I also had my school leather backpack, which I used to carry my learning books and things in at the Nest. It looked like the one Paddington Bear had in the movie, Paddington.

I was happy these came with me, as I didn't have many of my own possessions. Besides these, I had a few clothes, but I was told I would receive new ones on arrival at the large boys' home, to suit the area and school.

The best came last. I also got to take my ukulele, which was worse for wear with only three strings instead of four, but I still made music with it. I also had my old worn-out, discoloured, faded, and smelly rugby league ball, which I received for my fourth birthday, in 1962. It was a sad and sorry-looking sight.

The captain of the Salvation Army who had come to collect me, and he pulled up at a park in a little town, on the way. We walked across the road, where he brought some chips wrapped in the old-style newspaper. The smell is one you never forget—amazing—and filled with flavours you wouldn't dream of. Never in my life had I tasted anything like it. Being treated to them was a special moment I will always remember.

We sat in the park, and ate the chips, washing them down with a fizzy drink—also a first for me! Tiny bubbles raced up my nose as I drank and caught in my throat, erupting into a mad burp. The captain saw that the treat and gesture had relaxed and delighted me, as I smiled and thanked him for his kindness. I remember him explaining to me why the bigger kids are moved to other orphanages—the way he explained it seemed to make me feel more at ease.

He went onto say he also had a surprise waiting for me, which excited me and made me feel more at ease for the remainder of our travels to my new home. Being so young, some things don't always make sense. In the back of my mind, I kept thinking that, at some point, I would go back to The Nest, where I had felt so secure, loved and wanted. I never really let go and I certainly never got over the stark contrast of being at The Nest to Hodderville. Having learned to live with others, kids and adults that I'd never seen before scared me. It was a lot to take in and cope within one day.

I remember the Salvation Army officer saying, "Here we go, we are here" as we drove up a long driveway covered in grey gravel I craned my neck, to see a building with a massive entry to it that looked like it was straight out of a movie set, complete with a locked gate. The driveway leading up to it was surrounded by the tallest trees I had ever seen. The smell of livestock and the sounds of wild animals and creatures could be smelled and heard off in the distance.

Hodderville - aerial view

I looked up at this new place that I would call home for another six years, taking it all in, as we drove up its long stony road. It was cold. In fact, there was still ice on the lawns and across the stones that covered the driveway. The big, white building that was Hodderville Boys' home grew in size as we got closer—it made me feel so small. It stood majestically, nested on top of a hill with a commanding view of the massive property it overlooked. It was truly amazing. Breathing in the rich country smell, I began to feel a little more relaxed.

Hodderville's two stories stretched high into the clouds, from the thick, lush, green grass that was flanked by impressive hedges and trees, standing proud and tall. Seeing it for the first time, I thought it was a palace. I even remember calling it The Palace—I had no idea it would soon become a palace of pain.

The home had smaller buildings that appeared to be bedrooms, jutting out from the main structure of the building. The white of the building met the jade rolling paddocks, which adjoined a farm, at the base of which was a beautiful creek, where vegetables grew wild.

Hodderville

I stood next to the car at the top of the drive, in front of the main entryway and felt incredibly alone, as I took a look back in the direction from which we had just come—you could see for miles. Wide-eyed, I saw kids seemingly streaming out of the building from every angle. They were everywhere; playing, laughing and having fun. Seeing them running around and having fun, I thought that maybe things weren't as bad as I had thought they would be during my journey from The Nest.

I passed other kids my age and older, as I was led to the entrance of what was an incredibly large building. The kids all seemed to be dressed in the same drab colours, and all had the same haircut. Some just looked at me, and others took the time to say hello.

It was a new world to me, and something I never imagined or expected to exist. Coming from an enclosed location for young kids, to a now open field of what looked to be about 40 boys from five to sixteen was so much to take in. The truth was that I was apprehensive at first, after seeing so many boys. That feeling as if you're all alone in a big dark room enveloped me, and with that came the trembling of my hands and body.

"This is it," said the Salvation Army captain to me, as he guided me towards a woman in a bright, white dress and hat with the Salvation Army logo embroidered on it, who waited to welcome me.

Her name was Major Mertins. Over time I learned she was the senior female officer at the boys' home. She took care of the new arrivals and the kids aged from five years to seven years old. She was old, even back then I would say she would have been at least fifty to sixty years of age. I didn't know it then, but she would become one of the very few people I would trust at Hodderville.

I followed the captain and Major Mertins as I was led inside the main entrance, which I learned, later, was hardly used, other than to welcome new orphans and VIPs.

The building looked like a church in many ways; inside was timber from wall to wall, which together with the lack of windows and light made it look dark and intimidating. The floors were highly polished, and everything was impeccably clean. I felt that if I touched anything I would be in big trouble.

We passed three large dormitories leading to the dining room, which we boys called the hall. We made a left turn and then a right, into the main dining room and on to another entryway across the room, which lead upstairs to Major Mertins' office, where I was asked to sit down on a wooden chair. Major Mertins introduced herself formally and went on to explain to me what her role and responsibilities were at Hodderville.

Then, as if that wasn't enough to take in, she began explaining to me what a brother was. Already confused, I became even more confused and shocked, as she went on to tell me I had two blood brothers, who were living at the orphanage and who had been there for some time. I was also told I had a sister, but she lived in another orphanage, called The Grange in Auckland.

While my mind was still reeling, she announced she would take me on a guided tour and explain more as we walked, to give me some time to get more acquainted with my new home.

The Grange. All girls Orphanage in Auckland where my sister Teena went. She is pictured here—dark hair, smiling nearer to the top of the slide.

The boys' home was divided into four living areas. You were homed in a dormitory with kids your age. As I was only five, I was homed in what was known as "The Loft", which was the upstairs dormitory near Major Martins' office, above the dining room in the main building.

The living arrangement went something like this:

- Ages five to six years were in The Loft, upstairs in the main building.

- Ages seven to nine years were in Dorm 1, downstairs overlooking the front yard.

- Ages ten to twelve years were in Dorm 2, downstairs overlooking the front yard.

- Ages thirteen to sixteen years were in Dorm 3, downstairs overlooking the front yard.

Hodderville

To the general public, Hodderville claimed to be a children's refuge, operated by the state and church to help families in need. Going on that guided tour with the major, it seemed to reflect exactly that—everything looked to be exactly as they promoted the place.

Behind closed doors, I soon came to understand what Hodderville really was—a place where kids were raped, physically bashed to the point of death, and assaulted for the personal pleasure of two of the nastiest men who ever walked on the planet.

Like many other boys, I witnessed and became a victim to this horror, every day of my life there. The scars I carry are embedded in memories that are etched so deeply they pain me still, to this day.

CHAPTER 3

Brothers in Arms

Five years

After my grand tour, Major Mertins introduced me to another Salvation Army officer who I will refer to as O1[1] (Officer 1), whom I met in the dining quarters—a huge room with tables laid out in three directions. At the top of the room, in front of the kitchen door, sat one long table. O1 explained that was where the staff sat for meals with us. He told me he was one of three male officers-in-charge of discipline and activities.

I was led around to various areas inside the building where he briefly explained what the rooms were used for, before arriving back at the entrance area, where I had first come in, with its polished floors, and dark, private rooms.

---

1   Due to defamation legalities, as advised by Murray Houston, civil member of the government, who is in charge of Salvation Army complaints in NZ, the officers names have unfortunately had to be changed.

As we walked past the dining quarters, we entered a hallway, and he pointed to another three dormitories.

He said briefly "These dormitories are for older boys—you'll come here when you're older". Later, I learned, like a lot of things, that we were never allowed into the other dormitories—ever. The hallways near them were also off limits, unless we had a valid reason such as cleaning.

We walked into that dark space at the end of the hall. At this point, I was told that, unless I was asked to come into this area, it was out of bounds at all times to all kids. Some of the rooms looked like offices and all of them had closed doors. I later learned they were the private bedrooms of each officer.

The officer then led me into the office that I would later learn to fear, and which would be known to me as the punishment room. Here he began talking about my brothers, as I waited for them to arrive to meet me. He told me that my time would be spent more with kids of my age, and that brothers didn't really matter, because I would make new friends and play with them, mostly to ensure I stayed out of trouble.

It was hard to understand what a brother was back then, and I soon discovered many boys in the home also had brothers. I was still learning it all. It was hard to get used to a new place, new people, what we did, mealtimes, playtimes, that new thing called school, and local sports. There was so much to remember and take in.

Then, the door of the office opened and two boys walked in—the taller one had curly hair and was around ten years of age. The younger boy was skinny and shy, with the biggest black eyes I had ever seen and was around seven years old.

For the first time in my life, I met and stood face-to-face with two boys who were introduced to me as my brothers. I think it was as much of a shock to them as it was to me. Not too many words were exchanged, except for my eldest brother's awkward introduction: "Hi I'm Brian". Dale just nodded his head at me. We never got the chance to be alone or talk then, because they were quickly moved on and told to leave the room and go back to the others

It was strange and confusing to find out about my brothers and sister, and even more odd and upsetting to learn that Dale and Teena had also been at The Nest with me for many years, without my knowledge. I don't ever recall being introduced to them (neither do they remember meeting me) and it boiled my blood to think of all that time I had family within arms' reach. I wondered why I was not introduced to them earlier. Even now, that question remains a mystery.

Brian, the oldest of my brothers was the "MAN" of the home. He was older than most, was self-controlled and had many friends. He was very tall having got his height advantage from my father who stood at 6'2". He was liked by all the kids and was known at the home as a protector. His skin always seemed dry, as if ready to peel, because of a lack of nutrition.

Kids at The Nest. I am standing on the right of the table at the front.

Dale, my middle brother, was two years older than me, had an incredible sense of humour and an empathetic, caring nature. Standing tall in stature, like my sister and older brother, he had straight hair and darker skin. The twinkle in his eyes gave his ratbag reputation away immediately. He was a wild child, always getting into trouble; yet, he had an amazingly sensitive and caring side that was so beautiful. As a result, he was loved by everyone.

I didn't really spend a lot of time with my brothers, as the officer said to me we would each play and hang out with kids our age. Even though we went to the same school, on the same bus, and also had Sports Saturday and played for the same rugby club, we always had to sit with our age groups. At times, we would catch up, sitting on the eastern deck and talking; well, they talked, I just listened tried to learn more about them, more about Hodderville, and more about life.

We mostly talked about what it would be like to have a real life; a family, and a shared home together. Brian had a natural talent for music and taught me how to play the guitar, and Dale taught me how to get into trouble, which I quickly learned you didn't want to be in.

The Boys' home brought us together and gave us hope in the times when we felt there was none. It let each of us learn from each other as brothers, and we drew upon our strengths and shared them. I owe so much to these two incredible boys who never gave up on me and who became men I admired and loved.

CHAPTER 4

The Loft

Five years

In The Loft, we had one big room with about forty beds organised around the room. We had two showers and one bath, so it was shared arrangements at shower and bath time. I was to be bunked next to two boys the same age as me, Peter Schendler on one side of me, and Bobby Walker on the other. My bed was right next to a window that overlooked a fire escape. My ukulele, rugby ball, and backpack were stored under my bed. As for the clothes I had brought with me, I never saw them again and I was issued other clothing.

I was later moved to a centre bed for around four months and then to a bed on the sidewall with the older boys. There was wallpaper on the wall behind my bed of men in the scouts overlooking a fireplace. I would look at it for hours, hoping I would become a boy scout one day, too.

There was a single room off to the side with six beds in it. This room was for the older boys of around seven, who could not be moved to the dorms downstairs as there were no empty beds. We were mainly looked after by Major Mertins and one other Salvation Army officer. At that time the male officers would take shifts when needed.

Getting to know the other boys was wonderful and like all kids, I soon found friendship with the two other boys, Peter and Bobby, as well as Bobby's younger brother, Dennis, who often played with us. You rarely felt lonely; alone yes, but lonely no.

We had a fire escape slide at each end of the dorm, for evacuation, in case of an emergency. One escape had a slide we sat on and enjoyed the ride down to ground level, and the other had a walking ramp, down to the backyard area. We were never allowed to play on them for safety reasons (not that that stopped us from sneaking out and playing on them) and they were really old. The roof was high with the same hanging lights you saw in hospitals of the day.

I could smell the food that was cooking on the hot plates in the huge kitchen, as I was escorted down the hall towards an open door, which led into a much bigger, and better maintained, building. The floors were very shiny and nothing seemed to be out of place.

I received my first and last vaccination upon arriving at The Loft. I'll never forget it, because, within minutes of the injection, where the needle felt as if it had hit my shoulder bone, I became horribly sick. It was only later I found out that I had suffered an allergic reaction to it—the reason given was that my immune system was low and I was malnourished.

As such, I was to have no more needles for many years, only oral medication. While I don't have allergic reactions these days, to this day, I still suffer from eczema; and because of that first shot I was given, I never had the TB needle which today I am thankful of.

From the first day at The Loft, you could tell something just wasn't right.

My first night was exciting, but terrifying at the same time. I felt abandoned, alone, small, out of place and lost, for the first time in my life. As the days and nights passed, I learned about and heard many things; some good, but many bad. Many were the stuff nightmares are made of, as my carefree life as a little boy was soon stripped away and replaced with a life of fear and hell. Once it had you in its grasp, the truth behind the doors of Hodderville was quickly revealed.

Hodderville

Although I had been introduced to O1, my first physical contact with him and another officer, I'll refer to as O2, happened when I was outside playing with the other boys, about two or three weeks after my arrival. O1 had a medium build with wavy hair and a stiff smile that seemed to be stuck on his mouth. It never travelled up to his eyes, looked fake, and made you feel uneasy. Not tall, he stood around 5'10" and sported a perfectly pressed uniform, as all the officers had to. Apart from his body odour, you could tell that something about him reeked. He used to be on outside duty with one of the other officers, keeping an eye on all the kids playing.

The main role of the male officers was to watch and guide the kids, but I learned that they liked to do so much more. In particular, O1 and O2 were very intimidating and aggressive, whenever the female officers or staff were inside. O1 was mostly downstairs with the bigger boys, but from time to time, he used to come up and look after us little ones in The Loft, when the Major and other officers were on days off, or holidays.

I remember having an odd feeling about him when it was bath time. He would want to bath us, which the other officers didn't do. More strangely, he lingered on our private parts, which made me feel uncomfortable. Being so young, I didn't know what to make of it, since nothing like that had happened to me, before. All I knew was I didn't like it, so I spoke to my older brother. I asked him if he was allowed to wash and touch us the way he did. My brother said that was just what they did here. He said if you wanted to stay out of trouble, do what they say, when they said and how they said or else you would become a victim very quickly.

On his rostered time with us, his groping soon turned into trying to encourage us, boys, to play with each other, which I found sickening and wrong. Then he became more demanding—commanding and forcing us to lie still in the bath, while he played with us. Like me, the other kids didn't know any better—it pains me even to go back to those moments. It made me want to vomit back then and still does now.

Even though I had had no real dealings with O1, up until this point, other than bath time and outside playtime, you could tell he was a man little kids should fear.

About a year after I arrived at Hodderville, O1's real evil character showed itself. I can't remember exactly what we did to be disciplined, but four of us got into trouble for playing longer outside than we were allowed. We were told to have a shower and report straight to his office/accommodation room.

O1 made us stand in his office. He got out his strap and told us to hold out our hands. Not having ever been strapped before, I had no idea what was to come. He raised the strap and down it came, hard over the first boy's hands. He screamed out in pain.

Not satisfied with hurting us and inflicting that pain on us, he then told us to take our pants down and to turn to face the wall, as he strapped each of us across our bottoms. The pain was terrible and my bottom felt as if it was on fire, but we stood scared stiff, not moving, just crying.

He then went on for what felt like a lifetime, telling us we would all go to the children's prison if we mentioned what had happened. The first boy seemed to scream forever, it was horrible, and then there was a long pause. I wasn't game to move and terrified to turn around, but eventually, I did after I heard the little boy say "no, please, no". The sight I saw will never leave my mind. O1 had his pants down and had one of the boys standing in front of him. He had his hand firmly on the boy's head and was forcing the boy to put his mouth over his cock. He yelled at me to turn around and, minutes later, we were told to go back to our dorm.

It was, and still is, one of the most sickening, atrocious moments I remember and I wish to God I didn't. Appallingly, this and far worse was to follow through the years.

The number of times O1 forced us to masturbate each other's private parts were too numerous to say. It made all of us sick. I have no idea how long he'd been at this, but all of us living in The Loft feared the days he would be rostered on, knowing what came with it. None of us could do anything to escape him, or what he forced us to do. Even at five years of age, it was something that made you want to be sick.

We all knew it wasn't right. What we didn't know back then, was that it was criminal.

Being so young we questioned ourselves, and it felt wrong regardless, it wasn't until I went to school and mixed and talked with other kids and teachers who spoke about their lives that it became very obvious that the way we orphans lived was far from normal.

O1 preyed on us younger ones, intimidating us whenever he had the chance. I believe O2 wasn't born evil, like O1 was. Instead, I think he was as intimidated as we were and over time he had become conditioned to the abuse and gained the confidence, from O1, to do the same things.

CHAPTER 5

Palace of Pain

Five years

Fear was our constant companion.

The officers' abuse was constant. All children shared the fear, from standing waiting for the school bus to arrive at the bottom of the gravel drive, where we were regularly hit over the head for no reason, to the terrifying nights after the sun went down, and bedtime brought whatever O1, O2 and other officers wanted to do.

At times, we would be hit across the head for walking too slowly, from the home to the school bus pick-up point. Many kids had closed shoes, but some—like me— had to wear sandals (open plastic shoes) with socks. The winter days were freezing, so it only took a few minutes of exposure outside for your toes to freeze up and for walking to become painful. You couldn't feel your toes or feet, but the officers never understood. A quick smack across the head to remind us to hurry was the answer.

Hodderville's Bus

I was five when the intensity of the fear I felt became so great that I began wetting the bed. I clearly recall being so humiliated and insulted—it was as if my body wasn't even my own. Sometimes, I would be busting to go to the toilet, but the fear of being stopped, or called, or taken away by one of the officers to be hurt, paralysed me. No matter how much I tried to move and get out of bed to go to the toilet, I couldn't. The terror weighed me down like concrete.

I desperately tried to stop wetting the bed, until I figured out that the officers would mostly leave you alone if you had wee-ed in bed. As ashamed as I felt, I would lie in my wee-wet bed, stinking, cold, and frightened, just to escape the abuse. Thus, I started to develop survival strategies to get a reprieve wherever and whenever I possibly could.

After-school and weekend chores were taxing. We should have looked forward to coming home to the orphanage after school, to have fun, rest up, and rejuvenate ready for the next week of learning. But, we had to clean the yards, help wash uniforms, hang the uniforms on the line to dry, chop firewood, and attend to the vegetable patch, which was as big as, if not bigger than, a football field.

One night, we sat in a group of about ten or more on the open grassed area in front of dormitories one, two, and three. We began talking about the experiences we had lived through at the home. What was frightening was that for every true abusive story, told by one of the children, another kid would have another that would top it. We all lived the pain of our own stories and that of each other.

Peter talked about the belt and cane punishment, and how it hurt so much. Bobby spoke about the bashing he got from an officer for forgetting to hang the wet washing out one night. Another boy (I cannot remember his name) talked about being raped by two officers one day when he was too sick to go to school. That was one night, and one conversation out of the many we had as orphans at Horrorville.

The memories increased as we sat and shared the many moments, and times of sadness and shame. However, besides the sexual assaults and countless bashings, my most feared moment had yet to come. It was a day that made me feel as if I wanted to die for every reason.

> *We had every reason to want to die, several times over.*
> *To this day, I for one still can't fully understand*
> *why I am still alive.*

What may seem crazy is that out of all of this, we were able to unite and build a strong bond, one which we all understood as mates. We made a pact to stand by each other, and how grateful I was for that pact. I needed my friends so many times throughout my five-plus years at Hodderville.

Heaven forbid if you were caught putting your dinner knife in your mouth. I think every child has done this at some time in their life, but do it in the orphanage and expect a hard smack across the back of your head, whether the knife was still in your mouth or not. And don't take too long in the shower on a cold morning enjoying the warm water. If you were caught, it was cold water on for a minute and no towel to dry; just get dressed wet, as the officers took your towel from you.

CHAPTER 6

Numb

Six years

I was six, when I thought for sure my willy was going to die or drop off. I've never been so cold in my entire life. Today I can say that with conviction, having spent many years in the Australian Army, on survival training in the coldest and wettest parts of Australia. It was hard to the point where we felt as if the end was near, with an army officer yelling that he would break me, as I shivered in the freezing cold, thinking back to a colder night at the home. As he screamed at me, he would take any strength I had left, destroy me, and make me a man. "Well, well Mr. Army Officer" was the first thing that came to my mind—you're too late! Someone already beat you to it.

That night in The Loft topped all of that.

It was nearly time for bed, and the last story was being told by one of the volunteers, mostly farmers' wives who used to come in and read to us. I can't remember her name, there were so many over the years, who came and went. As the story came to an end, we started to get up ready to hop into bed. I had a blanket over me just like some of the other boys as the nights got cold fast, really fast, in New Zealand.

I didn't realise it at the time, but another boy next to me had fallen asleep on the edge of my blanket. As I got up with my blanket, I pulled it out from underneath him, rolling him onto the floor where he woke up screaming, after hitting his head. One of the male officers came over and asked what had happened. I explained it was an accident and was about to tell him what happened, when I could see a look on his face, which stopped me in my tracks. Unknowingly, I had just said the four words this officer detested—'it was a mistake'. The other boys looked at me with fear on their faces, knowing he hated those words and knowing what would follow. I on the other hand did not.

"Get up!" was the first thing he said, and "follow me" was the second. As I walked behind him, I felt scared to death and began crying. I was led to the door leading to the rear fire escape. He opened it and the freezing cold air hit me in the face. "Stand here" was the third thing he said, and then he stood and looked at me.

At six years of age, and as tall as a mushroom, you tend to do as you're told, and fast. I stood there waiting for him to speak, not knowing what to expect. Then he said, "Take your clothes off". At first, I hesitated, confused, until I saw his face begin to redden in anger.

At that time, I thought, "Are you for real?—it's winter, maybe minus zero and you're asking . . . no telling me to take my pyjamas off?", but that flew from my mind as quickly as it came, when I realised he was deadly serious. I understood full-well this was no joke, and confusion gave way to fear, as I looked at him glaring at me.

I began taking my PJs off and stood, there, naked in front of him. I watched the rage that bristled in his eyes transform into an evil look that pulled the corners of his mouth into a sinister smile.

Cold was an understatement. The freezing temperature engulfed me as if I'd just been dipped into the core of an icicle. He took my pyjamas, went inside, and closed the door, leaving me out on the platform at the top of the stairs of the first landing. I could hear the other kids saying to each other, "He will freeze outside". Trying to keep warm was impossible. I was too scared to move, in case he did anything more. I just had to face it and hope like hell he would come back to get me, soon.

It was fifteen minutes before he finally came back. He looked at me as I stood shivering and holding my manly parts to prevent them from dropping off—already they were frozen and solid like ice balls.

I think my dick had gone inside my tummy at that point, as all men will understand when cold hits their manhood.

He said, "Get back inside you little black shit and get into bed". Being so frozen, my legs and feet wouldn't function, but not wanting to be left out there any longer, I somehow shuffled as quickly as I could up the fire escape and back inside.

"Pick up your pyjamas, and put them on" he barked, and followed me as I desperately hobbled towards my bed.

The rear landing. The lower platform where I was left to stand naked in below zero temperatures.

He turned and left the room. I was immediately relieved because my hands were so frozen, I couldn't put my PJ's back on. I was terrified he'd make me go back outside again if I didn't get them on. I stood there helpless realising it was impossible in the frozen state I was in. I also couldn't see clearly, because my face had frozen and the tears that had run down my face had stopped halfway down as they froze.

I tried to wipe my face and eyes to see, but it hurt, and my hands were also frozen so they weren't much help. I felt every eye in the room on me as I stood there, so terrified and lonely.

Peter and Bobby snuck out of bed and rushed over to me. At first, I told them "No! Please go back to bed." It was bad enough that I got the punishment, but I didn't want them to get in trouble too. Peter shook his head at me. He walked over and held me.

Taking one look at me as the tears melted and began to roll down my cheeks, made them start to cry as well. They tried, and finally got my PJ's on and helped me get into bed, My whole body was convulsing, and I couldn't stop shivering as I began thawing out and the numbness turned to agony. I was crying so badly—the pain was excruciating as the blood ran through my body again.

As I laid there shuddering in pain, Bobby and Peter knelt by my side and held me close, trying to help me get warm. The other boys, who were still wide-awake, softly said "You will be ok, Daryl". But the truth was I wasn't. As a now-sixty-two-year-old man, I have felt many forms of pain over the years but none as bad as that night.

My body was locked and shaking. I was sure no blood was circulating through my body and the pain was something else. It felt like I was being burnt by heat. As I managed to move my arms, I realised that the officer had hurt me, and broken me to the point I would always do and say what he wanted. Anything, so that I never had to face anything like that night again.

Even now, writing this, and remembering, I burn with intense hate for that asshole. I hate him for everything he did to me and everything he did to the other boys. He crippled me for life that night and for no reason other than to wield a fake sword of power over the powerless; over young boys. If I faced him, today, I would KILL him without a second thought, no matter the outcome.

I must have fallen asleep, because when I woke up to another day in Horrorville, I saw and heard my relieved-looking friends say, "You made it Daryl. We are so proud of you. Don't let him beat you with his silly games". I thanked them and the others for being my friends. The little boy who had fallen asleep on my blanket and hit his head turned out to be Bobby's little brother Dennis. He came up to me and gave me a hug, saying how sorry he was about what had happened. He went on to say he had begun to explain what had happened to the officer, but he had told him to be quiet and go to bed. I knew he didn't mean it, and told him it was ok and that I didn't blame him. It must have been one of those nights when the Salvation Army officer's demons were at play.

A strong friendship grew between Peter, Bobby and I that night, one that would become even stronger as the years passed in Hodderville together. Dennis, Bobby's brother also eventually became part of our circle of friends. That connection of friendship and the love we had for each other was embedded deep inside me, where it still sits today.

Those memories of our bonds are the good memories and the ones I've treasured over the years. Far better than the sudden and unwelcomed flashes of abuse, such as that night when I almost froze to death.

I was recently watching the movie, Frozen, with my daughter and throughout it, I was bombarded with memories of that night. You never quite get used to moments like this invading your everyday life, you just get better at not allowing them to take over or bleed into your normal day-to-day.

They live with you forever.

CHAPTER 7

My Passion

Six years

At the big boy's home, as I called it, there was so much going on every day that finding time to fit it all in was back-breaking. From cricket to making wooden toys, from soccer to donkey rides, with adventure walks around the farm and down the creek. It was busy! Another amazing introduction was pocket money. I'd never had money before! Each week we received an allowance, depending on our age. Ten pence, or ten cents today, was my first allowance which climbed to two bob (which would be 20 cents today) over time. It was a lot of money back in those days. We could bank our allowance for later, which is what I did. I saved mine from the age of six, to take on the annual holidays I got from the age of seven, with a foster family who took me during the holiday breaks.

A lot of us boys had a foster family we would spend our holidays with. I always spent my holiday breaks with the same family, the Lewis's from Beach Haven, North Shore Auckland. Mr. Lewis and his son, Darrell, (who funnily enough had the same name as me and with the same spelling) would pick me up from the home and off we'd go! I do recall a few of the boy's holidaying with different families, but I can't recall why, now.

Like most homes back then, we had chores, such as cleaning the floors, toilets and showers, as well as cobweb removal from the windows, mowing, hedging, raking, and the general upkeep of the yards. We also had weekly chores, such as gardening which included cropping on weekends and weeding during the week. At night, or on a Sunday, we also had lessons in Christian culture.

Just as at The Nest, I was selected for the choir at Hodderville. From the age of five through to the age of eight, when my voice broke, I sang in our choir group. The group consisted of between fifteen to thirty kids, mainly boys but with a few girls, and the children of the local farmers. On Sunday, we would add a further ten or more adults, who stood behind us as part of the church choir. The choir was always led by the Salvation Army priest (if I remember correctly, his last name was O'Donnell) and a little old lady always sat on the organ as the music provider.

I enjoyed the time with the choir, but the one thing I loved and would always make a bee line to watch was RUGBY! I had decided to branch out and to enjoy my sports more, so instead of watching it, I soon began playing it at school, after school on the paddock in front of the home, and on weekends for a local team. I had a passion for the game. I can't say whether it was In my blood, or I was just a sucker for contact sports, but my first choice when it came to sports was always rugby. I could not get enough of it as a child.

I always seemed to get picked to play in the team that had the biggest boys. They did the hard yards hitting the ball up like a good forward does and would then offload to me—the little, skinny kid with the fastest legs to post a try. Their strategy worked, and I soon became known as "The Dart" among the players, which gained me a little more respect from the other boys, along with more protection, which would later be invaluable at times. Rugby definitely kept me going and I lived for it! I played every chance I got—at the boys' home, at school, outside of school for the Putaruru League and for the regional side as well. I couldn't get enough of it.

CHAPTER 8

Christmas at the Home

Six years

Over time, I learned that Christmas is a time to share, enjoy, and reflect on your happy memories from the past year, leading up to the celebration of the New Year with family and friends. We celebrated at the orphanage, too. It was one of the two times a year we all got to see and experience the most amazing things—presents, lots of food, and numerous celebrations with music and dance.

The boys' home had a huge hall, which was used for many functions, such as theatre nights, awards, dinners, and events such as Christmas and Easter. I can still recall the smells wafting in from the hall as we entered it at Christmas. The Christmas season was particularly wonderful. The gardeners would chop down a big pine tree and set it into a big shiny bucket, where it stood proudly next to the pot belly fireplace for show. The decorations and lights will always stay in my mind, but the one thing I will never forget was the aroma. Leading up to the big day, the smell teased us with the promise of a special day to come.

We practiced pantomimes to present, such as the story of the Lord Jesus and his birth, as well as carols and speeches. The tables would be filled with the best foods from our nation and from lands far away. I can remember the happiness on the faces of all the kids. It was amazing. These are things many kids take for granted, but as an orphan, they were far and few between for all of us.

Christmas Day would come, and the hall room lights would be dimmed—the only lights giving us a sneak peek of the room came from the tree. Then we would hear the sound of bells followed by happy shouts of "Merry Christmas!" What a sound! We all looked forward to that moment every year. The main door would open and Santa came into the room. He was tall and colourful with a big white beard and a fat belly. I just loved his boots; they were so shiny, and when he spoke you felt the love and happiness pouring from him. One by one, every boy would have his name called. When it was my turn, I would go up to the big red seat where Santa was, and receive a present and stocking filled with so many goodies that my eyes popped!

I later learnt that the local community made it all possible, along with a collection from the church. I got a wooden army tank one year, a ukulele another year, and one year a basketball which was exciting, but I didn't really know what to do with it, since we didn't have a basketball hoop at the home. The stocking was filled with yummy treats that filled my belly, and small puzzles, games and toys that filled my time. I swear that stocking was as tall as I was!

Christmas was the one day a year we could forget the pain, suffering, rape and abuse so many of us faced every day, at the hands of the officers. However, the one thing that I missed, as I grew older, I heard about from the kids at school, who talked about their Christmas Day and holidays with their families—it was knowing I didn't have a mother or father to enjoy this special day with. That was hard.

The old Hall where we celebrated many festive events. To the left of the Hall stood the Dry Rooms and Laundry. At the top of the photo near the trees, you can see the back yard we would play.

CHAPTER 9

School days

Five–Six years

School for us boys consisted of onsite learning. Hodderville had four classrooms with two adjoining rooms used for changing into sports gear. These rooms were arranged three down one side of the hall, leading to the back-area shower block, and three on the opposite side of the hall.

The four classrooms were set up with a main black board at the one end, with large windows, which could be opened, along the side and that allowed natural light in and gave a clear view of outside. Along the other side were personal lockers for our books.

The remaining two rooms were set up more like a sports club changing room for players. They had steel lockers for training clothes and there were back-to-back long benches to sit on when getting changed, in the middle of the room. These two rooms were closest to the shower block, so that we could undress and walk directly to the showers, after our return from town when we played sports away from the home such as rugby, cricket, and athletics. In later years, these shower blocks also served as extra shower facilities for the home, after the numbers increased.

During my early years, schooling at the home was primitive, with little education involved. I assume was because of the cost of employing full-time teachers available. So, most of the education was carried out by the officers of the Salvation Army and local community members. The main academic subjects were English, mathematics, social studies, history, and craft. Together with these we also studied music—in particular, singing—Bible studies and games (sports).

We also had spare time to do whatever subject we wanted, I chose cooking. I don't know if it interested me, because I never got enough food (I was malnourished for the most part of my young life until I was around 17 from having little or too few nutrients in my food). So, anything to do with food interested me.

To my surprise I had quite a natural flare for preparing, cooking, and arranging food. I would spend two hours a week, helping in the kitchen, watching and learning from the in-house cooks, learning how to make everything from porridge, soups, stews and broths to desserts, slab cakes, scones and prepare school lunches. It used to fascinate me, and I enjoyed it, plus it was a safe space away from the officers, most of the time.

Our normal school and studies at the home started at 8:30 am and the last class was around 2:30 pm. This would change, daily, to suit the officers in charge. I wasn't sent to the local town's primary school (Oraka Heights) until 1966. There I completed Standard 4, 5, 6 and my first three months in Standard 7, before my move to Australia. In New Zealand, we had eight standards at primary school, before college. In Australia, it was the same as doing Grades 1 to 7 at primary, followed by Forms 1 to 6 at high school, followed by university.

We didn't receive homework at the home, which showed in my later years, at Oraka Heights. On my arrival at the local school, I was handed homework for the first time and was told we needed to do extra studies at the boys' home to catch up with the class's level of education. This was a shock for me. It meant no after school-rugby training or playing with the other boys.

The class hours were taxing, with our wake-up call being 5:30 am, to do our chores before we got on the school bus at 7.15am, to travel a good 30 to 40 minutes. Sometimes I was exhausted even before I got to school, after the morning routine of bed-making, cleaning the shower and recess, and sweeping the outdoor balcony, or the main internal floors. After school, we'd have the afternoon chores, such as the garden beds, vegetable garden, feeding the animals, and cleaning up the hedge clippings. It was hard yakka. School was from 8:00 am to 3:00 pm, in class, with breaks and PE before that same 30 to 40 minute bus trip back to the home and our jobs. For a kid of my age, it was challenging that's for sure.

Peter and Dennis also attended the same primary school with me, that year and to them, it also felt as if all hell had been set upon us. To think; no games, free time or—God forbid—rugby. It was more than we expected and we soon found we were failing many assignments with poor school reports. We were seven years old, yet learning to read, learning to count from one to ten and learning about places around the world was too much.

My grades were falling and something had to give. I just couldn't sustain it. It's strange to look back in time to those decisions, but I do, and I am not disappointed at all with my choices. Yes, it took me more years than an average person to complete my education, but I did and with a degree; a Master's and a diploma which have all built an amazing life of employment for me. In 2010, I was able to gain copies of my school reports and was shocked to read what the teachers said in those reports.

They said I had the ability to be an incredible teacher or leader, with good examples of my quick ability to learn and my good information retention. They said I was naturally creative. As for science, my theory might have been on the low side, but I made up for it in my understanding of the components.

CHAPTER 10

A glimmer of hope

Six years

Remembering these events in my life, to write this book, has hit me hard. So many emotions; happy, and sad. I'm grateful to have a few photos of the happy moments, to remind me of the special memories that helped keep me going throughout the years.

Something all of us boys hoped we'd have was a forever home. Back in the early days of my life, adoption seemed to be a word that many people didn't want to talk about, and it was also a word, and world, that many still don't really understand. Like all the boys at the home, I had opportunities to be adopted. For me, it's something I find hard to talk about, and even all these years later I still can't accept why I wasn't.

Being an orphan was hard enough. Throughout my life, I cannot even count the number of times I have had to explain to others that I was an orphan—such as when I tried to further my education, or to gain employment, among others. It was difficult to risk people judging me for something that was beyond my control. No one likes being judged, least of all me. I didn't want people to see me as a NO body.

Many times, I wanted to write down that I was an orphan, in documentation, but with it came the thought of all the questions that would come, such as:

Why…. Would a mother leave her newborn child in an orphanage?
Why…. When the chance came, she would not allow
a family to adopt me?

It was too much, and I didn't have the answers until many years later. Even now that I have the answers, I still struggle to explain or talk about it.

My first opportunity to escape the orphanage and to become part of a family came at the age of six years old. I was taken to the major's office and introduced to a lady, whom I was soon to discover was from an adoption agency. At that age, I didn't really understand the full impact of what that visit meant exactly, but I later learned what it meant. She was around thirty to thirty-five years of age, of medium height and dressed in a suit with a little hat that tilted to one side. She smelt very sweet and had a beautiful smile. Her words were spoken softly, and I remember how she always looked me in the eye when she was talking to me, which made me relax and trust her.

She had come to the boy's home to find a son to adopt, and I was the one from all the boys of my age that she had asked for. At the time, I felt scared, lost, and breathless, once I knew why she wanted to see and meet me—it was a lot to take in.

I didn't know it then, but she had been keeping track of me for some time, receiving information on my upbringing as an orphan, my schooling, and the other things I did, such as sports, music and my love of animals.

We sat and talked for a long time and she asked me so many questions my mind was spinning. The major tried to explain to me what an adoptive parent was. She went on to say that if my biological mother agreed, this lady and her family would be able to take me from the orphanage and take care of me. I was nervous because I had never even met my mother, and I had no idea whether she would agree. After some time, the lady asked me if I would like to come and live with her family in Hamilton, a town that was not too far away.

At first, I said "No". I was truly confused by what it all meant. In addition, I had just found my brothers and I didn't want to leave or lose them again. She assured me about many things which I am sure she meant at the time. The lady told me I could come back and visit my brothers, and they would always be in my life. I was still undecided, so, she asked me to think about it, and let the major know within the month, if I wanted to start a new life with them. Then, she left.

That night I told my brothers. They were really happy for me, even knowing I would be going away to a new place with strange people, to live a life as a foster child. Brian, my oldest brother held me and told me I had to go: He said that if I didn't, I would never have a good life. I stood and looked at Dale, my middle brother, who had tears running down his face. It pained me all through to my body to see him so sad. If hurt could be in you, then I felt it with every cell of my being.

I remember Brian asking me if they had kids and where they lived. I could only tell him I would be moving to Hamilton, which was not that far from the boys' home and that the lady and her husband did not have any kids. The thought of leaving my brothers behind did not seem like the right thing to do, and seeing Dale's face, I pretty much knew what I was going to tell the Major. I had made my decision— my family, and the ones I knew and loved were where I wanted to be. However, I didn't get the chance to tell the major, because little did I know at the time, I didn't have a choice anyway. Although the lady had applied to adopt me, my biological mother had other plans, no matter what decision I made.

Around three weeks later I was asked to go to the major's office again. I sat for a while before the Major and another lady walked in. I had never seen or met her before, but she looked official, as she was neatly dressed and she was carrying a bag. As I sat there, the major introduced the lady to me as being a representative of the adoption board. She spoke to me, explaining that the adoption paperwork that the first lady, who had come to see me, had submitted had been denied because of a court injunction from my biological mother in Australia.

At the time, I didn't understand what all that meant, other than for some reason a person (whom I had never met), and who was apparently my biological mother, had denied the lady's adoption request. My mother had said that she was going to apply to have my brothers, sister and I returned to her by the time I was seven.

That birthday came and went, along with many more lies and broken promises that she made during my lifetime.

As I was slightly older and wiser, I asked, "How can this person, who keeps saying she is my real mother, leave us here alone?" The lady from the adoption place said that being my biological mother meant she had every right to deny adoption. She went on to tell me that, like Brian, when I turned sixteen, I could leave the orphanage to work—but that, until then, I was stuck in the orphanage, to live a miserable life and knowing there was a family out there that wanted me.

I still ask myself to this day, what gave my biological mother the right to give birth and then to take away all of her children's rights to a decent, loving, happy life? My biological mother had started a new life, in another country, which the adoption agency told us was the reason she had never come to see us or called or written to us.

CHAPTER 11

Wide Awake

Seven years

The years in The Loft passed slowly and my seventh birthday arrived. I thought life was about to start because I would be moved to the big boys' dormitory. I was excited and thought it a proud moment at the time, as I saw this as recognition that I was growing up as I would be living with the older boys. Additionally, being close to my brothers (Brian at the end of the hall in Dorm 3 and Dale next door in Dorm 2) meant having a family had never felt so real. Knowing I could spend more time with my brothers meant the world to me, and having my two best friends, Bobby and Peter, to grow up was an extra bonus. I thought nothing could destroy the happiness I'd found—sadly, nothing could have been further from the truth.

I will never forget what I endured and witnessed at the orphanage, in the years that followed. The screams at night, from boys aged seven to eleven years of age, chilled and kept me awake then, and still do to this day. They are the sounds I will never forget, that explode into my consciousness unannounced during moments when I least expect it, as I go about my regular life as a sixty-two year-old man.

I had been allocated a bed next to the window, over-looking the green playing field on the veranda side. Bobby was next to me and had come down from the loft a few weeks before me, so having him next to me, from day one was amazing. Peter followed about a month later, as he was younger than I was. His bed was across from me and to the left as I looked at the sidewall. I remember the day he came down from The Loft. He was so excited, as he walked into the dorm. He smiled and jumped from bed to bed down one side of the room.

The first week was hit and misses, as I learnt new chores and rules. I stayed low key as I was not sure about what to do, or what would get me into trouble. Bobby had warned me about the officers, O1 and O2, and he gave me the heads up that their abusive activities downstairs were even worse than we'd experienced upstairs.

It would have been a few weeks after I moved to the 1st dorm, when I was lying in my bed, a little after lights out. I heard talking in the hall, and then all went quiet for a moment. As I had in the past, I pulled the sheets over my head for protection. I heard the sinister voice of O1, and could hear him saying things to the other kids, such as "Close your eyes", "Roll over" and other muted words, you couldn't make out or maybe tried to not hear.

I didn't really know the other boys that well, as I had only arrived in the dorm a few weeks before, but they were between seven and nine years of age, and they were as terrified as I was.

I recall being told to get out of bed and stand in the centre of the room and wait. Three other boys were already standing in the centre, looking away, towards the shower blocks, which could be seen when you looked out the windows, at the end of the room from the internal hall. I was told to follow the other boys as we were taken away.

Four other boys and I were led to the dark rooms at the end of the hall; the ones we called the punishment room. We were told to sit down on the long timber bench against the wall, inside the room, and were also told that if we ever mentioned what we saw in this room to anyone, we would be sorry, very sorry, and sent to another boys' home. In fact, we were told it was a prison where kids were sent to live for the rest of their lives, and that we would never see our family or friends again. We didn't know it, at the time, but from the very first days, the officers had been grooming us for what was to come, and to instil fear firmly within us, to guarantee our silence and their safety.

For us orphans who didn't have anything other than our friends and maybe a brother or two at the Home, this was enough to make all of us petrified. For me, the threat of being taken away from my brothers the only family I knew, and my two best friends to yet another, possibly worse place, was enough to paralyse me with fear and prevent me from reporting it afterwards or talking to anyone else about it. I was so scared I could not even talk to my brothers about what was going on.

Being told that at just seven years of age was a very frightening thing, so from that day onwards I closed my eyes to whatever I saw, no matter how painful it was, just so that they wouldn't come for me, and so that I could stay with my brothers. Most nights of the week, I would see boys being taken to the dark rooms and hear them crying out in fear and pain.

I learned that if you had brothers in the home, you had a good chance of being left alone; well to a point, as I soon also learnt. In many ways, this was my saving grace, and the reason I was not sexually assaulted by the Salvation Army officers as often, or in the same way, as many of the other boys were. We were beaten with sticks, belts, and fists. We were forced to do things no one should in their lifetime—for no other reason than to satisfy their sick personal pleasure, as they watched us little boys drop to our knees begging for forgiveness, just to end the pain we were suffering.

I'll never forget the first time I got the cane. Four other boys and I were running down the hall and sliding on the waxed floor, trying to see who could slide the greatest distance. It was something we all did, often, and on that particular day, Robbie Hamilton, Dennis Walker and two kids whose names I can't recall were playing the game with me. (Robbie had also moved down from The Loft to be with his brother, even though he was only six, but they needed the bed space upstairs.) O1 just happened to be doing his rounds and came into the hall to catch us having fun. In his mind, we were damaging the floor which others had worked hard to polish and he became enraged. We were taken to the punishment room where we were told to turn around, pull our pants down, and bend over.

One by one I heard the boys before me scream and start crying, and knowing this only made me more anxious. By now, I had already experienced several bouts of abuse, none of it pretty, and none of it without suffering a great deal of pain; so hearing the other boys scream the way they were only intensified my fear. Then, without warning, pain hit me like a bolt of lightning—that cane hurt so much.

I jumped in pain, and my bottom immediately started to burn as it began to welt up. I couldn't sit down for hours and remember saying to myself, never again! Unfortunately, that wasn't to be. I'm not sure how many more times we received the strap and cuts with the cane, during my time at the boys' home; O1 and O2 found any excuse to flog us.

From that day on, I decided to try not to show the officers how much it hurt, wherever possible. I would hold my breath so as not to cry and walk out with my head held high, which became my sort of trademark among the other boys, a lot of whom followed suit. What they didn't see however was me escaping to lie behind the big tree on the edge of the playing field, to cry in pain.

We boys were so sick of the treatment we received, but with nowhere to go and no one who cared about us, we also knew there was nothing we could do about it. I think the officers knew it, too. The abuse was relentless and always cruel.

I remember one night I was passing my rugby ball across the bedroom to Peter for fun. O2 looked in, and saw it happen, but walked out of the dorm. I was just thinking we had gotten away with it, when O2 came back in with the cane in his hand and told us to get out of bed and stand in the centre of the room.

This was the first time an officer had told us to do this, outside the punishment room. I thought that he wanted to make an example of us and show all the other kids his authority and power. I got up and walked towards him to the centre of the room; when, without warning, he grabbed my shoulder and flung me around and hit me with the cane right across my bottom, while I still had my PJ's on. Peter then copped the same.

We stood there as he continued, out of control, to whip the other kids, while yelling at us. Truth is I just didn't hear what he was saying, because the pain from the whack was so intense. The other boys and I were screaming out in pain and crying. It wasn't easy to get back into bed with our hands holding our bottoms. Trying to reduce the pain never worked, and there was more to come that night.

I was sick of being hurt, so I waited in bed, in pain, until I thought all the other kids were asleep, and then I got up and went to the shower block. I pulled my PJ's down and saw a long, angry, red welt across my bottom. It was about the thickness of a pencil. As I looked at it, I decided enough was enough and I pulled my PJ's up. I walked out of the shower block, and turned right, to go to Major Mertin's room, up in The Loft.

I was going to tell her what O1 and O2 had been doing to us, but it proved to be another dire mistake. To get to The Loft, I had to go through the dining room. I didn't see O2 sitting in the room, having a cup of tea or coffee. The kitchen staff always left a pot on the stove to stay warm for the night staff.

As I walked through the room, the first I knew that he was there was when I heard him roar "Te'Nadii! Where do you think you are going?" I froze in fear. I had been caught and I had no answer, as he got up and began to walk towards me. I nearly took off, hoping to get to the stairs first, but he was standing between them and me.

All I heard were his heavy footsteps and angry breathing, as he marched me out of the dining room, down the hall, past Dorm 1, towards the punishment room. I was already crying and trying not to shake. I couldn't know I was about to get it worse, because of my effort to get help.

The window 5 from the right of the picture was the window the Salvation Army Officer pulled down onto my legs leaving me unable to walk for two days.

As I stood in the punishment room, he told me to take my PJ's down which I did with a lot of effort as my hands were shaking so badly, and I couldn't see my PJ cord because of the tears in my eyes. I undid my PJ's and because they were about two sizes too big, they dropped to the floor.

He stood in front of me, looking at me. I tried to avoid eye contact with him, because I knew that would enflame him and make things worse. That's when I felt him touch me for the first time since the Loft.

He held my testicles and penis in his hand and said, "You like this don't you Te'Nadii?" as he started to play with me. I stood there, so scared with my eyes closed. This went on for a few minutes, which felt like hours. I hated him and every minute he sadistically abused me. When he finally did stop, he told me to get dressed and go back to bed.

I don't even remember pulling my PJ's up or leaving the room. I was so scared and I ran back while trying to pull them up, feeling sick. He came back to the dorm a short time after and came over to me, lent over me and, glaring at me hissed, "If you ever go upstairs again, you will get it!" Then he walked out.

From that night on, we boys banded together to give each other support, after we were assaulted. Normally it was for no good reason other than we were just being boys and having fun, which didn't hurt anyone or anything. I am not saying, for a minute, that we were angels—with so many boys under the same roof, there were arguments or disagreements here and there, of course. But there was nothing that warranted the level of the beatings, or the punishment and abuse that we got, all too often.

We sorted out our disagreements amongst ourselves, as often as we could, to escape punishment, but if the officers were around and we were caught in the act, we never got that chance. They would just step in and punish us regardless of how big or small the issue. This was their way, the Salvation Army way, and the only way we knew.

It was never a shock to see one of the kids with a black eye, a fat lip, welts on their legs, or red eyes from crying from the punishment, beatings, and abuse. I recall sitting with Peter, on the deck in front of our dorm, one day after playing rugby and talking about who between us had been hit the most and how many canings we had received. We laughed about it, at times, just to ease the stress and pressure we felt. We also cursed those officers for what they had done to us and other children, to vent the rage we felt. Talking to each other was our only emotional outlet.

By the time I was seven years of age, I had been sexually abused so many times I'd lost count, beaten breathless, caned, strapped, and kicked across every part of my body. I had walked the hall of shame in pain, with black eyes, fat lips, and with all dignity stripped from me, on more days than I hadn't.

While most kids my age were out riding their bikes or playing happily in their front yards with their mates, I had been broken-down, beaten, shamed, and hurt and terrified in ways I know would make kids today curl up and die, and adults commit murder over. I never had a say and had to accept the Salvation Army's manner of childcare.

My mind rages as I try to write this, through tears of pure anger, and amidst the many memories. I agonise about telling this, to set we boys free and to get justice. I also worry about the fear of shaming both myself and my family and friends, who I know will read this one day. I can only hope that they understand the eternal fight I've had; that my brothers had, and thousands of other boys have had. I hope that they will see us not as the boys who went through what we did, but rather as the men who we fought against all odds to become.

I just wanted out as I sat there with Peter, sharing our worst moments, and feeling so fucking scared, petrified, and lonely. I wore the word God out asking Him to just take me to fucking Hell! I didn't want to live any longer. Peter's thoughts echoed mine, but I'll never forget him looking at me saying, "We are brothers. Darryl. Please don't leave me. I need you". His words still ring in my ears fifty-three years later. His steadfast friendship helped me to stand tall back then, and even taller in all the years since, as I held on to the belief that one day it would all be over.

Until then we just lived every single day, one day at a time, never knowing what would come, and hoping for the best but preparing and expecting the worst.

CHAPTER 12

Oraka Heights

Seven years

At Hodderville boys' home, I was introduced to the education system by attending Oraka Heights Primary. I spent just over five years there learning under the NZ education system, before I was moved to Australia. I loved going to school, if just to get away from the boys' home and the abuse.

Every morning we would collect a paper bag from the side door of the dining room, to take to school. Our lunch bag would contain a sandwich and piece of fruit—normally baked beans on bread, tuna paste, or cheese and vegemite. As part of the government-run health programme, we also received a small bottle of milk, each morning break, but other than that we drank water from the school bubbler.

School was what you made of it, and I loved learning everything from English, and Maths, to Art and Music, as well as taking full advantage of the PE program, to play sports and do dancing. I was never the best dancer, I have to admit, but I did entertain others with my out of control moves that resembled an out of control helicopter.

For some reason, I was gifted with singing talent as a young boy, and quickly advanced to leading a group in song presentations with the school choir. Sadly, that amazing voice left me as I went through puberty, and today I can honestly say I sound like a tin can rolling down a windy street.

The school also offered so much more than cultural learning, music classes etc., and once a year we had dental checks. Mind you, even as a child I had the biggest whitest teeth, just like my father—a gene I thankfully passed on to my children.

My first teacher at primary school was Mrs. Baldwin, an older woman who really spent time with me and the other kids. She was so kind and lovely. I remember her passion was making and decorating wedding cakes and some of my fondest memories were the days she would bring icing mould leftovers. These were treats we never forgot, and probably the reason I have a sweat tooth today.

I had Miss Baldwin for one year, before heading into Grade 1 with Mrs. Wallace and then Grades 2, 3 and 4 with Miss Hayman, who was the most amazing teacher I ever had. She also used to bring icing leftovers in.

During winter we would spend the best part of five minutes every morning, doing hand exercises to warm up and to help the flow of blood. The hallways leading into our classroom had wall-mounted heaters, but the truth was they never gave us any warmth.

Another thing we did every morning was earthquake drills. Putaruru was on a fault line, or so we were told, and such safety drills were mandatory in all schools around the area.

It was only a small school; but, even so, we boys from Hodderville kept to ourselves in a small group of kids. Although you didn't see much of it, we were known as outcasts. I remember playing sport at school on the oval, and hearing parents tell their kids not to play with us which was crushing. It wasn't our fault we were in the boys' home.

Hypocritically, they were mortified if their kids played with me during or after school, but when it came to outside school sports, they all wanted their kids to play with me there! Already back then I showed natural sporting talent and was high achieving.

Regardless, I still found, and loved playing with any, and all other kids from the local town who were happy enough to play with me. Like all kids around that age, I had a sweetheart too. Her name was Rebeca Ramera, and she lived right across the road from the school. If I had time I would walk her to the gate at the end of the day. We would sit and talk a lot, unless some kind of sport or game was on, then you'd find me on the sports' field. I lived every moment waiting for the next sports' event to come along.

I remember entering a sports challenge at school and had to loan borrow a bike from a classmate because I had never had one. The event required riders to begin at the start line and ride a bike to the 100-metre finish line, whoever went the longest distance without falling off or touching the ground was deemed the winner. Surprisingly, since I had never had a bike, I won this event and many other sporting events in my school years.

Sitting to the far right in the bottom row was a very shy Daryl. This picture was taken in the year 1966 at Oraka Heights Primary School

Playing sport was an outlet for me; a way to escape the life I was living. Unbeknown to me then, it would also be the basis of my future career. It also attracted the respect of others. Early on, I learnt that if you succeed in anything, people look up to you. As I was only five foot nothing, they wouldn't be looking up at me physically, so I was thankful for my sporting talent which earned me respect and was a great way to meet new friends.

Twice a year there was an athletic sports day carnival. I would count down the days until it came, so I could run like no other; the wind in my hair, and the freedom to go my hardest, winning and receiving recognition, rather than the reprimands we got at the orphanage. I became a middle-distance runner, racing mostly in the 800-metre events. Years later, that training served me well and I began marathon running as well.

It's crazy, but of all the amazing things I remember from my school days, it was the smell of meat pies that was one of the most significant. When lunch time came the local kids whose parents had treated their kids (or who were too lazy to make their lunch that day), would collect a lunch pie. The smell made our mouths water as we sat outside where the little tuck shop truck parked, and just breathe in that amazing aroma. I would look on and think how lucky those kids were, telling myself that one day, I would eat my first meat pie and I would devour it!

That day did come, years later. It was my first winter in Australia and I went to the AFL grounds in Geelong to watch our home team play Carlton, with Dale and my younger brother Darren. The treat of the day was a meat—Four and Twenty—and a Coke. Ironically, I discovered later in years that I didn't really like them—it was more the smell and not the taste that excited me.

When I returned to visit the school in 2010, one of the first areas I went to was the outdoor lunch area. I could still smell those meat pies, and the other amazing food smells were in my mind. I was shocked to see just how small the school was. Back then I would have been so small that anything and everything around me looked huge. The second area I made a beeline for was the field I played sport on. It looked so big back then, but in reality, it was only about 50 meters long, and around half the size of a footy field, give or take a meter.

The last place I went was to my classroom. Just walking in brought back so many memories—ones I never want to forget. Those times were happy times for me; it was such a relief getting on that school bus and escaping the daily abuse. I was able to be myself for the day and did not have to live in fear for five wonderful hours a day.

CHAPTER 13

The Lewis's

Seven years

I got a reprieve from the hell of my life when I was lucky enough to meet, and be fostered out to, the Lewis family from Auckland, just after I turned seven. I didn't know too much about foster families and how it all worked. Brian and Dale told me about the times they shared with their foster families, and from that, I was looking forward to having one of my own. Now that I was seven years of age, I was counting the days until I got a foster family too.

The day I found out I had been paired with a family, I was in church. I had been told I had been asked to share time with a family in the next holidays. Honestly, I didn't have much bloody faith in the whole experience or in God anymore, but I still hoped for the best. We had returned to the home for lunch, when O2 asked me to come to the office. "Here we go" was the first thing that sprang into my mind. Anytime that he or O1 summoned you to the office it was never a good thing. I had tried to be good and to stay as far as possible away from them, so I automatically began to get nervous.

But, surprisingly, this time the talk was a good one. I was given the brief of a foster family, who wanted to take me for the holidays. O2 said they lived a few hours' drive away in Auckland, and they would come to pick me up next Sunday, after the Easter church service. I would be spending one week with them.

My holiday bag was packed by the service staff, as they did for all the boys heading off to foster families. They always made sure that we had clean clothes and toiletries in a shoulder knapsack. I was thrilled I was also allowed to take my cool rugby ball.

The Lewis family consisted of Mr. Lewis, who would have been around thirty years of age then, not overly tall and always unshaven; Mrs. Lewis and Darrell Lewis, their son. Darrell and I were not only the same age, but we also had the same name spelt the same way. Stranger still was that years later my biological mother would go on to marry a man with the surname Lewis.

Mr. Lewis was an everyday hard-working husband and father and also an extrovert, firm but fair. When he came home from work, he'd have a shower, as he worked in a foundry, and then he'd ask us about our paper-runs, grab the rugby ball and say "Come on boys, let's have a throw!", or he'd grab the fishing rods and we'd go for a fish, bogan. We loved hanging out with him and listening to the many stories he shared, over countless afternoons on the back deck. I can still see him sitting there with the three-day beard he always had. He loved spending time with us, recounting tales of his childhood and memories of growing up.

Mrs. Lewis was always so nice and caring. She had a softly-spoken way, and was polite with impeccable manners. Even though she was a nurse, she had chosen to stay home to look after Darrell. She always dressed neatly and had her short hair well-groomed in the same manner as the Queen's. She always included me in everything, and would take Darrell and me out to do the grocery shopping and the errands that she needed to do.

The Lewis's lived on Lancaster Road, in a suburb called Beach Haven on the north side. Beach Haven was a suburb of Auckland, the biggest city on the North Island of New Zealand, and the place the Lewis family called home. It was not a busy place, but more a settlement for those wanting to get away from the thriving city life. It was a great location as there were parks to play in, and a fantastic local water way. You could see the navy base from the jetty, where I loved to fish. It was an amazing spot.

I don't remember a lot about the surroundings, we had to stay close to the house on our adventures. I'm not sure why, maybe because you never know what's out there, and who? If only they knew, I already lived with the worst kind of people at the orphanage.

I enjoyed the opportunity to work, while I was at the Lewis's and had two jobs every time I visited for the holidays. The first was a paper run which we did every Monday, Wednesday, and Friday for the local News Agency. I earned around $3.18 for the three days' work, which consisted of about two hours on each of those days.

The second job was at the foundry, where Mr. Lewis worked. I'd go there every Saturday morning, from 6:00 am to 12:00 noon, with his Darrell and we'd help prepare the sand moulds for dye casting. The smell was amazing, I just loved it....why, who knows. When we were done, we pushed the trollies to the casting platform, and stood back as Mr. Lewis poured the hot molten steel into the cast. Darrell and I really enjoyed those mornings, and we also got to make castles from the left-over sand, which would set hard, thanks to a resin used in the mix.

When the day was done, we would all go for chips and freshly-baked bread. I earned $1.50, for that work, not much really, but I would have done it for free. I loved it that much and was very grateful that the Lewis family were so kind to me. The Lewis's were incredible and treated me just like their own son, always making me feel so welcome and part of their family.

I remember and miss them still and wish I could find them to say thank you for everything they did for me. After Christmas came another term at school, then Easter would arrive, more holidays and more wonderful times that I remember so well. It was a time when I felt safe, and miles away from the cruel and sick officers at the home. It was also a time to do many things that lots of we boys at Hodderville couldn't do, such as going to the movies, fishing and shopping.

The Lewis family home.

The Lewis's had a large back yard to play rugby, cricket, and hide-and-seek on. The yard was great, had its problems, as it had a downhill run. Like me, the family were die-hard Kiwi supporters when it came to rugby. We never missed a game and also went to local draw days, when the local team played at home.

The family were also fanatics when it came to eating healthily, so I would always find tasty food on the table. Breakfast was a mix of cereal, toast and a boiled egg. Lunch was mostly salad and sliced left-over meat or a packed salad sandwich. Dinner was always a surprise, which made the waiting worth every minute. Mrs. Lewis was a great cook and made the best home-baked cookies for us, which were always on hand.

My first Easter/Christmas with the Lewis Family was in 1965, and would create some of the happiest memories I had as a child. Learning to do things like a normal kid and feeling safe meant so much to me. I never told them about what happened at the orphanage, afraid they would judge me or think I was telling lies. Worse, they might bring it up with the officers at the home, who would then not let me come and stay again. I just loved being with the Lewis', even if it was for short periods of time, and nothing was going to take that away.

It was during these visits with the Lewis's that my confidence grew and I felt truly accepted. I was thankful I could spend the holidays with them, and still get to live with my brothers. I was born Darryl Te-Nadii, and later changed the spelling of my first name from Darryl to Daryl.

For years to come, I went on my holiday breaks with the Lewis family, enjoying every moment and receiving the love and care any child got from their parents, except they weren't mine. They were truly very special times.

CHAPTER 14

Torn

Seven years

As a child, you assume going out to play with friends would be times you remember fondly. Times when you can look back and say to others, "I remember that game, OMG I played it when I was a child back in New Zealand with other kids my age!"

I remember one such occasion when I was coming up to my eighth birthday. It was a Sunday; the day we all went to church in the morning. I was a member of the choir, and like all the other members of the choir, I sang in front of the congregation. After church, we would go back to the orphanage for lunch, normally a roast which we all looked forward to, and pudding with custard. After lunch and chores, we were allowed to go outside and play.

This was a day that started off so great, but soon ended as a nightmare. Fun turned to fear, happiness turned to hurt.

I was playing and enjoying the moment with my friends, yelling in laughter as all the other boys were when we decided to play a game of Cowboys and Indians. In our spare time, we had made wooden guns and pistols out of wood and bows and arrows from twigs discarded from by the old tree at the back of the property. As we played, Dennis and Bobby Walker, Peter, the younger Moenoa brothers, the young Edwards' brothers, a few other boys and myself, made up mock games, deciding on the events, to make the game as real as possible. All of us were having so much fun, when, without warning, O1 turned up and told us to throw our toys—the ones we had excitedly spent days making—in the bin, and wash up for tea. This man hated seeing us have fun and whenever he showed up, we would immediately pretend we weren't having fun so we wouldn't be abused. It was still early in the afternoon and nowhere near dinner time.

I made the perilous mistake of saying "but it's still day time". A harmless plea kids make every day, but one that I would regret as he walked over to us. He had a full-on look of anger, and I could hear him beginning with "You little bastard…," what else he was trying to say I just don't remember because it was at that point that he lunged for me. When he came at me, I was in a huge acorn tree, on a lower branch above an old tin-sheeted fence that ran along the back of the property behind the main hall. He lurched forward grabbing me by the legs and pulling me down with force, intent on throwing me to the ground. The problem was I wasn't going anywhere as I was stuck, as my finger was caught; wedged between the two sheets of the old tin fence.

With the pressure on my body and hand, from his pulling me down, I couldn't lift my hand to free my finger. The more he pulled, the more the tin sheet dug into my finger wedging it even more. He totally lost control and began raging, yelling at me to let go and get down. I was screaming from the pain, as the sheet ripped into my finger. I yelled until I was hoarse asking him to stop because my finger was caught.

He just kept pulling and pulling, raging even more. Another boy, Dennis, and Peter, one of my best mates, were yelling at him, 'Stop!!! He has his finger caught between the tin sheets!"

He kept pulling me and the pain ripped through my body as my finger was finally dislodged and I came flying down. I thought I'd lost my finger. All you could see was white flesh raggedly ripped all the way to the bone and blood pouring out. It covered my finger and hand and was racing down my arm. The pain and the sight were so bad, I fainted. When I finally came to, it hurt so much, I couldn't breathe or cry. I gasped for air, lying on the ground and trying to hold my finger. I was taken to the first aid room and treated for what he called a minor cut. In fact, I needed a whole heap of stitches to put it back together and then they wrapped it up in bandages to hide the truth of what had happened and said it would get better in time.

O1 said it was my fault and that next time he would deal with me as I sat fighting the pain. I did pluck up the courage to try to tell one of the officers what had happened but they didn't believe me or the other boys, who also had tried to report it. I remember the smell that came from the wound, for months. It was sickening. Every day the treatment and replacement of bandages would hurt because the bandage was stuck to my open wound. In the end, I used to soak my hand in water, to loosen the bandages, before going to the first aid room for my daily treatment, just to avoid the pain of them removing it. The scar is still evident today, and is a reminder of that day, and the hate that I have for that bastard.

Nothing was ever done about it. No report was made. It was just another one of the hundreds, if not thousands of cover-ups of the abuse, neglect, torture, and torment that the Salvation Army were very good at sweeping under the carpet. It was always our fault for everything, according to the Salvation Army.

To this day I look back and think how insane O1 must have been. I was only a young boy, having some fun in a tree with his mates and who made a harmless plea for it not to end. Any child would have said the same, but not many would have suffered the same consequences I did.

CHAPTER 15

A Birthday to Forget

Eight years

The first time I had any idea about birthdays and which was also on the date of my birthday was when I had to leave The Nest. We were always told that as soon as we turned five we had to leave. Up until then, we had no idea what a birthday was, or even that we actually had one. I guessed mine was the week of the 11th of June, for no other reason than that was the week I was told I'd have to move to Hodderville as I had turned five.

There was never any celebration, birthdays came and went without us even knowing that we had turned a year older. It didn't mean anything to us, because we didn't receive presents, cakes, or even good wishes. We just weren't conscious of them at all. It wasn't until my eighth birthday that I even thought about my birthday again, since leaving The Nest. I was asked to stay back after book reading, to receive a present that had come in the mail for me. It was a card from a woman in a place called Australia. Inside was writing, wishing me a happy birthday and signed love "Mum".

Accompanying the card was a letter from the same lady. As I began reading it, I grew even more confused. Receiving a birthday card from a stranger was one thing, but to get a letter filled with words that hurt was another. I still clearly remember seeing those first few lines through tear-filled eyes. The letter started off with "Hello Son, this is your mother. It's been a long time since I have had the chance to write to you and your brothers. A lot of things went wrong, and you were taken from me at birth. I am hoping to visit in the near future"... ... ... that's as far as I got.

I was confused, and I felt hurt and betrayed. The words seemed shallow, from a stranger who professed her love, but whose actions spoke otherwise. It raised more of the same questions I'd always asked, but having this contact from her seemed to raise a deep ache and pain in my soul that I couldn't comprehend.

Why would she contact me now?

Why had she sent me to an orphanage, if she loved me?

Why would she claim that I had been 'taken' from her at birth?

Why did she never come to visit me and my siblings?

Why would she say she wanted us back in her life, after eight years?

Really? ….visit me rather than say.

Talk to me rather than write to me.

Show me rather than talk.

I threw the card and letter onto the floor, held my head in my hands, and cried. O2 held me briefly as I sobbed. I accepted it thinking he was being genuinely comforting until I felt his hand on my groin as he tried to rub me. I jumped up and yelled at him, telling him I would tell the matron. He warned me and said in a menacing voice that if I ever mentioned a word, I would be sorry. I knew he meant it. Even at that moment, I knew I was lucky to get off with a warning.

Many of the other kids he had assaulted would get the worst duties, such as cleaning the toilets, halls, or yards, even after they had had to endure his abuse! Their weekends were ruined by having been abused and then having to do chores, as others played sports and other things. O2 was a nasty fucking man. Many of the boys did complain, but nothing was ever done. They were untouchable, as the other officers turned a blind eye to their obscene behaviour.

The next day I spoke to Brian and Dale, and asked them if they had received a card and a letter from our mother too. They confirmed they had as well. During all my years at the orphanage, we only heard from our mother twice. All of our mail was opened by The Salvation Army, prior to our receiving it, but there was never any mail withheld to our knowledge. So her promises were a mystery to us, since she had never acted on them, to date.

CHAPTER 16

The Drowning

Eight years

One of the many days we all looked forward to was the opportunity to go down to the creek and collect some of the vegetables we had growing alongside the creek bed, which was situated behind the back fence, at the end of the boiler rooms. I am not sure who started the planting, but if veggies could grow this was the place. The creek had so much to offer, long reeds to protect the water and keep it clean, rolling slopes that allowed the rainwater to flow naturally into the creek, which would also flush the cow manure but nourish the water, and eels that also helped to keep the waterway clean.

Now I must admit I was very good at having fun and, at times, doing things just to get a laugh out of the boys, as many other eight years old's did. Bobby Walker and his little brother were my partners in crime, when it came to playing games, whereas Peter was reserved, and more concerned he would get into trouble. Like me, Peter had had many run-ins with the Salvation Army officers, which always ended in some kind of abuse. A beating was never far from our minds on any given day. It was always random and never predictable. It was a little like, pick a number… you lost, your turn to feel some hurt, Te'Nadii. I got used to my name being called out, and that went for the other boys who tried to stand up against them.

I'd had a good run and hadn't been in trouble, abused or received any punishment for two weeks, which had to be a first, as I always seemed to be the pick of the group for punishment. I will admit that this was our fault, as we always tried to get our cleaning or duties done as quickly as possible so that we had more time to play. However, if O1 or O2 saw us rushing through our jobs, we would get extra work to do.

It was veggie collection time, and about eight of us boys decided to go down with the cook to collect some veggies for the night's soup. Robby loved to be the leader and he assumed the role often. As a leader it was up to him to decide, which way we took to get to the creek. He loved taking the long way, which had to be at least five minutes longer and which was frustrating for me, as it meant that was lost playtime.

I think a lot had to do with the time he got stung by some bees. Because of that, he took other paths to get to the creek, to avoid the same thing happening again. For me running, rolling and falling down the slopes seemed more fun, and I always took the first opportunity I got on the long walk, to break away and have that extra bit of fun. Truly, who could blame me? I loved rolling and laughing on the way to the veggie garden. It was the only chance we got to do it.

On that day, we found out O1 was to accompany us. I don't know why, but what I do know is that if I had that time over again, I would have stayed back at the home and done chores. It's not as if there was never anything to do. The endless chores always kept you busy.

Did I leave the group and take that adventurous roll down the slopes? Yes. Did I get covered in dirt from head to toe? Yes. Did I care that I also tore my shirt? Yes, of course! I rolled, spinning around and around down to the bottom of the creek bank. I got up and shook off the dizziness from the roll and looked back up to see O1 standing over me. My throat filled with a big lump as, he grabbed my neck, without warning. All I could do was tense up, knowing my lucky number had just been picked out of that random box.

The slope finished at the edge of the creek, so that was the direction in which he dragged me. Truth was I thought he was going to beat the hell out of me, which he could have easily done without anyone seeing, as the reeds were so tall, no one would have seen a thing. Instead, he dragged me to the edge or the creek.

All I remember was being told to clean my face and wash that dirt off my shirt. OMG… I thought, G-wiz. Is he not going to hit me, for the first time? I started to splash water over my face, cleaning off the dirt. I must have hoped for too much as he said, "That's not how you do it", and without warning, he pushed my face under the water.

I don't know how long he held me under. All I remember is losing my thoughts, as I gasped for air that wasn't there, while he began drowning me. The next thing, I heard yelling, then his grip on me was released and I whipped my head back. Peter, Bobby, and Dennis were screaming at him. Peter held me as I tried to draw in a breath. They were terrified at the scene and crying so loudly that the cook came to see what was going on. I wasn't aware of it at the time, because I think I passed out, but the boys said she scooped me up and carried me in her arms back to the home, with the rest of the boys following behind.

If it hadn't been for my best mates screaming blue murder and attracting the attention of everyone around, my life would have ended that day. I will never forget the feeling and sound of my own choking, as I began to feel my life slipping away.

I spent an unknown time in the first-aid office and then I must have been put to bed. The next day I woke up to find my boys, Peter, Bobby and Dennis standing over me and asking was I ok. Not really was my reply. They asked me what had happened and I told them how O1 had grabbed me and pushed me into the creek and began to drown me. Brian and Dale, my two older brothers, had been in town when it happened, and with them out of the picture for the day, O1 had thought he'd take advantage of my vulnerability and lack of protection.

When they came into my dorm, I lost it seeing them and cried, as I began recounting the story of what he had done to me. Before I was even able to finish, O1 came in and yelled at them to get out. Brian stood up and gave him a look of pure hatred that unnerved O1, who slowly walked out. The look on Brian's face even scared the hell out of me. Brian hated these men. I had no idea how much, until years later.

Later that day O1 came to speak to me and warned me about doing things my way and what can go wrong, as was the case apparently. Lying in my bed, my eight-year-old body trembled as O1 neared me.

The story he'd been told went a little like this, I decided to go on my own adventure, and rolled down the slope while the other boys walked along the track, following Robby Hamilton our leader for the day.

He looked at me and said aggressively "You slipped and landed in the creek, and I was trying to pull you out but I had difficulty because of the muddy bottom". So that was it, the 'official' story he had told, and that I was forced into going along with, or else.

I shake my head over that lie today—really? I slipped and put my head under the water and into the muddy bottom? Really were the other officers really that naive? It was a great story, but all lies. I am sure that even though it was a lie, it was yet another incident that was never entered into my personal file, just like all the other bashings and abuse that I suffered over the years. Years later, I did try to tracking down the reports and sourcing my file, but had no luck. Funny that.

Yet another escape from justice, nothing noted, nothing is done to protect us kids from the evil hands and abuse of the Salvation Army officers. No one cared, we were the un-wanted ones.

CHAPTER 17

Dances and Pinecones

Eight years

For the many things I went through during these years I always tried to find ways to be positive, and things that I could focus on; that I was grateful for. I would lie in bed and push the fear aside, visualising living my life without fear and what that would look like. I treasured the times that did become memories that make me smile, such as my first school dance night.

School was such a fantastic outlet—we loved the special activities that were planned and which gave us moments where we could relax, have fun, and truly be ourselves.

One night the school had organised a dance night and we had been looking forward to it for ages. The big night came and there must have been at least 200 kids at the dance, with parents as support staff. The kids from normal families looked great in their smart clothing and polished shoes. We, on the other hand, looked all grey in our school uniform of black shoes, grey socks, grey shorts and white shirts, since none of us Hodderville boys had any good clothes to wear. We arrived at the school dance hall in the old raggedy home bus. There were no Cinderellas amongst us, but we all felt on top of the world.

I can't remember the songs, but after Rebeca walked into the dance room I also forgot about many other things such as dancing, eating, and enjoying myself. I just wanted to sit and talk to her. I finally came to my senses and asked her to join me on the dance floor. At first, she said no, which took me back a bit, but then she said she couldn't dance, not that she didn't want to, but she just couldn't. I lightened it up by making some jokes about not being that flash on the dance floor either "Let's look silly together, hey?!" She smiled and got up to join me on the floor.

It was messy and my moves and groves put Brad from the Rocky Horror Show to shame. I just never had, or found, my groove that night. Rebeca didn't mind, she got lost in her own moves, most of which I had never seen before, either. I've never seen someone trip over their feet as much as she did that night. We didn't care though, we laughed, and we danced, and had the best night. Two really bad dancers just having fun.

The night came to an end and, as always, I walked her to the school gate. As we got to the gate, some 50 meters or so from the dance room, she looked at me and said, "You are special" and she leaned over and kissed me on the check. I stood in silence with a big goofy smile on my face. My first dance and my first kiss.

We never got another chance to be alone, again, so that I could pay her back for that kiss. Without warning, she was gone. I remember saying have a great holiday to her and when the New Year came and school restarted, I learnt her family had moved. I never heard of her or saw her again.

Life went on, and we always looked forward to the annual school dances that always had a theme to them.

Another annual event that I loved was the pinecone collection day. Once a year we would be taken out to collect pinecones in the big paddock down the end of the driveway, next to the home. Because we only went to the paddocks that sat directly along the boundary of the home, the older boys would be the leaders and the officers would stay up the top of the hill. They were too lazy to walk down the great big hill, which was fine by us. We would collect as many pine cones as possible, for hours, and pile them up in one area next to the side gate leading back to the home. Once we had a large enough pile, we would sit down and start sorting them into four different sizes. Then, we would carry each pile back to the back of the laundry and wash them to remove any spiders, bugs, and dirt. When they were all washed, we would place them outside, to dry. The next day we would collect them and take them to the activities room.

This is when the fun would start! After school, we would go down to the activities room and select one pinecone of each size. We would then tie a piece of string around the butt of the pinecone and tie all four pinecones onto the same string. We would write our names on a paper tag and attach it to the end of the string so we always knew which ones were ours. Over the weeks, leading up to Christmas, we would find time to paint and decorate our pinecones in readiness for the Christmas tree decorating, and Celebration Night which would be held around ten days before Christmas Day.

Those days were like other times when life felt good being an orphaned boy. A great thing about these times was that those two nasty men had nothing to do with these activities, so we were left in peace for a short time.

CHAPTER 18

Mealtime

Eight years

I was a fussy eater and, try as I might get some foods down, for whatever reason I just couldn't. This posed all sorts of problems and landed me in trouble more times than I care to think about.

Many nights, the food was literally indigestible and one particular night O1 came over to me and asked me why I wasn't eating the food. I naively told him the truth, that I just couldn't eat it because it tasted so bad. I tried but couldn't stop gagging. O1 saw red and dragged me out of the dining room by my collar, and into the hall, where he pulled back his arm and let it go like a slingshot.

His hand slapped me so hard across my face that the force of it knocked me off my feet and sent me hurling towards the ground. He then kicked the shit out of me with his big boots, repeatedly in the stomach, chest, and my little legs. I lost count of how many times he kicked into me. My body began going numb as I desperately tried to roll away from him and protect myself. I remember looking up at him as he vented his rage upon me and seeing his enjoyment of belting me in his eyes and the ownership he had of me.

Badly bruised, with a cut lip, and hurting all over as my body began to feel the searing heat and pain, O2 came into the hall and laughed, calling me a little girl. He said "get up Rugby Boy, let's see how big you are now!" and kicked me as he passed me, walking away still laughing.

I lost count of the number of times I watched as other kids were bashed, hit across the head, or forced to stand in the corner of the room during dinner times. Many times, I had to stand in the corner of the dining room, while the rest of the kids ate dinner, all because I would push part of my meal to the side of my plate. Of all the foods, I just couldn't swallow mushrooms. The taste alone made me physically sick and I always knew that when they were served, it would end in trouble. It got to the point where I didn't want to eat, or even go to the dining room, and I used to make excuses just to avoid eating— until I ran out of them.

One night I recall we had tripe with white sauce, the smell alone made you want to vomit and I just couldn't get it down my throat. When the officers weren't looking, I stuffed it down my top. Bad move!

As I stood up after dinner, one of the officers noticed my wet and stained shirt and dragged me outside behind the scullery and threw me against the wall. He told me how the cooks had worked all day, to feed me as he bashed the back of my head. I fell to the ground.

I am not even sure how long I lay there; all I remember was feeling dizzy and numb. I could vaguely hear voices in the background and to protect myself from further bashing, I pretended to be out to it. I think that may have saved me from an even worse beating that night. The kitchen staff helped me up and took me to the first aid room, where I waited for treatment.

That night I lay in my bed with a concussion. I was bruised and battered and in pain everywhere, inside and out. My punishment for not eating my dinner, in addition to the flogging I got, was to clean all the toilets the next night while dinner was being served. I was not allowed any dinner and wasn't allowed into the dining room—a reminder not to waste food.

My best friends snuck out a slice of bread and an apple for me, so I had something in my belly. Great friends are worth their weight in gold. As I gratefully accepted the food, Peter and Bobby said that's what friends were for, and we will get through this, and one day we'll all get out of this hell hole.

Although the years passed, I would often sit silently and shed tears, wishing I had said something, back then and stood up to them, or even run away to escape the hurt, pain and disgusting things I witnessed. I still don't sleep well, today, remembering how I lay half-awake, those days, dreading each night, and not knowing who would be next. I never really understood just how many boys were being abused back then. Many of us were too scared to say anything to anyone.

A rear view of the old home showing the Fire Escape that lead to the Loft. The window below housed the Dining Room and the Kitchen.

So many of the boys lay in their beds crying, during the night. I would go over to talk to them, to let them know they had a friend and thinking they might be lonely, but as the years went on and I got older, I realised it was more than loneliness. The abuse infected all of us. All the boys had been sexually assaulted, raped, penetrated, and abused in some way. Many of them were crying from the pain of their ripped and bleeding bottoms. It was sickening.

I was in Dorm 1, and my bed was the second from the window facing the outdoor yard. Like many, I slept lightly, in fear of the footsteps in the night. Any noise would wake me. Once or twice a week, I would hear those footsteps walking into our dorm and I would open my eyes, halfway, while holding the sheets over most of my head, to see one of the Salvation officers leading a boy away.

This went on the entire time I was imprisoned at Hodderville. I can't tell you the pain, guilt, and shame I still carry for never saying a word. It haunts me. I wonder if the other boys, who have survived as long as I have, feel the same. I wonder if the officers who didn't abuse us boys, but worked there knowing what was going on, feel any remorse, shame, or guilt for seeing these atrocities every day and not doing a thing?

Some things, I will never understand, and even in my adult life, I can't make sense of them. Mental and physical scars are embedded like pictures etched in stone—not eroding, and not erasable.

If there was such a thing as something out of a living hell, the Salvation Army officers and in particular O1 would have been it. I have hated him for all of my life, with every ounce of blood. You can't go through what I did and forgive. My eyes burn and brim with tears, my head hurts and my heart aches, reflecting on what we all went through.

CHAPTER 19

The Burning

Eight years

School days were great as we got to escape the abuse, at least during the daylight hours, and I loved Saturdays as well because it was rugby day! I was a very excited eightyear-old on Saturdays! I would wake up, get dressed for breakfast, and do my chores in super quick time, so that I could catch the bus to Putaruru, in time for my rugby game.

One of my chores on this particular Saturday was to collect wood and chop kindling for that night. The time was passing, and I heard the boys talking as they stood in the drive waiting to hop on the bus. I looked around the corner and saw they were getting onto the bus. Not wanting to miss out, I put the tomahawk axe down, and ran to the bus. Dennis Walker, the younger brother of my friend, Bobby, had grabbed my boots and socks, so I climbed onto the bus, sat down and we were on our way. We played a fantastic game and won. I was so happy and excited; I couldn't wait to get back to the orphanage to tell my brothers.

As we pulled up to the home, I saw O1 standing at the top of the drive. One by one we hoped off. As I stepped down from the last step of the bus I felt a sudden push, and then I was being dragged along the stones. The other boys ran as they knew standing around would only get them into trouble as well. My knees started to bleed as the gravel ripped into my skin. He dragged me over to the wood pile, where I was pulled upwards and told to stand up.

O1 asked me why the chopping was not all done. I was so scared and tried to explain that I had rugby, which just wound him up even more. Trying to say sorry was impossible. I was so terrified I lost my breath and could not even get a word out.

After the first hit across my head, followed by a kick to my stomach, I knew I was in for one hell of a belting. At eight years of age and no more than a measly 40 kg, I couldn't do a thing to stop the tall, 80 kg forty-year-old wildly swinging at me, hurtling his fists and feet into my body and head.

Finally, he finished, at least I thought he had and I struggled to my feet with so much pain, from so many places, I didn't know where I was hurt. It was excruciating. Blood was running down my face, legs, everywhere as I stood up to face him. He started to laugh and said "This is only the beginning" as he threw something wet onto my face.

The first couple of seconds I thought it was water until my eyes started to burn, and my skin began to scorch. My legs buckled and I fell to my knees in agonising pain. The burning intensified and my eyes, oh God, felt as if they were on fire. Panic set in, as I could smell the liquid on my face and realised it was the gasoline, which we used in the mowers.

I couldn't believe it. The evil bastard had thrown gasoline into my face! The fumes stole my breath, and the liquid charred my tongue. The taste is entrenched in my memory as if it had happened an hour ago. I tried gasping for air, but the fumes and burning would not stop. I was howling in terror and pain when he grabbed my face and thrust it into an old water trough that was behind the timber and storage area sheds. He left me spluttering, as he walked away with a sinister parting statement "Next time I will light you up and let you burn in hell!"

I returned to my dorm and knelt next to my bed praying to God to take my life. I ran outside and screamed, as I ran down the gravel driveway, to the main road. All I wanted to do was jump in front of the next car or truck that passed. Just my luck, not a single vehicle passed, and I returned to my dorm in absolute despair. Dennis came in and knelt next to me. He cried with me, held me, and told me not to give up. That's all I wanted to do. Why would you want to live, when all you were was a pawn, tortured, humiliated, and shamed by people for their own sick entertainment?

Every night, from that day on, I knelt with my hands closed tightly and tears streaming down my face, before a God I hoped was there, pleading with him to take me. I remember one night even yelling, so he would hear me, "PLEASE TAKE ME! I HATE THIS PLACE, I HATE THE OFFICERS, I HATE MY LIFE, I WANT TO DIE, PLEASE TAKE ME!!!"

I wondered often why I was even born. I wondered why I hadn't been born with chains on my shoulders instead of arms. That way they could hang me up like a boxing bag and do what they did best; hitting, hurting, and abusing kids.

Today, I don't feel the physical pain of what happened, but I will always carry the scars of the event that took place that day. Once again, I never told anyone as I was more scared of the repercussions that nasty man my start. I HATE that man.

CHAPTER 20

Shame

Eight years

There was only one day I missed rugby in my childhood, the reason still haunts, hurts and shames me today. It was without a doubt the worst out of all the sick acts I'd witnessed since my arrival to Hodderville.

It was a Saturday morning. I know this because it was RUGBY day: the one day in the week I looked forward to. I just loved that sport so much that even if I had broken my leg or arm, I would still have turned up to play. Before roll call and hopping on the bus to go to town we had to do our chores. This day was different as we were told to collect the eggs and feed the pigs, which was normally done by the older kids in Dale's year, as the pigs could be aggressive at times.

Peter Schendler, Bobby and Dennis Walker, Russell Mann, David Jones, Robbie Hamilton and maybe another four or five boys and I headed off through the back paddocks, behind the home, following the tracks to the chicken coops and sheds. I decided to be in the group, to feed the pigs. We seemed to have had a few more helpers than the group collecting the eggs and feeding the chooks, so I walked across to the shed to help the other kids out. As I walked around the back of the shed to get some seed, I heard someone crying. At first, I thought someone had been hurt, so I ran around and in through the rear barn door. I stopped fast, frozen in shock, fear, and revolt.

O1 saw me immediately and yelled at me to get out. I don't even know the little boy's name. He was quite new to the home, and maybe around seven years of age. When I saw him, he was looking up at me crying, shaking, and reaching out with his hands towards me. It was a look I never want to see ever again in my life. I felt his pain plunge into my heart, as he stood naked and bent over with his pants down and legs apart. O1 had penetrated him from behind and was hurting him. I felt so sick I told the captain, I couldn't play rugby because I was sick, and he sent me off to bed.

That was the first and only rugby game I did not turn up to play in my life. I lay in bed shaking and scared. I heard his footsteps getting louder as he came closer to my bed. Petrified, I looked up. He was there looking down at me.

He said, "You are lucky you have brothers here, or that would have been you!" My blood stopped pumping through my body I am sure. I felt the beat of my heart take over as I tried to breathe.

I was just waiting for the beating; but, instead, he went onto tell me my name was in the book to go to the child's prison if I said anything to anyone about what I had seen. With immense shame and guilt for that little boy, I regretfully have to say that I have held that secret in my head, until now. Today I don't feel any better talking about it, to be honest, but if that little boy had a family they need to know what took place that day.

As crippled as I was from all the abuse I felt, it was even worse seeing him standing there with no place to go and no one to turn to. He was a boy, small, young, and scared, and his face was frozen although the tears just kept coming. There is no forgiveness for raping someone like that at such a young age. His entire life had just been taken away and all I did was walk away in tears. All I can say to this day, is I am so sorry.

I did try to find that little boy, but he had been moved to another orphanage. That's what they did, the Salvation Army, when incidents were reported. They either moved the child or moved the officer, to hide the evil act that had occurred. I wondered if the boy had been severely hurt during the rape, and the nurse had reported it or perhaps he had escaped the hell hole we lived in. At the very least, that's what I hoped for that little fella. It just broke my heart and still does to this day.

Evil fucking bastards.

CHAPTER 21

Rolled

Eight years

Just two weeks after nearly being blinded, with gasoline, I found myself at the wrong end of the stick for something I didn't do.

It started as a normal Sunday. After we arrived back from church, we sat down for lunch. During our meal, a few of the boys and—as always—Peter, Bobby, Dennis, and I decided to go eel catching down at the creek. It was all set. We had asked for permission to leave the area and, so, after lunch, we collected the eel lines we had made for past catches, grabbed some hessian sacks, and bolted excitedly down to the creek on our great adventure.

We grew lettuce, leeks, radishes, turnips, and parsnips along the creek bedside. The running water gave lots of nutrition for the plants to grow from. We would harvest these and take them to the kitchen for broths or soups—the ladies in the kitchen loved it when we brought them sacks filled with vegetables.

We only needed two boys, one to set and hold the line and another to stand by with the wire net we had made. Bobby and I were the ones to fill these roles while Peter and Dennis sat on the edge of the creek talking to us and telling stories of what they would be when they grew up. This was something we did quite a lot. It made us happy to think of the future. The creek was amazing and provided so much fun for all the boys. It was also our private area, a place we would go and sit, and talk.

Dennis wanted to be a singer and who knows maybe he is today. Bobby just wanted to be a fireman, so that he could drive the big red truck. Peter never really decided on one thing and changed his mind all the time, but I am sure today he is a living memory of what he talked about the most, a teacher. Me well I just wanted one thing . . . to play for the New Zealand All Blacks. Well, I did play, but not at that level.

As far as eels went, I didn't like to eat them, but loved the catching and cooking part of it. A few hours passed and we had a good catch of about eight creek eels. We decided to return to the home, to wash, boil, and skin the eels. We took them to the scrub room, which was at the end of the laundry, where the two copper boilers we could use to cook them were, along with the old-fashioned roller style washing tubs.

The washers were basically big tubs with a set of two rollers on the top of them that you fed clothes through to squeeze out the water. You would be lucky to find one of these today as they were dumped after newer models became popular.

We would fill the copper tubs up with hot water and heated the base of the tub, this boiled the water, at which point we would drop the eels in. The eels would jump and slide around for a few minutes then go to sleep (cooked). We would then cut and peel the tailback and hang them on the line. From here we would peel the skin off slowly to expose the flesh which we could eat.

I don't know who put the eel in one of the old-fashioned roller style single washing tubs, but someone did and it definitely wasn't me. O1 came into the laundry, noticed it, and went right off! Of all the people to come in it had to be the one person that had made my life at Hodderville the worst. He didn't need a reason to hurt me, he revelled in it any chance he could drum up.

He spotted the eel in the washing tub and immediately grabbed hold of me and began yelling top note, as he always did. He gripped me tightly around the back of my neck and squeezed the hell out of it, before dragging me across the room. He screamed at the other boys to get out; a sure sign I was about to cop it and cop it good. Once alone, he turned the washing tub rollers on, grabbed my left hand, and shoved it in between the two rollers.

The old free standing washing machine Salvation Army Officer placed my hand into and turned it on until the safety lid released. This left me unable to use my arm for over 2 weeks.

I was eight years of age and tiny, but I soon found my arm being pulled and squashed into the roller machine. He was laughing all the while and saying, "This will teach you, you little shit!" Thankfully the rollers had a safety mechanism and it automatically stopped as soon it got to my elbow. The top cover automatically flew up and released the pressure from my arm but the damage was done.

The pain in my arm lasted for days, and I could not use it. There's an old saying that goes "it feels as if I have been through the wringer", well I know exactly what that feels like. At that time I just could not understand why this bloody evil officer had it in for me, but I found out later.

I found out that my older brother, Brian, had become sick of taking his punishment, and stood up to him, one day. I was told he struck the officer to the ground and told him if he ever tried anything again, he would beat him up. It seems I was his payback. I reported that day's abuse to the matron, something I usually didn't do, for obvious reasons, only to be told to go away and stop lying. It seemed that I just had to accept being bashed and tortured as the normal thing in my life.

This also brings back another memory, but this time not about me. It must have been a few weeks after the roller incident that we were told we were going on a field walk. This time all the kids from the home came along, but we still all stayed within our dorm groups. It was more of a friendship thing that we had built over time, mind you; Dale was there which was great: Brian may have been working at the sheds milking the cows. Truth is I am not sure why he and a few of the older boys were not with us on the walk.

We had only just walked out through the side gate, about 50 meters from the veggie gardens, when we were stopped. O2 told us that the old stump, to the right of the edge of the embankment, had been struck by lightning many years ago, and all that remained was the stump which stood maybe a little short of a meter in height. We were also clearly told never to go near it or to touch it as it had become a hive for wild bees. As long as we stayed clear, we would be safe. As quick as a breath we all stepped further away to avoid the bees.

As we walked on past the stump, I noticed one of the Moenoa brothers pick up a long branch. Straight away I realised what he was going to do. I shouted at him to stop, but it was too late. He poked the stump, laughing, and then gave it a whack a second time. O2 was 40 to 60 meters ahead and too far away to stop the boy.

All hell broke loose as the bees came out in their thousands and attacked the closest kid. Within seconds Robbie was on the ground screaming, crying, and rolling in a fit of pain and panic. The sound he was emitting was frightening as he cried out for help. For the first time I'd ever seen, O2 actually showed some compassion and empathy. Realising what was going on, he ran back to us trying to shoo the bees away. Seeing the bees all scoot away from his flailing arms, we all started to help as well, by waving our arms in the air, too.

O2 scooped Robbie up in his arms and raced towards the veggie garden where he grabbed a garden hose and started to hose Robbie down. The bees cleared off to avoid the water damaging their wings and O2 began shouting at us to go on ahead back to the home, as he carried Robbie in his arms, behind us.

Poor Robbie ended up fainting from the pain. As I looked back I could see his face, arms, and legs had big red, angry stings everywhere. We all got scared, at the sight of him, and many of the kids were crying as Robbie was rushed to hospital. I tried to comfort the rest of the boys and hold in my own tears.

Days passed, even though it felt more like weeks until Robbie was finally brought back from the hospital. We ran to him and huddled around him asking a million questions about the bee attack, what they did for him in hospital, and how he felt. He recounted the whole amazing story, until he was called to go to O2's office where he was given some good advice I'd later recall, after finding out that Robbie was highly allergic to bees, and that many kids have died from bee stings.

CHAPTER 22

Crushed

Eight years

At the home, having any type of fun, as any kid did growing up, was fraught with danger and consequences you wouldn't wish upon your worst enemy.

Things, such as sliding down a hill when it rained, were the best fun, but the repercussions from doing it were another thing. We were forced to strip where we stood and were flogged at least twice, with the strap, across our bare butts leaving two long red welt marks. The officers just loved seeing us in pain, the evil bastards. One day, not content with that, they made us put on girls underpants (bloomers) and stand outside for all the other boys to see, just to humiliate us—all for sliding down a hill in the rain.

My leg throbs, as I sit here writing; a ghostly reminder of the Hodderville days when playing rugby was literally the only thing sometimes that kept me going. My bed was against the wall, under a window overlooking the lush green expanse at the front of the property. I loved looking out at the oval and I spent many hours playing rugby and imagining myself playing rugby.

I was lying on my bed having a rest one day, when I swung my legs out through the window and propped them up on the window seal to feel the fresh air flowing around. Bang! The window came slamming down onto my shins. I thought the windowpane had cut them off and screamed out so loudly the whole place must have heard me. Through my screaming, I heard someone laughing. O1 was standing over me with his vile smile saying "That will teach you, you little black shit! Windows are for letting fresh air in, not hanging your legs out of."

He walked off, leaving me to struggle to get the window open to release my legs. Blood was gushing from the cuts where the window trim had hit my legs. Too frightened to say anything, I laid there in agony feeling sorry for myself, and wishing I was dead, while cursing the officer.

At dinner that evening, I could see him looking at me. I tried to hide my face, so he couldn't see me and froze when he strode towards me. He announced himself with a sharp poke of his finger into my back and said in a hushed voice, "That was an accident wasn't it? The window must have come down on its own". I gazed hesitantly at him meeting the eyes that burned into me, with his threat. "Yes Sir" I obediently said as he walked off, to tell another boy off.

Peter looked at me and said, "Daryl did he hurt you again? Go and see the Matron". I shook my head and Peter understood. If I did, I would just get worse from him later, or on another day.

You have to wonder how some people can be so evil. I wondered a lot about that man. I later learned, through the boys, that he had had a girlfriend at one time, of Maori descent. The word was that she had left him for another young Maori boy. The older boys said this is why he hated Maori boys so much and anyone with dark skin. I remember thinking, "Lucky me—I am a half cast Maori boy and I also have dark skin", a double whammy.

It was as if he was on a mission to do as much damage as humanly possible and to as many kids as he could. As a young fella, I hoped things would change, but I knew they never would. From then, until the day I left Hodderville, I kept one eye out for him, regardless, of where I was or what I was doing. I would hide when I heard his voice, or walk the other way when I saw him, and stay close to my older brothers whenever possible.

In doing this, I kept myself safer, but his rage boiled over and he turned his attention onto other kids—venting, raging, and assaulting them. I didn't escape it either, I still coped a whole lot more abuse, but not as much as I had before.

CHAPTER 23

Night Terrors

Eight years

I must have been around eight or going onto nine years of age when one night out of curiosity after hearing O1 walk into the dorm and start talking to Robbie Hamilton, I looked up to see O1 leading Robbie from his bed, shaking and not sure if I should go or not, I got up and followed them.

To this day I am not sure why I decided to get out of bed, or why I had to see what was going on, I just did.

O1 took Robby to his room which was at the end of the hall. This room was the staff accommodation area, and the officer's rooms were here.

I could hear Robbie crying, and the officer savagely telling him to be quiet and do as he said, or he would go away to a children's prison forever. Hearing that, I ran back to my bed in tears, petrified of him ever coming to get me. I didn't know at the time what was happening, but the threat of going to prison and leaving my brothers and friends was frightening enough.

Robbie came back on his own, crying and in pain. He lay in his bed with his head sunk into his pillow to hide the noise. I looked over at him seeing him hurting. I could not let him lay there alone, so I got up and went to his bedside.

We had all faced many terrible things over the years and I knew this time would be no different. I asked Robbie what O1 had done to him, I heard his words, but taking them in made me loose all time and space as concern turned to a wave of intense anger learning Robbie had just been raped by O1.

I wasn't sure what to do, I told Peter who was in the bed next to Robbie what had happened, and that I needed to help Robbie, so he had to keep watch for O1 in-case he came back.

I took Robbie to the shower room and helped him clean his bottom and the blood that was running down his legs. I helped him back to his bed and knelt at the side of his bed holding his hand and trying to tell him he would be ok all the time, knowing he wasn't, and never would be.

Robbie was around my age and had a thin build with bright red hair and freckles to match. From stories, he told us his parents did not want kids. To me, he seemed more to enjoy being on his own—a bit of a loner.

As the years passed, he did come out of his shell, and mixed more with us kids and even became a bit of a leader in his own way—much to our annoyance sometimes when he'd let it go to his head.

He was a great kid though, like all the boys who lived there we had our ups and downs—a scuffle here and there and on occasion we were too much for each other, but I liked him, he never deserved the treatment he got from the officers—none of us did.

CHAPTER 24

A second chance

Nine years

As with past years, it was the time of the year that meant so much, when I got the chance to holiday with my holiday foster family, the Lewis's. Even though we had only spent a few holidays together, I had become well-attached and connected to them. The time I had spent with them, in the past, had been incredible. I had done more with them than most kids at the home could only dream about. I had learned a lot, too.

As each holiday came up, Mr. Lewis and his son Darrell would travel to the boys' home to pick me up for around four fantastic weeks, with them. These times and weeks always went by way too fast, but we did enough to fill a year in the time I had with them.

One of the many adventures we had together was going on a trip to the observatory. The location was also known as, and still is, "One Tree Hill". Here, we got to gaze out into space and see things, which seemed beyond real to me —but they were real. Today of course I know them to be stars, planets, and clusters etc.

We camped in the back yard, just for the hell of it, since Mr. Lewis worked most holidays. Not that it bothered me; every day was like another best day ever, especially being away from the home.

I was nine years of age and had just returned to Hodderville, from having a wonderful Christmas holidays with the Lewis's, when I was asked to go to the major's office. I sat waiting in her cold, dark office, with its wooden walls and furniture. It wasn't a warming or welcoming room, that's for sure; more like an authoritarian type of room that showed the occupant had control and power.

The major walked in and sat behind the wooden table. She asked me if I had enjoyed going to the Lewis family for holidays, and I replied saying "Yes, I did". She said, "That's good because they want to adopt you". She explained that because my biological mother had not collected us within twelve months, I could be processed for adoption as a child of the state. Processed—what a word to use. It made me feel as if I was something that was made and sold for the enjoyment of others.

I sat there as she talked but, to tell the truth I didn't hear a word she was saying. I was already worried that I would never see my brothers again. I really cared for the Lewis Family in Auckland, and wanted to be with them, but I also knew it would mean leaving my brothers, which I just didn't want to do.

This time was different to the first time that I had been up for adoption, because I was told I had to wait for an interview with the adoption agency, first. In the meantime, I told my brothers about the adoption request and that I had to wait for more information. Brian told me the same thing as he had the first time—to go and live your life brother, play rugby, and learn. He also told me then that he was leaving the home to work on a local farm, because he was old enough and he wanted to, so he would be going soon, too.

Dale was Dale, and I could see in his eyes what he wanted to say, but he didn't. He told me to go. He said I would never get another chance like this because I was getting too old to adopt. Dale had also had an adoption request for him, a year earlier which had also been denied by our biological mother.

Sometime later, I can't remember exactly how long after the meeting with the major, a woman from the adoption board came into the room. She started to talk to me about the adoption paperwork, submitted by the Lewis family, and said that unfortunately it had been denied through a court injunction by my mother again.

It felt as if my gut had been torn out and. that no matter how many times I was given a chance in life, she—my biological mother—always prevented it. I could not understand why. I dropped my head as a few tears trickled down my face and fell on the floor between my feet. Feeling empty is never nice, but the emptiness that you feel is caused by your own mother is nothing short of painful.

I did get to spend another two holidays with the Lewis family, before finding out more about why my mother had not wanted to sign the adoption papers. The matron said that she was completing her arrangement to have Dale and I reunited with her. At that point, I was not even aware that Teena had already been sent over to Australia, and had been living there for just over a year—they kept that quiet when Easter came and went that year (1969) and she didn't come to visit us boys.

CHAPTER 25

Boys' fun

Nine years

Looking back while writing this book, I've noticed that a lot of the worst abuse happened on Saturdays. I wished I had noticed that back then and made myself scarce!

Another Saturday, and we boys had returned from church, done our chores, and had spent time in the garden, in preparation for the harvest, as there was no rugby on outside the winter months. After lunch we played and, like all boys, took it in turns deciding on which games to play. That day it was decided to play with the donkey we had named Arnold. For some reason we called him The Pig, I can't remember why, maybe because he ate everything or grunted, who knows.

We built steps out of wooden boxes to get the height we needed to climb up onto Arnold's back and took turns riding him around the paddock, with just a piece of rope loosely tied around his neck, and an old blanket to sit on. Old Arnold had the worst smell, I can't begin to tell you, but we put up with it because the fun we had was worth more to us than a little stink.

Time passed, and boys being boys, we decided on a game change. We decided on stilts. If you have ever built stilts you will understand the enjoyment of making them, and then walking around proud, at a height well above the windows, and in some cases above the gutters. From those who may not know what stilts are, they are the long legs you see clowns wearing under their pants, which allows them to tower over everyone and everything. You've probably seen them at fairs and sideshows.

This day, we made our own stilts, which took around 15 or 20 minutes of work. When we were all ready we carried our stilts to the landing outside the woodwork room, stand on the edge, and climbed onto the footrest of the stilts, while holding the upper leg frames for balance, before slowly walking away from the buildings. At times one or more of use would fall, but over time we became good at mounting and dismounting the stilts.

Those of us, who had decided to make higher than normal stilts, needed to stand at the top of the walkways leading up to the carpenters' workshop. It was more of a ramp, but served the purpose of giving us that extra height needed to step up onto the stilts. We climbed on to the stilts and walked around proud and happy, laughing, and at times trying to knock each other over, but all in fun. I can still see the many smiles in my mind, as we played and joked with each other.

An image of what the walking stilts looked like. We would make them and play for hours.

The moments we got to play meant so much to us. Picture twelve to fourteen boys trying to show off their best-made toys and talking rubbish just to have fun . . . all boys do, harmless fun and so important for us, because it let us escape the abuse in the home for a while. Sadly, that freedom and fun didn't last long as HELL rained down upon us in the form of the fun police and the cruellest, nastiest man alive, showed up from around the corner of the laundry.

What next? was all I could think, as he walked towards us with a look on his face that could boil an egg. I remember thinking what have we done, or what did I do, that had him walking towards us in such a rage. He was throwing his arms up wildly in the air and yelling. I was shocked, as for once, it wasn't me; not that I wanted to see another boy hurt but I was relieved it wasn't my turn. It was a boy with the last name of Neilson, I can't remember his first name . . .maybe Glen or Neil? I do remember there were two or three of them (brothers). It seems he had not finished his daily chores and had left three bins in the officers' quarters filled, which should have been emptied that morning.

As O1 approached the Neilson boy, he kicked the leg of stilts out from underneath him. The boy lost his balance and fell, but not in the direction the officer expected. He fell into Peter and me, which sent us tumbling to the ground also. Peter hurt his shoulder badly and was taken to the first aid room, and then to the dorm to rest. I, on the other hand, fell awkwardly and landed on the upper ramp area that we used to get on the stilts. At the time, I thought I was lucky to get away with so little suffering, but that wasn't to be the case.

I felt pain in my right leg and I looked down. I could only see blood and lots of it, from a huge gash down the other side of my right leg. It was running down my leg and onto my foot, and then the pain set in. It seems that when I fell onto the upper ramp my leg struck the outer boards, which were old, and had nails sticking out. My luck, my leg struck and pulled against a nail which left a gaping hole in the side of my leg.

He blamed me for being in the way, while attempting to talk and get stuck into Glen Neilson, another kid who hadn't finished his chores. I told the other officers what had happened only to be told that if I lied, I would go to hell. Can twelve boys get it so wrong? They just never listened or tried to stop all of the hurt, as most of them were as bad as each other, and seemed to love seeing us hurt and crying.

Once again, I got medical treatment and another cover-up to protect that officer. I still have that scar, which is as long as my little finger and as wide as an average pen, so imagine the wound on a child of only nine years old. The hell was building, and so too were the many scars I would carry for life.

CHAPTER 26

Eyes Open, Mouth Shut

Nine years

It all seemed so innocent at the time . . . a normal craft class, where we learned the art of needlepoint and stitching, along with gluing things onto material. Sitting there talking and stitching things together, we decided to play doctor and stitch our fingers together. Something many kids do, at one time in their life, and really harmless, but the officer in charge was the one man who never saw the fun in anything. His whole purpose in life was to inflict as much pain, suffering and terror in people's lives as he could.

As he walked around the room, he noticed what we had done to each other fingers. Playing doctor and giving each other stitches was fun, but he wasn't having a bar of it. In a split second, he flew out of control and struck me across the head with the ruler that he had in his hand. I felt the blow but tried to put on a brave face and take it on the chin. It bloody hurt, but I thought I was ok until Dennis said to me, "Daryl you're bleeding on top of your head". A minute later the blood began sliding down my face.

I was taken to the first aid room for treatment and asked what happened. When I tried to explain, I was stopped and told not to lie. Like every other occasion, it was my fault. No one ever believed us, and I was left with another scar to add to the growing patchwork on my body, from being at what we began calling "Horrorville".

A few other times I tried to report an assault to the Salvation Army, through our school, but I was disciplined for doing this. I had told my teacher the Salvation Army officer was hurting me and other boys. The report was taken to the school headmaster the same day. That afternoon I was asked to report to the headmaster's office, not knowing that O1 would be present. He forced me to say I was lying for attention. If I didn't he was going to send me to the boys' prison, it was a place that frightened the hell out of us, even though none of us knew whether it existed or not—the threat of such a bad place was all it took to keep us quiet.

On returning to the boys' home I was taken to his office and given the strap. The strap was a brown leather strap about 400 cm when folded. This punishment was something that took place, quite often. We would be told to hold our hands out and to open them. The officer would swing the strap in a full circle before striking our hands.

The pain was only with you for a second or two, but our hands would swell from the impact, and after about 30 seconds they would go numb. After a time, the numbing would go away, and the pain would set in again.

Normally if you received the strap, you would get up to three blows (normally two and three, if more serious), and you could hear the boys yelling as they got the strap: It truly hurt, and left long red painful marks on your hands or bottom. That day I received three straps for telling the truth, two on one hand and one on the other.

Along with the strap, we would also receive the cane which in many ways was much more painful than the strap. We would be struck across our naked butt, and it left one or two red welt lines that burned for hours. To make it worse, he always made us bend over, to stretch the skin out, so there was no padding to soften the blow. God, it killed.

CHAPTER 27

Head High

Ten years

I was obsessed with the sport of rugby, and after a year, I was picked to be captain of the rugby team, a role I held for a further three years until I moved to Australia.

At ten years of age, I got an amazing opportunity to play in the opener for the All Blacks, which only highlighted my pathway in sports. To stand on the same sports field as so many of my sporting heroes and legends was, without question, one of the most memorable moments there was.

The night before, it was early to bed for us, as we prepared for what was to become a moment in history . . . well for me anyway. On the day, the excitement was high, as were the nerves of all the players in the team. We were new and hadn't played together before. Our coach gave us a quick talk before it was time to head out to the ground. Being a squad that had been put together, only days before the event, made things hard, and running on as half-back I knew I was in for a challenging time. We had managed to meet each other as a team the night before but names were always going to be an issue.

Minutes out and on the field, I looked around to see people everywhere. The sound was incredible and the truth was I felt as if I was way out of my depth, for those first few moments. The stadium was intimidating. It was then, as I turned around, that I saw him standing with the match-ball—it was Chris Laidlaw, the All-Black team captain. He shook my hand and said, "Do the game proud". He handed me the match-ball and walked away, as I ran onto the field. That was my big brush with a celebrity athlete and my first claim to fame.

We won the game and walked off, our heads held high, to the roar of thousands. I was given the match ball, as I scored three tries, defeating the team from the South Island. I looked after that ball, until I left New Zealand, as if it was a pot of gold.

The All-Blacks were preparing for their pre-session game, as we came off, so we were directed to a back room to change. Some of the boys came from the suburbs around Waikato, where the big game was being held, but another kid and I were from Putaruru, which was about two-and-a-half hours' drive away, so after our game, we had to leave. I never even saw the game, would you believe it.

I think the All-Blacks played France that night, but I'm not entirely sure as there was so much going on and the excitement so great, we didn't even think about their game.

I spent endless hours telling the boys all about it that night, back at the home. They were all so happy for me and kept asking question after question, about the stadium; how many people were there, and did I get a hot dog. I told them all about how exciting the night was. As for the hot dog . . . no, I didn't get one but we did stop for a snack on the way home at a gasoline station.

We must have brought the food along with us, because I don't remember getting anything special to eat. I think that I was too tired to think or remember much of anything on the way home.

CHAPTER 28

A Special Easter Visit

Ten years

Easter is a special time for kids around the world and this was no different for the boys and girls in the orphanage homes. There were so many good times to be had at school leading up to Easter, such as Easter egg decorating, which was followed by the egg rolling events. Thinking back, it was so cool to get an egg, boil it till it was hard, and then paint it in many colours.

We always made two eggs, one for the weekend events at the boys' home, and one to take to school for the annual Easter fair. We would display our craft, and then see who could roll their egg along the school oval the furthest. I don't think I ever won but I always enjoyed it nonetheless.

Back at the boys' home, we would just roll the eggs down the back-paddock hill, leading to the creek, hoping our egg would break open before it hit the water. No prizes, no rewards, apart from the laughs we had doing it. You can only imagine seeing one hundred plus eggs, rolling down a hill at the same time with the sound of forty to sixty boys yelling, screaming, and filling the air with laughter.

A single moment of happiness while it lasted, and hardly tarnished by the officers, as only a small number of staff worked at Easter. We made the most of these days knowing it would all come to a shattering stop and we pretended we hadn't had fun when the bad officers came back on duty.

All up, Easter was the greatest time of all, because it was the one time of the year Brian, Dale, and I would get a visit from our sister, Teena. She would travel four hours from her orphanage, The Grange, and would spend two-and-a-half hours with us. It was a long day for her, but we all treasured the small amount of time we got to spend together as a family.

After I grew older and had arrived at Hodderville, I had learnt I had a sister, but I didn't really understand too much about what a sister was. I had to rely on what the other boys and my brothers told me. It wasn't until I was around eight that I started to realise how important and amazing having a sister really was. It was strange those first few visits, I was a bit confused about why she would come and visit me, and shower me with hugs, and kisses all over my face.

We never spoke about our parents: I have no idea why—maybe she was asked not to, I'm just not sure. For my part, I was just so happy to see her that I always forgot to ask. I clearly remember those days when her bus would pull up, and her tears would begin as soon as she hopped off. By the time she had to leave, they would be streaming down her face and mine too, knowing it would be another 365 days before we would be together again.

I remember the first time I saw her. She was so pretty and had tanned skin just like me. Teena was a skinny girl from the time I first met her and right up to her passing. Her hair was wavy and curly and her voice was sweet and soft, which made me feel so wanted and relaxed.

On her visits, we would walk together, holding hands and talk about many things—her friends at The Grange, and the music class she was part of. I would jabber on about the boys and rugby as always. We would never sit down; we just kept walking and talking . . . I miss those days with her. Our connection was formed all those years ago and weathered the years, the distance, and across countries. Our bond remained as strong as ever the whole of our lives.

One of the most amazing memories I have is when all of the boys' sisters came to visit was the watermelons. The girls would bring these huge watermelons with them and the kitchen staff would cut them into slices and hand them out. The taste was incredible. I'd never tasted it before and the taste just exploded in my mouth. It became something of a tradition each year and an annual treat that we enjoyed immensely.

The strange girl, who first came to visit, became a sister as the years went on and I became more familiar with her. Years later, she would also be the one person who was able to change my life, when all I wanted to do was take my own. Love's a powerful thing and when it finally becomes a part of you, it seems nothing can break that bond. Teena was my only sister and, many times in my future, she would be my saviour.

CHAPTER 29

Hopeful to Hopeless

Ten years

I was excited to be heading off to stay with the lovely Lewis family, for the Easter holidays. It warmed my heart how much I had become a part of this amazing family unit. I loved being there and felt as if I was home when I was with them. Every time I had to go back to the home, I would cling to Mr. Lewis, holding on for dear life to the one father figure I had ever known, until the Salvation Army officer would pull me away from him, and put me in the car bound for Horrorville, once more.

It was Easter Sunday, in 1969, and we had just left church. I can still remember the music and songs, and the kind gifts handed out to all the kids at the church. We arrived home only to be told we could not go out and play, which I found very strange, as playing was the one thing the Lewis family knew how to do and did it well. Instead, Mr. Lewis asked me to come into the house and to sit down as he had something he needed to tell me.

Darryl to Daryl, we sat across from each other as he spoke—five minutes later, I was sobbing so much that I ran out of the house and sat under the willow tree in the front yard. The whole Lewis family came out, and as they approached me, and said "It will be ok, we thought this is what you wanted, and we wanted it, too". I ran to them and hugged them asking them not to let go.

Inside, Mr. Lewis had shown me a piece of paper stating it was an application to adopt me and said to me "We want you to become part of our family, Daryl". My heart was bursting. Yes! I was beside myself with joy. What do you say, and where do you look when you have the most amazing family of three who wanted you to join their family for good and become a family of four? Knowing someone wanted me, an orphaned boy as their son and brother was a huge moment in my life.

We all went back inside and all I could do was read and try to understand the contents of that application, over and over. The terms, conditions, and statements were way over my head at that age, but I understood the most important thing—they wanted me to be with them forever! I was elated. The only question I had was about my brothers, Brian and Dale, and sister Teena—"Would I ever see them again?"

Mr. Lewis told me I would get to see them every holiday and during the year on weekend trips to the home. He said Teena's orphanage was only a twenty-five-minute drive away and I jumped up, excited, knowing I could go visit her at least once a month. Things got even better as the holiday passed. We enjoyed chocolate eggs, and fishing days, did our paper rounds, worked the two Saturdays at the foundry and just played.

We decided to buy a tree for the front yard, with the money Darrell and I earned over those ten days. It was something to remember those special holidays by, and one that we hoped would one day remind us of how the Lewis family of three became one of four.

Was I happy? Yes.

Could anything destroy that moment? No.

Back at the boys' home, I waited to hear those final words that would change my life forever, "Daryl, your adoption has been approved by the courts, and you are now free to live with Mr. and Mrs. Lewis in Auckland". I imagined those words over and over. I sat happy, with a face filled with smiles. Not even the worst pain could take it away; well that's what I thought.

In just one second all hell broke loose and pain worse than anything I'd ever experienced at Hodderville, blasted through my head and heart, as I was told the courts approved the adoption, but my biological mother had contested the application and refused to sign any adoption forms or release me to the Lewis's. Shattered beyond words, I went back to my dorm and grabbed my rugby ball. I ran from end to end of the grassed yard all the while screaming in my head "WHY?".

How could anyone person take away the love and life of a child as she continually did? She'd never shown any interest in me. I'd heard from her ONCE in my eleven years of life, two years earlier. Since then, there had been no visit, no call, no birthday cards, or Christmas presents, nothing! It was as if I didn't exist. She had never wanted me; so WHY?

I went over and over these questions and more, as I sat, sadder and more destroyed than I ever had been before. I felt like giving up. I asked God to take me so I could live free in another place, away from the pain of what I would have to endure in the hellhole of Hodderville, for another fifteen months.

The only impact my mother had had on my life, up until then, was one that had resulted in pain. It was such a big blow to cope with. The hardest thing was knowing that in just nine weeks' time I would once again be on holidays with the Lewis family and I would have to face them. I felt betrayed by my own mother and deeply wounded for both myself and the Lewis's.

CHAPTER 30

Release

Ten years

I went over and over the good times—any good times—to get through the despair I felt. Doing this brought me strength. I focused on great days that I had never forgotten, such as rugby days, school carnivals, eel fishing, and Guy Fawkes Day.

Rugby became my great release and helped me heal, as I threw myself into the game to channel my anger and to deal with the sadness of not being with the people I had come to love. I lived for rugby. Even when we didn't have games on and it was out of season, I used to spend hours and hours training and playing rugby. Not only was it my passion, but doing it kept me up in the paddock, away from the home and, more importantly, away from the officers who hated walking up there.

Rugby days ... now these were the most special of days, besides holidays with the Lewis family. They were so incredible that I would wake up before the birds and count down the minutes to the game. The one thing that saved my soul throughout that period was knowing that every Saturday morning, during winter, I would be able to escape the home and the officers' abuse, to play the game I loved so much.

I was always up, with my shorts on and breakfast done early. The Saturday choirs were done as quickly as we could and then we'd race off to the pickup point on the old gravel driveway. Our boots tied together with their laces, we would hop on board the old bus and sit waiting to arrive in the local town, Putaruru.

Our rugby coach, who was also a teacher at our school, would be standing, waiting for us, to lead us onto the field. We talked and chatted before the game and then it was time. Jumpers on, bodies warmed up, boots on. A quick swig of water which we held in our mouths and out from the dressing room we'd go. I really came alive on the field and felt most like the person I truly was.

I mainly played in the position of fly-half, but at times the coach would swap me into the scrum-half role as a half-back. My game plan in that position was all about looking and deciding which player to place the golden egg with.

I was one of those players who never accepted losing. With every breathe, I gave my all—we had an amazing team and the four years of playing with them not only kept me going but were also among the most incredible times of my life. I loved the game, the friends, the sport, and the escape.

I must admit that some of the boys in my team were intimidating. Back then, the grading was done on height, so as most of us were full, half, or a quarter and mostly short, which meant playing against younger boys in the other teams. The rules changed in my last year, and I went up a grade which was a challenge that I loved.

There was one year, in particular, I can't forget. It was 1968 and the end of the rugby session. Like all clubs, we had our end of the season team break-up where all the kids would attend a night of awards. The night started, like all presentations, with plates of food on the tables, and music playing in the background. It was a big night for us young kids, as we listened to the adults talking about the year.

The small awards were first, to start the night off, and they seemed to take forever, as every player received an honour award with a few exceptional awards passed out in between for the older grades. I received one for being a member of the winning team in my grade, and an award for player of the year for our grade also.

Then the big award was announced that was given to players in the top grades, the presentation for club player of the year across all grades, which was normally given to one of the senior players. I can't tell you how shocked I was when they announced the award for player of the year was me! Stunned, I made my way up to the stage. All I can remember is the clapping and cheering from the players of all grades. This award was a cup and I also had the honour of having my name on the club's MVP (Most Valuable Player) shield which hung in the clubhouse.

I was selected as the club's MVP for 1968. Rugby was truly my calling in sport, and one that paved the way for me to realise that although I was small in structure, I could turn adversity into an opportunity. This moment was to be the foundation of many sporting successes throughout my lifetime.

I also learnt my challenge was not to be as a player, even though I did well, but more as a teacher for others. A leader, or coach; my destiny was born at that moment.

Apart from rugby, I held on to memories of times that helped me survive back then and which held me level emotionally and mentally for years to come, such as the school carnivals. Carnival days were rewarding because we got to challenge ourselves in the many activities over the day's events. Our teachers were amazing and even though we were orphaned boys, they never treated us differently. I enjoyed running.

Ironically, it had become part of me as I grew, because I had to run away from the abuse so often. I loved attempting the 110- and 218-yard sprints, which are today's equivalent to the 100 and 200 m distance races. Truth be told, I wasn't that good, and when I was running I looked awkward as my head and shoulders tried to keep up with my legs.

I always thought that I was fast, because not too many could catch me on the rugby field, but on the track that all changed. Over time, however, I found my little niche in middle distance events and did quite well, before venturing into cross-country and later to marathons. I was eventually running around 70 kms each week, as well as cycling, swimming, and weight training. One of the many things I loved about running was the total freedom; the wind, and the fresh air and knowing I had NO one to challenge but myself.

Times that I enjoyed like that, while under the care of the Salvation Army, were major events for me. I always felt safe when at school knowing I was away from those mongrel officers.

Another activity that I still recall fondly was eel fishing . . . there were many creeks surrounding the property, which was amongst the hills and many valleys. These valleys left the creeks highly populated with many living water creatures—but particularly eels and freshwater cray. When the days came calling for a hand up to going eel fishing—which were few and far between—I think my hand nearly hit the ceiling.

It was so exciting, knowing I would get to leave the home for four to five hours and walk through the paddocks to the creeks, which were covered in reeds. We would pack a small lunch and a canteen with cordial and water as well as an old towel. Then we'd collect the eel nets and old sacks and be on our way. The journey normally took around forty minutes to return, but it was worth every minute. On arrival, we would set up a cleared area, just above the edge of the creeks, and lay our sacks down after dipping them in the water, first. We tied some string to the top of the sack and fixed a rope to a tree, so we could put the eels in it and keep them alive.

The older boys would place the eel nets into the creeks and use heavy rocks to keep them submerged just under the waterline. From here, we would sort through the weeds and fish out freshwater crays and take them back up to the sacks for keeping. We would then place three or four of the crays in the nets, along with a little fresh red meat we got from the kitchen staff, to entice the eels.

The raw smell of the red meat would travel in the water, attracting the eels into the nets through a small looped entry hole. It had an overlapping fold inside so that the eels could enter, but somehow could not find their way out. The nets would be left for thirty minutes or so before we checked them. The fact that the creeks in the area had not been hunted or fished during the winter months, for up to six months, meant there were abundant eels and it wasn't long before we would have two and up to five in many of the nets.

A few of the boys were great at telling which eels were laying eggs, so we sorted them out, along with any that were undersized, and returned them to the water to keep growing and populating. Once we had about twenty or more eels, we'd head back to the home.

On our arrival, we would fill up big tubs with freshwater in them and sit the sacks that carried the eels in them to keep them alive. The copper boilers would be filled and turned on to bring the water temperature close to boiling point. Once the water began bubbling, we would take one eel out at a time and place it into the copper. The eel would splish, splash and thrash for a few seconds and then it would fall asleep—as we were told back then. Around ten minutes later we removed the eel and took it outside to the clothesline, where we would hang it up and nick a ring in it, cutting around their tails, so we could peel the skin back and down slowly exposing the meat.

The older boys would fillet the meat of the eel and place it into clean containers, and the meat was taken to the kitchen. The kitchen staff would cook the meat on the hot plate and bring it out to all of the boys to share later in the day.

As for the freshwater crayfish, we would catch hundreds and give these to the kitchen staff, also. These would also be washed and cooked on hot plates for the boys to eat. These are times I remember so well. I loved our eel and cray catching days; they bring back a lot of good memories.

We had Guy Fawkes Day every November 5th . . . the day was also known as Bonfire Night or Cracker Night, and was an annual English tradition going back over 400 years. NZ and Australia also celebrated it, because of our history with the British colonies. We loved Cracker Night which continued until about 1980, when many countries began cancelling it for safety reasons. We would prepare the most incredible bonfire—it would take us a week preparing for that one night each year, when thousands celebrated it together, all over the world.

As the day drew closer, we took some time to make a special man, like a dummy, but made from wood for the frame, old sacks filled with rags as the body parts, and which included legs, arms and a head. We would rake Arnold's tail to remove some hair and attach it to the head of our man-made dummy. Good old Arnold, every year, he would be brushed. All so we could get just enough hair to make our man-made dummy look real.

The night finally arrived and all the boys and staff sat or played around the stacked wood. We always got a few crackers which made for an interesting night, especially when it came to lighting our Tom Thumbs. These crackers were the smallest of them all, so as boys do, we would challenge each other to hold the cracker in the palms of our hands and light them. Whoever held the cracker the longest and let it explode in their palm was seen as a hero . . . crazy I know, but God it was fun!

Being where we were, out in the sticks, with the nearest town 30-40 kms away, all you could see were a million stars, the light from the crackers and the flickering from the burning bonfire. We would celebrate for hours, once the fire was lit. I can truly say it was the one night of the year that all of us boys had lots of fun.

CHAPTER 31

The Ice Block

Ten years

The shower blocks are reminders of so many sad times at the home and of all the hurt and pain we went through at the hands of those Salvation Army officers. Like many other children at the Salvation Army boys' home, it was a place we called the room of pain or the ice block.

On my return, with my wife, years later I found it very hard to walk into this room. The memories were just so hard to face—every moment of pain came flooding back, knocking the wind out of me even fifty years later.

In the mornings during winter, the shower blocks were ridiculously cold. The nasty officers would open up all the windows allowing the coolness of the night-time and cold winds to freeze the room to ice. They'd then force us to shower naked, in front of them, all the time waiting for the water from the boilers to reach the taps. But the officers would not give us that amount of time, so we had to shower with the cold water. The tiles we stood on were so cold our feet and toes stuck to the floor and would go numb. Some of the kids had slippers, but not all of us were that lucky.

Chores week in the shower blocks was not a nice time, either, on your knees scrubbing the floors and walls with cold water. By the time the cleaning was done, you would be wet, freezing, sore, and shivering.

After football, we would be told to shower, but before we did, we had to clean our knees with scrubbing brushes in the lower trough, to keep the dirt out of the shower areas. God it was painful! Our knees were full of cuts and abrasions from the game and the stiff bristles of the scrubbing brushes just tore into our raw flesh. It didn't stop the officers from forcing us to scrub our knees though—no matter the pain it caused. We would go into the shower, bleeding, and they would laugh and make jokes, calling us sooks or little girls, finishing by saying you know what we do to little girls don't you—their sick and perverted way of telling us they were going to enjoy some time later with someone.

I spent many hours, sitting with other boys at night, after they had been abused in the shower blocks, by O1 or O2. I am sure that, like many other times, we boys will never forget them. I and many kids after me faced horrors in the ice block that twist into and tug at your very being. So many terrifying moments—too many to write and some you just can't write. I recall one night trying to sleep, but I could hear crying in the distance, the worst thing about me back then was not minding my own business. I cared and cared deeply about others and always wanted to help in some way.

This particular night I got up. It could not have been too late because the yard lights were still on and they were turned off around 9:30 pm. I slowly snuck out into the hallway and down to the shower blocks. I could hear the cries and mumbling words as I got closer.

The young boy in the shower was from the first dorm and new to the home, so he would have been around eight or nine years of age. When I saw what they were doing to him, I got so scared. He was crying and in so much pain. One officer was holding his hands over the back of the sink while laughing, and the over one had penetrated him from behind and was forcing himself on the boy. I felt sick as I ran back to my bed.

The next day I looked for the little boy, but he never turned up to catch the school bus. I was later told that he was sick and had to stay in bed for the day. When he finally came out, I asked him if he was ok. Sadly, he told me to leave him alone and walked away. That boy became an outsider. Every time we tried to get him involved in anything, he would walk away, or tell us to leave him alone. It was clear the attack had affected him. It was heartbreaking to see this happen to such a young person. I can only hope he moved on from all the abuse, later in life.

So many boys who were affected back in these days turned to drugs and alcohol or suicided later in life, to drown out the pain and humiliation they went through. It's seriously painful to me to think about that. These were boys I lived with and was with 24/7. Knowing I survived and other boys didn't hurts me deeply. It's devastating to know there was no one there to help any of us. I know how strong all of us boys were, but it's beyond gut-wrenching and heartbreaking.

That was the impact those Salvation Army officers had on many of the young boys. That night was only one of many nights in the shower block that would forever change little boys' lives. Because we were all so scared, no one ever complained, and no one ever did a thing—terrified we'd be next.

CHAPTER 32

Heartbreak

Ten years

The biggest bombshell of the year came when I was back with the Lewis's at their Beach Haven home in North Auckland. We were playing after completing our paper run. That day we had earned about $1.06 each for one hour's work and were allowed to go to the local shop down the road to spend it. Not that we could spend it all. In those days $1.06 would be worth close to $15.00 today in buying power. We did, however, buy a few lollies.

On the 28th of May 1969, a day etched firmly in my mind, a car pulled up outside the Lewis family's house. It was the Salvation Army vehicle and a tall, skinny man in a Salvation Army uniform hopped out of the car, as Darrell and I stood watching. I didn't know what was happening and thought it strange, since I still had one more week of holidays left with the Lewis's.

He approached Mr. Lewis and introduced himself and his position with the Salvation Army and he asked if he could talk with Mr. Lewis and his wife in private. As I played in the front yard with Darrell, I overhead the officer tell Mr. Lewis that I was to be reunited with my biological mother in Australia. Mr. Lewis turned and looked at me, and I could see he was not happy. I couldn't hear the rest of the conversation so wasn't sure what was about to happen. I thought it was just another periodical visit that we had from time to time, and didn't think too much about. I kept playing with Darrell.

Mr. Lewis walked inside as the car drove off, and after a few minutes, I was called in. Mrs. Lewis was sitting in the dining room and was crying. Mr. Lewis came over to me and held me while saying in a soft and forlorn voice, "I am sorry Daryl, we have done all we can, but sadly you are leaving us tomorrow". At first, I thought it was just for the remainder of the holiday period, but as he spoke I soon learnt it was for good.

He said my biological mother had applied for returned custody of Dale and me, and that my sister, Teena, had already been flown over. I had no say in the matter; it was that simple . . . I was leaving the next day, to fly to a foreign land called, Australia.

All my belongings, awards, and personal items were left behind at the boys' home, never to be seen again. It was so hard knowing that Mr. and Mrs. Lewis had applied to adopt me three times and every time the woman I knew as my biological mother had refused to sign the court documents, arguing she wanted me back one day. For years I'd heard this and was stunned that it was actually happening.

I sat in the lounge as if I were in a cloud, I just could not understand, and worse I could not even look at Mr. and Mrs. Lewis. Darrell was sitting next to me and I could see he didn't know what to do or say. I sat with my head dropped down and couldn't stop the tears as they ran down my face and onto the floor. I remember looking up, looking for hope but that had gone. Mr. Lewis left the house and Darrell, who I thought would one day be my adopted brother, would not stop crying which made things even harder. Mrs. Lewis went about doing things just to stop crying. It was horrible—I felt terrible that my own mother had inflicted so much sadness on this wonderful family, and I felt incredibly lonely.

Mr. Lewis came back and walked into the house with a big black case and came over to where I was sitting. He sat me down and said, "This is for you Son, we were going to give it to you to take back to have until we came to pick you up for good" as he handed me the case. I opened it and was shocked. As I looked up at him, I could see his emotions brimming over as the first of many tears ran down my cheeks. Inside the case was a brand new six-string guitar. It was the most beautiful gift I had ever received. I sat and looked at it and the truth was I was too scared to pick it up and take it from its case. He knew how much I loved music and would play his old guitar every night to me before bed.

I absolutely loved it, and for many years to come it would be with me, lovingly looked after until it had finally seen better days, and the body became too dented and it lost its sound and pitch. To preserve the love and memory of it, I had a kind of little memorial for it and broke it into a thousand pieces and burnt it in the back-yard incinerator, sitting and reflecting on all the joy and good memories it held. I just couldn't bring myself to just toss it in the bin and discard it like that—it meant more to me than anything. I am now on my fourth guitar and I still play, remembering Mr. and Mrs. Lewis and Darrell.

I never went without it when it came to this family and the love they shared. They were wonderfully generous and had showered me with many gifts including socks, tops, shorts, and new school shoes. At the time it seemed to be an every-day thing that families did, but as I grew older, I realised just how special they were and what they had really done for me. No doubt, Mr. and Mrs. Lewis have passed on by now, but I would love to find their son, Darrell and show my thanks for all they did for me. How incredible would it be to stand in-front of each other after fifty years and to think about the many times we shared together, and to talk. I'm sure they must have wondered what became of me.

Several times, I've wondered what my life would have been like, if I had been given that opportunity of being adopted into their family. What my education would have been like, where I would be working, what my family would look like, kids, everything.

If I ever did meet them, I would say this first though:

With my deepest thanks I thank you for your love, and the amazing care you gave me. From the many gifts you shared, the one that I will always remember the most and with the deepest of gratitude was that single piece of paper requesting my adoption. Although it never came about, I will never forget that you did that for me.

My love and thanks always Daryl Te'Nadii.

CHAPTER 33

Then There Were Two

Ten years

In the early months of 1969, Brian moved on to work on a farm not far away. He had reached the age of sixteen, and if employment was offered you could live with the family who owned the farm and learn the skills of a farmer.

The day that Brian left the home was sad, but at the same time, I was happy for him. I would miss sitting and talking, and sitting outside his dorm, listening to him and his mate Jimmy playing music together. Brian had talent far beyond his years and would spend hours humming music. It was as if he was writing songs in his head. He was a left-handed player, so I never got to play his strings, as I was a right-handed player, but it didn't matter. I just loved hearing him play.

I would also miss his support and cheering me on—I could always hear him yelling from the sideline when I played rugby "Run, run faster!". He was proud of me and my sport. I always saw him as a rugby player—he was naturally gifted with the good physique most athletes had to work hard for, with broad shoulders and great strong legs—but he never wanted to go in that direction. It was the music that was in him and that would be his future.

As he walked down the drive towards an old truck, Dale and I looked at each other. We gave a little shrug and waved good-bye. Even though we were brothers, we weren't like other brothers were in families, in homes all around the world. We didn't see each other every day, travel in the car to school together, eat together, or go to social functions and family gatherings with each other. Our time together was brief and haphazard with chance encounters. We were always so busy with home chores, school, and playing with our own group of friends, that even though we had a blood bond, we still didn't have a brotherly bond—not until many years later.

I am proud of him for his love, protection and the life that became so much of mine.

I would still see him at times. He would ride the work motorbike up to the boys' home and wait until the school bus arrived, once a week, for a few short minutes as he whizzed by to check on us. We would talk and tell our stories of how things were if time allowed. I would ask him what his days were like, and if he ever got to go to town. He explained his days started early, seven days a week.

After waking he would be required to go across the paddocks and let the chickens out followed by the pigs. He would have a warm, hot chocolate and then go and herd the cattle with the farmer, ready for milking. After the milking had been done for the morning they would herd the cattle to new paddocks for the day, and clean the sheds down.

On their return, a hot breakfast would be waiting for them made by the farmer's wife and a female worker. The day would see him repairing fences, topping up feed troughs and cleaning sheds. After a full day, they would do the second milking run which would end as the sun went down. Brian would have dinner, then a shower, and a little spare time before it was bedtime, to get as much rest as possible for the next day. This seemed to be his life.

As for going to town, those days were far and few between, as the farm operated seven days a week. He did get Sunday off, however, when he would get his weekly supplies from town, and work on his music, which he dreamed would take him places. I was sure that with his talents that would be the case in time.

He seemed happy but deep down I could see he wanted to move on and he was only at the farm to escape the boys' home and to save to travel and play his music.

CHAPTER 34

Last Days in NZ

Ten years

My last day in New Zealand was spent with the Lewis family. Counting down the hours was hard. I never returned to the boys' home, so all my belongings stayed at the home. In a way, I was hoping Dale would bring some of my belongings as he did return to the boys' home before coming to meet me at the airport in Auckland.

On Thursday, May 29th 1969 the time had come. A white car with a big badge on the side pulled up. It was the same Salvation Army officer who had come a week before with the bad news, and another officer who was female and younger than the male officer.

I stayed outside, watching, as he talked to Mr. and Mrs. Lewis. As he returned to the car, the female officer opened the back door. Mr. Lewis walked to the car with my bag of clothes and my guitar. He placed them into the open boot. I just remember trying to hold on to them with every bit of strength I had, but it wasn't enough, and before long I found myself sitting in the back seat of that car. I saw that Mrs. Lewis had turned away with her hands held across her face. My heart started to beat fast and my tears flowed, as I looked at Darrell who had taken hold of his mother and buried his head into her side. Mr. Lewis just stood motionless, as I waved goodbye, he raised his hand and did the same. That was the last time we would ever see each other.

I am not sure if you have felt the inner linings of your gut being pulled out of you in a single jerk, but that was how it felt to me and it stayed with me all the way to the airport. Dale was at another foster home, where he was also told, but instead of going from his foster family to the airport, he had returned to the boys' home as his foster family only lived fifteen minutes away, whereas mine was more than three hours away.

PART 2

From the Pot into the Fire

CHAPTER 35

Reunited

Eleven years

I was ten as I walked through the Auckland airport on May the 29 1969, with my brother Dale, destined for a new life in a new land.

In only a few hours time, we would be reunited with a woman I'd never met, but who called herself our mother. I knew very little about her, other than she had divorced my biological father eight years earlier and re-married an Australian man by the name of Gerald.

I still don't understand, at that time (or ever), why my mother took back custody of me. All I can say is that from the day I arrived at Essendon Airport in Melbourne, my life got worse, and over the years to follow, it left me more broken and hurt than I ever thought possible.

The flight was like any other flight we take today, with a few exceptions. I was given a first-class tour of the cockpit and a few treats to keep me entertained during the trip. Dale sat looking out the window. I am sure it was all a frighting time for him. I think being picked up and moved in such a short time would scare any child and he was still young, being only one-and-a-half years older than I was.

I played games with the hostesses and went for walks. I think it was the staff's way of keeping Dale and I entertained, and it all seemed different and exciting at the time. On our approach into Australia, I recall looking out of the window and seeing a mass of land that was burnt and black. It was so different to the sight I had seen flying out over NZ, as we flew over lush green lands. I later learned this was the result of the great 1969 Lara fires, which ripped through many acres, destroying anything in their path.

Departing the plane was very scary. I had my only possession— my guitar —in one hand, and I held on tight to my older brother Dale's hand with the other. Halfway across the tarmac, I started to struggle. Dale could see me carrying my guitar but losing my grip on it while juggling my luggage, so he took it from me and carried it the remaining distance.

We were led straight from the tarmac, through the airport to a lounge area under the control of a flight attendant and a security officer. We didn't even get off with the other passengers. The security officer asked us to sit and wait and the hostess said, 'OK boys, I'll leave you here now with the security officer' and she left the room. Dale and I sat and waited a short time before a woman came into the room and introduced herself as social services. She then escorted us to a group of people waiting outside the room, in a hall. There was a tall, thin man standing next to a woman who was very short in stature, and a boy who seemed to be younger than I was.

It was all so unfamiliar to me, but I did recognise one familiar face standing there with them—it was my older sister, Teena. Unbeknownst to us, Teena had been reunited with the family one year before our arrival. It was so nice to have her there and gave me some hope that everything would be ok.

She looked at us and said "Hello" but didn't say anything else, Reflecting back, she was definitely awkward and didn't really know where to look, and knowing what I know now, I assume she was told to stay quiet and stay back until things settled with Dale and me.

The woman, whom I had never seen before in my life, came rushing up to us and grabbed Dale. She started crying and said "I love you, Darrell" while holding him tightly and looking at me. OMG . . . she didn't even know who I was! At the time, it was all too much for me and I held tightly onto Dale's hand, not wanting to let go. Who was this person? Why was she trying to hold onto him? I wondered why she was crying at the same time as she was trying to talk to us? Truth is I felt scared.

The social worker looked at my mother, a little taken aback, and not entirely impressed with the error. She said, "Mrs. Lewis, that's not Darrell you have, it's Dale the older son". Embarrassment, number one, all-round, as the hostesses then also knew this was the first time my mother had seen us in just-under eleven years. She brushed it off and carried on as if it was an Oh well that was a bad moment.

I could only assume she got us mixed up after being told her son Darryl played guitar. Seeing Dale carry it for me, she was confused.

She hugged Dale and me, tears running down her face and she said that she missed me. I had no feelings whatsoever for the strange lady claiming to be my mother. I had no real concept of a mother's role other than what I'd seen and experienced from Mrs. Lewis. I remember thinking to myself watching her gush all over us, "really? How could, or why would you say that when you hadn't met me before, and don't know me at all?" It just made me cringe.

The boy who was with them just looked at us, not knowing what was going on either, from the look of it. Thinking back on that day, in a way I was angry at this woman carrying on, while knowing she had left us to live the life we had, for ten years in the hands of the evil officers and the pain we had to live with daily because of her.

The lady—my mother, and the man who had been standing next to her, completed some paperwork and led Dale and me out to the open-air car park. Between the airport and the car, we were introduced to the little boy whose name was Darren and told that he was eight years old and our little brother. We were in shock. How could this white-skinned boy, who looked nothing like the rest of my brothers and sister, be our brother?

We didn't know where to look, or what to say, and I held onto Dale even more tightly, as he bent down and whispered that things would be ok and he would look after me.

I didn't say much, except "Hi". At twelve-and-a-half years old, Dale was also wary of what was going on and stayed close to my side. As we walked, we looked at each other time and time again.

CHAPTER 36

Down to Earth

Eleven years

It was so weird going from being by myself at The Nest, to finding I had two brothers at Hodderville and a sister at another orphanage in NZ, and then arriving into Australia being reconnected with Teena AND learning I also had a new half-brother!

We arrived at a light-green car in the parking bay. The lady—my mother, then turned to the man who had been accompanying her and introduced him to us as Gerald—her husband. He didn't say a word to us, didn't even acknowledge Dale or me, he simply looked at us and got in the car.

To this day, I still remember that walk from the Airport to the car. All the love she had showered upon us in the terminal vanished. We were directed to the back seat of the vehicle and the atmosphere was cold. We could tell the man (Gerald) had no feelings whatsoever for us. We quickly felt as if we were not wanted there. I sat next to the car door, and Dale sat in the middle with Teena on the other side. My mother sat in the front with Darren in the middle and Gerald driving. It was an awkward trip that seemed to take forever. I didn't think we would ever get to our destination.

I didn't even know where we were going until we began driving away from the airport. Teena began talking to us, but very quietly, explaining that we were going "home" and what it was like to live in a family group. I didn't really listen, to be honest. I was overwhelmed and just kept looking out of the window.

I still remember the landscape on that car trip from the airport so well. There were houses along the roadside that seemed to go on forever. The roads were filled from side to side with every possible vehicle. This soon changed to open green paddocks for a short time and fewer cars on the road, and then, wham bam, the scenery turned into something out a Stephen King novel. Every bit of land was burnt black or brown and whole trees were destroyed.

As we drove through the mess, we were told the area had not long been devastated by a fire that had raged through there, and which had burnt everything in its path. I didn't see any animals or birds, just lots of large burnt-out paddocks, and the odd grey and melted car or truck, as well as houses that looked more like fire pits of old burnt, blacked wood than homes. It was really strange. I'd never seen a fire other than our Guy Fawkes bonfires and definitely hadn't seen such destruction before.

Darren, who had turned around a few times, from the front seat to look at us, held out a bag out to us and offered Dale and me what looked like food. I couldn't be sure of what it was, because we very quickly got to see Gerald's true colours. Before we could accept, he grabbed Darren's hand and pulled it back saying, "I brought that for you to eat, not give it away to others!"

All at once, memories and feelings of Hodderville came back in a rush— the unrest, the ill-treatment, the feelings of dislike from another person who you didn't really know. I felt all the hate that I had for the Salvation Army officer come back at that moment. I had thought that when I left the home, for a new life, that it would be with people who would care. How wrong I was to think there was anyone other than my brothers and sister who would care about me or what happened to me.

My first home upon arriving to live in Australia on the 29th of May 1969.

After a very awkward and almost silent car ride, we pulled up at a little white house across the road from a playground. I say little because the boys' home was so big, it made any house seem small in comparison. I liked the fact there was a playground with an open field, across the road. I was excited that I would have somewhere to play rugby, and also meet other kids, because from what other I'd seen I wasn't that impressed so far. It's not easy to say good-bye to your homeland and to face uncertainty, but I also owned it and was willing to give it a try.

As we got out of the car, an older boy and two girls walked out of the front door of the house. Dale stood silent and I mirrored him, as we wondered who they were. Our mother introduced them to us as Graham, Fairlie, and Heather—they were Gerald's children from his first marriage. "So here we go," I thought; seven kids and two adults under one small roof. The only sibling who wasn't there was Brian, who was back in NZ, working on the farm. I missed him, even though we weren't that close. I asked why Brian hadn't come over with us and got the abrupt reply that he would when he was ready. It wasn't spoken of again. I couldn't contact him and it would be many years before I got to speak to him again.

As we were led inside, we were given a quick tour of the house and our new bedroom which we shared with Darren, and then taken outside to see the yard. There was another building outside and which was called a bungalow—this was Graham, the oldest of Gerald's kids', private bedroom—lucky him.

Back inside, we sat in the lounge room. I didn't say too much, just listened to how the house was run, and the shower and meal arrangements etc. The room was filled with smoke; my mother and Gerald were both smokers and we lived in a cloud of haze from it, every day. My mother's smoked Park Drive cigarettes in a gold-coloured pack, and Gerald's smoked Rothmans, non-filtered in a red package. I got to know these pretty well as, most nights of the week, I would have to go up to the local shops with a hand-written note and money to purchase these, as well as bread or milk. My mother took me up there, soon after I arrived in Australia, to introduce me to the local shopkeeper and to set up an arrangement where the shopkeeper could sell me cigarettes when I came up there with a note from my mother.

I also soon learned Gerald was quite the beer drinker, sitting there without a care, drinking from a glass. He really never spoke to me other than the odd "Behave and listen to your mother" statement here and there. He had a terrible tic of shaking hands and was consistently rubbing his left knee.

Down the track, I learned that Gerald was a retired navy pilot. He had been injured during a combat mission and had taken a bullet to his knee, which was the reason he was no longer in the service. At the time, I believed it, but like so many other things I learned that the lies built on top of lies from my mother and him were unfounded after I spoke to his parents, many years later. They said he was briefly in the Navy but the extended stories were all false. I should have guessed, I suppose, as I didn't see any mementos of his service days; uniforms, pictures, service medals—nothing.

When I arrived in Australia, he was a designer for the Ford Motor Company in Geelong and was highly involved in the design for the XA and XB model Falcons.

Graham, the eldest of Gerald's kids, never said a word. It was like pulling teeth trying to have a conversation with him. In fact, he seemed very reserved, as if he was the kingpin of the family. Gerald praised him endlessly, for being a top student and athlete. I noticed that my mother seemed to have a very close bond with him too. To me, Graham had the appearance of an athlete and he was tall. He had well-built calves with strong legs. He looked after his appearance and stature incredibly well and later in life became a company warrant officer second class in the army, which made sense.

He was naturally sporty, and although he didn't play any contact or ball sports, he competed in athletics and was a swimmer. He could run like the wind and swim like a fish, but he preferred solo sports. He was also very smart and an A-Grade student. He didn't ever seem to have any girlfriends, at least none that came over and if anything he kept his distance from girls, which I saw as odd.

The two girls, Heather and Fairlie seemed nice but didn't say much in the early days. You could tell that Fairlie, the older of the two girls, was definitely the terror out of the three kids, though. Heather was quiet like Graham. I had more to do with Fairlie than the other two, and we became quiet close—she helped me during the time we shared the same roof, which I appreciated.

Day one at my new home with strangers, other than Dale and Teena, was very confusing. People kept talking; asking questions and explaining things such as the address of the house, where we were allowed to play outside, and the direction to the local shops. We were also told that we had to go to the Salvation Army office in the city, the next day, so that the final paperwork could be completed and processed. Luckily for me, Darren asked if we could go and play in the park across the street.

The house stood out from the others, as it was very well maintained and clean, with a green lawn and a single tree in the nature strip and centre of the front yard. The gardens around the edges were very well kept with flowering plants, which gave life and colour to the house. It was just a pity that those happy colours didn't bring their joy to the people in the house, namely my mother, Gerald and others.

As we walked across to the park, Darren pointed out a few houses and named the people who lived in them. These same homes had kids around our age, so over time, I got to know them and play with them. Although they didn't play, or even know what rugby was, they gave it a go, but soon walked away after a few man-sized tackles from Dale and me.

Teena and Dale came over and sat on the swings as I did loops on the high bars. A girl, around my age, came over to the park. She was the sister of a friend of Teena. Her name was Pam Plunket, and she later became a friend of mine. In fact, we spent the next two years in the same class at school.

It was time to go in and wash for dinner. The table only had six chairs, so it was eat and leave to let the others sit for their meal. This was strange to me, as in the home, I sat with many at the same time to eat. I returned to my bedroom and sat on the edge of my bed, which was the lower level of the bunks. I played my guitar softly, wondering what my friends were doing. Suddenly a few tears found their way from my eyes, as I started to realize that all that friendship and more had been taken from me.

Dale came in to see what I was doing. He looked and said, "Let's see how it goes Daryl, it will be OK". Over time that became a statement he wished he had never made. Dale helped me pack our clothes away in the drawers of an old wooden high boy. We got our PJ's on and went to the lounge.

There was only a three-seater couch and two single seats, so it was floor time for me. As we sat watching TV, we were also told about some of the customs and culture of the Australian people. We were told that kids like us, with dark skin, were different to many of the kids around, and that we would be seen as ethnics.

I soonlearned that was true and more, at school where I was bullied for the last part of that remaining year. I also had to attend school on a Saturday morning to learn about the culture of the country. Hardly any of the other kids in that class with me spoke English, as they came from many foreign different countries.

The next day we got up for showers, breakfast, and got into the car to go to the Salvation Army office in Geelong. After a short time of sitting and looking, we got out and walked down the street. The buildings were tall, with people rushing all over the place. We made a quick shopping venture into a store called Myers, to get a few things for school, and it was off home again. At that time, every trip became a new adventure, looking and learning my way around. I also went for many runs, not just to maintain my fitness but also to see the local area with my own eyes.

One of the many great things I had was Dale. Over the weeks that followed, I spent countless nights asking him questions. I think he might have gotten sick of my constant questions—I am one of those people who are naturally curious; I always have been. We spent many days talking about the boys back in New Zealand and how we missed them. The weekend wasn't the same any more, with only Darren to play with, and daily trips to places such as the movie theatre, the beach or other people's places. Dale and I just took it all in. What they saw as family outings, were more of an excuse to show us off and that didn't appeal to me at all.

As the months passed, I soon made friends from around the local area, but not too many, as most of my time, at that point in my life, was spent going to athletics training, rugby training and—for a single year—AFL junior football. I enjoyed AFL – but, truth be told, I'd have played any sport. I didn't play it for long because I was told I was far too rough on the tackles for it, so I had to stick to rugby.

Fortunately, my mother and Gerald weren't short of a quid, as they got incomes from their jobs and also the Australian Child Benefit and the NZ Custodian Payment, for us, which enabled us to play our sports.

CHAPTER 37

Life in Australia

Eleven years

When I arrived in Australia on Thursday the 29th of May 1969, I was told I would soon turn eleven years of age. At that point, in New Zealand, I was in Grade 6 and doing fine with my education. I did not go to school, directly after I arrived in Australia though and, in fact, it wasn't until after my eleventh birth that I finally attended school.

There seemed to be so much that had to be done, before I could attend school, such as uniforms, medicals, school assessments, and orientation days. As part of my first year, which only had five months remaining, I was also going to be required to attend special school activities, on a Saturday morning from 8:00 am to 12:00 noon. The aim was to help children from other countries learn a little about Australian culture and customs. I was surprised that I would be required to do this, but had no choice. I felt it was a waste of time, and we learned bugger all, since the teachers' time was spent on the Czech, Russian, Italians, or Croatian, kids who couldn't speak a word of English.

My educational assessment deemed I would suit going directly to high school and, as such, they asked my mother if I could wait until I turned eleven, as the school felt that having a boy of ten might have raised questions. This was agreed and I started attending Geelong High School on Monday the 16th of June 1969, at the ripe age of eleven years.

My first day was one to remember, firstly Dale and I met with the headmaster. Mr. McFarland, who welcomed Dale and me to the school, with the vice-principal. After a short time of listening, I was separated from Dale, to be taken to my classroom. Every kid will get this if they've changed schools. Walking into a new school, and a new classroom and being small and a Maori definitely ensured I wasn't going to blend in.

You cold have cut the air in the room clean in two pieces. It felt like a thousand eyes were upon me and looking at the boys in the class, I soon realised just how small I was. I learned the kids in this grade were twelve or thirteen years of age, as I was eleven, this didn't do me any favours.

I noticed Pam sitting in the class, which made me feel a little better; but as for the rest, well let's say the first few days were anything but comfortable. I took the time to become friends with as many of the other kids as possible, as I had learned to build numbers at the boys' home.

I became close friends with three boys in the class, in particular, who were also from other countries, so we had that one thing in common. Elea Maroso was one of those boys who had a good understanding of sports, so we hit it off very fast as we showed our personal strengths in PE classes and the school sports' days.

The second boy was George Morrisofe. He was a living freak when it came to sports. He, his older brother George, and the Stefanovic brothers won nearly every possible sports event there was. They were all incredible athletes and one of them—George, became a close friend. Both Elea and George attended the special Saturday classes with me and many other kids.

The third boy was called Minka, I just can't remember his last name, but the one thing I do know is that out of all the other kids in the school, he was the only one shorter than I was. Our friendship grew and soon I found myself having lunch at his house every day of the week, since he just lived up the road. We'd race up there during lunchtime, for the most incredible lunch.

I didn't have that luxury of school lunch, as neither my Mother nor Gerald ever made school lunches for me. I was told to get it myself, but every time I tried to, I would get into trouble for taking food that was apparently for Gerald's kids and was called a thief. In the end, I had enough of it and gave up, drinking water at school or I would take a piece of fruit from the neighbours' trees when it was in season.

Minka's mother and father were just amazing, and so supportive of all three children living under their roof. Minka had told them I didn't have lunch food, which might be the reason he always said his mother had cooked lunch for me as well. Wow, the food was hard to take in at first, but within days I fell in love with the amazing taste and flavours. It was typical Russian food, from a family that was still so generous, even after the battles that they had faced just to get out of their country and to escape to Australia, because of wars. They were awesome times and funny! Minka's parents didn't speak English, or it was restricted to "Hello", "Goodbye" and "Eat Dawal!"—that was the way they said my name, it used to crack me up.

Over time I made many more friends, who lived locally to my home and these would be the ones I started to spend more time with on the weekends, such as Stephen Purnell, Tony Rarpertony, and a girl called Angela Robinson. Stephen was the son of a golden-gloves boxer from England, so he liked to spar in the yard with gloves. I seemed to be a challenge, as I never took a punch lightly, rather I would throw two in return. We quickly built up a bond and respect for each other.

Sadly, I had to walk away from this friendship, after Stephen brutally bashed another boy, for personal reasons, and that boy took his own life less than four hours later. This shocked the community and caused Stephen's family to pack up and move. We never found out where. It was a horrible time.

Raps, as I called him, was a loose goose. He had a canny knack of getting into trouble and me with him! His parents were from Poland and hard workers. Raps got whatever he wanted, always taking advantage of his Dad's, love which used to upset me at time. He was so disrespectful and expected everything on a silver platter. I used to pull him up on it all the time, but it made no difference. He had two sisters, Maria, older by a year and Victoria, younger by a year, and they were total opposites.

Both girls were incredibly attractive, with blonde hair, blue eyes and fully-sculptured figures, well ahead of time, which everyone—well the boys at school—admired. To their credit they never played on their beauty, rather they just wanted to be normal girls. We had many great times going bowling, to the beach and the local pool and just hanging out. Mind you the pool and beach days did put a smile on my face.

Years later in life, Raps found me, only to tell me he had been involved in a car accident and to relieve his pain and suffering he was required to take medication. This medication had really affected him on a mental level. I took the time to visit him as much as I could around work, but it was very hard to sit with his parents and talk to Raps about the old days, and what he was doing in life. He had been more badly affected than I had first thought, and it left him impaired in many ways, but mostly mentally. He would forget conversations and revisit times we shared over and over. Raps' sister, Maria, told me that day, that they were going to place him in care, at Grace McKellar hospital for the mentally disabled. I felt so gutted when she told me and the only thing I could do was talk with him and leave knowing that would be our last day together.

Angela was one in a million, at that time in my life. She was incredibly attractive and physically well-presented, also ahead of her years as a teenage woman, but her friendship was always that and nothing more. We built a unity of trust and mateship that I thought only boys had. Angie, as I called her, did not feel comfortable with other girls, mind you they all wanted to be part of her life. She was smart, and built a solid friendship with all and was always ready to have fun; even if it was boy-fun, such as kicking the ball, climbing trees, and just wrestling around. What's she is doing today? I have no idea, I only hope she is happy and still the girl I knew as my friend.

The teachers were what I expected, over-bearing and never wrong, or so they thought. For the first five months, my journey to school was crazy, until I got a bike for Christmas, that year. Until then, I was dinked[2] by friends, Pam, her older sister Sheryl, or my sister Teena.

It was about 3.6 km to school, so not a hard ride. After school, I would run home as extra training for my rugby and athletics. Pam would come over to my home, just to make sure I made it back ok. She was a great friend and very pretty, but I needed a friend, not a "girlfriend", if that's what it is called, and that upset her a bit when I told her. Happily, we stayed friends, which was good.

Most of my spare time, when I had it, was spent training and playing rugby for Geelong. The club was small, but dedicated, with mostly away-games. My coach, Derick Costello, was a full-time police officer. He had respect for all the team players. I did try to convince some of my school classmates to come along and learn the game but they preferred AFL.

---

2   Dink: Australian slang for to give someone a lift on your bike.

The hardest part of wanting to be a player for the rugby team was that I had to use my weekly pocket money to catch the bus or run to the fields, which were around 10.4 km away. The run home from school, at just 3.6 km, was a whole lot different to running home 10 km after a rugby game on eleven-year-old legs, that's for sure!

I decided to bus it, so I only needed to run and walk home on a few occasions. My mother or Gerald never took me to training or attended any games I played.

In fact, I got no support in anything I did. They only spent their time with Graham and Darren with sports. I'm not going to lie, it was upsetting at times. I'm not a jealous person and I didn't feel like a victim, but it was more the injustice that bothered me than anything else. But there is a saying that goes, the proof is in the pudding, and I was that pudding. In the years that followed, I became the most successful family member in sports.

I'm not saying that to blow wind up my own butt, but I do have to say I have a great sense of pride about that. After no support, and having to cover all of my own costs; after making my own way there and back and weathering the constant barrage of emotional abuse, telling that I would never make a good athlete in any sport, was bloody hard work I'll tell you. Well, how's this Mother and Gerald? The son you didn't believe in, and belittled and abused, did ok without your help thanks . . . I went on to represent Australia, not once but TWICE and won TWO gold medals as well.

I didn't stop there. I won another 18 athletic titles in cross country and marathons, 9 swimming titles, rugby and touch Football awards, the North Queensland Iron Man in 1989 and 29 more international, national, state and regional titles.

How's that for a NO hoper son?

Ironically, my mother had married a man named Gerald Lewis, which was the same last name as my host family in New Zealand. When I arrived in Australia I was taken to Australian Customs and the Court, where my name was changed from Tenadii to Lewis, on my passport and civil documents. I didn't want to take Gerald's last name: I saw it as disrespectful of my NZ Lewis family. In 1978, at the age of eighteen, I went back to the courts and had my name changed back to the original family heritage name I had: Darrell Keith Tumori. These days, I use and am known as, Daryl Keith Te'Nadii with an apostrophe and capital N as I found out that was how it was written on my father and grandfather's birth certificates.

CHAPTER 38

Mother

Twelve years

Going back in thought, I didn't know much about this woman who was my biological mother. However, it wasn't long after I met her that she showed all the signs of being a selfish person, who didn't care about anyone other than herself and the way she looked, or how she was seen by others. I was already beginning not to like her.

My mother was a very short and stocky woman some thirty-five years of age when I was reunited with her. She had middle-length hair, was always well dressed, and wore far too much cheap and nasty perfume. Five days a week, she worked as a cook/staff member at Geelong Grammar School. I didn't know much about her job or that place. I do recall asking what it took to be a student there, only to be cut down, and told I would never be good enough for a school like that. Ironically in addition to smashing it in sport, I too am the only child from both my mother's side and Gerald's side, to have a degree!!! I bet she loved digesting that!

Everyone (including me), really wants to think well of and be proud of their mother. But the truth is my mother was just all bad. She was one of those people who gained power by pushing others down. She LOVED seeing people fail and couldn't stand anyone being better than her, or Graham my step-brother—for some very strange reason she had a real fascination with him.

She was like a smiling assassin. She'd get to know as much about you as she could, but not to get to know you. It was to use whatever she could against you, or to use as a base for a personal attack. She revelled in other people's misfortunes and weaknesses. She was a disgusting person—cruel, selfish, cunning, manipulative, and narcissistic and she didn't give a rat's ass if she hurt you. She would merely turn and shrug her shoulders as if to say 'Oh well'

Because she was incredibly manipulative, she could turn absolutely anything at all in a scenario where she was the victim and you were the bad guy. It was like a sport to her. She would take great delight in humiliating the hell out of me, in front of my new friends or anyone, she didn't care and had no shame. She loved an opportunity to pick out something you said or did, just to be able to get that release of having a shot at you, so she could get what she had been busting to say to you out of her system.

She would manipulate people in ways they wouldn't see coming, and worse wouldn't know about for years to follow. I've come across handfuls of people she has told that I wanted nothing to do with them! No wonder some of my letters went unanswered. I wondered why people, with whom I'd tried to get in contact, would never return my calls. No wonder when my mother had been running around telling everyone I hated them! She really was a piece of work.

She and Gerald would scrimp and save on essentials, such as food, in all sorts of ways, in favour of their weekend partying and grog. My mother would bring home the leftover food from the Grammar School, where she worked, in alfoil trays or plastic containers, five days a week. Because it was live-in accommodation there, meals were provided and she'd lop all the leftovers into a tray or container and bring it home to feed us. It was horrible. A chaotic mess of cold, often unrecognisable food that was tasteless. There was often a lunch stew that looked like a quagmire of mud with a few vegies through in. It was ghastly. The potatoes would have been boiled to death so even the starch had escaped. However, she always reminded me how lucky we were to have food even this good, saying many kids around the world had no food for days.

I had to wonder where all their income went and what they did with it, because the house we lived in was a government-supported army house, so the rent was very low compared to normal families' rents. They had multiple benefits coming in from government agencies, and their two jobs, but that didn't stop them from charging me on board at the age of thirteen. My pocket money most weeks was for doing the lawns, cleaning the house, and whatever my mother asked me to do and I was given around 10 cents a week for it.

My mother's weekends were spent with friends, day and night, and Darren and I would be left to find food wherever we could, on those nights or days that she enjoyed her time, eating and drinking at the local pubs with other men and women. Gerald would go out for a while, but soon tired of it and would come home early.

It was pretty dysfunctional, to say the least, living as we did with a lot of strange things. One was the segregation; Gerald's kids had a different set of rules to us and got what they wanted. We got what we needed, if that. Every morning was a joke, and you never knew how you were getting to school. It was pandemonium with one bathroom and seven people sharing. I can't ever recall going to a grocery shop to do a weekly shop, we only ever visited the corner store, each Monday.

Most of the time, Dale and I drifted along, as if we didn't exist. On the rare occasion, she'd have a change of heart, and give us a cuddle, it was awkward and lasted a nano-second. She saved what she had the capacity for and showered Graham and Darren with all the love, kisses, and attention. Dale being Dale, pushed it to the side saying, "Mate, we will be out of this house soon. Don't worry about what they do. Our mother is a liar and never had any intention of wanting us back".

We were a dollar sign for her to claim the government entitlements until each of us reached sixteen. I didn't understand back then, but Dale was right as always. What really annoyed me was that I later learned from Gerald that she continued to claim those entitlements for two more years, after I was left to fend for myself out on the street, eating out of garbage bins and off people's fruit trees.

Dale was always so relaxed. He coped with it better than I did by just taking it all in his stride and fobbing it off. He used to say to me "Oh well, if you don't like it find somewhere else, Brother". He never cared the way I did about what was happening. He just wanted to end the few years he had with this family and move on. It used to upset me no end, when he said that I had been lost for years and without him, I would be lost again. If my big brother Brian had been around, it would have been different though! He would have had a completely different reaction, and he would have been like "If you do that again, I'll frickin' hit you!" ha ha ha ha—chalk and cheese those two!

You could tell my mother wasn't right. I got a really uneasy feeling early on in the piece, watching her cuddle Graham and the way she looked at him and interacted with him. Years of being in an abusive home, and watching the officers; I knew what she was doing. She was grooming Graham and it made me sick to my stomach, and angry! Watching her also brought up every bad memory I had and I burned. Slowly she was transforming Graham into what she wanted in every way, and many years later this would be proven to be true.

I felt sorry for Graham, he had no self-control. He couldn't manage his own life, ever, so she did. She manipulated him until he sat around the house lost and lonely, with only a few friends, no girlfriend and nothing much outside of that house.

My mother was good at her craft. I later learned, from her family, that she was no stranger to control, deception, and destroying other people's lives. Her wave of manipulation and demolition began at an early age and she used, intimidated, and strong-armed her own sisters, lying to and thieving from them. She never stopped. She would even coerce us, boys, out of the little pocket money we had, with promises to pay it back. We'd fall into her trap time and time again, believing she would pay it back, but she of course never did; not once.

I don't know if it was because I was gullible or just had a big heart, but I kept on falling for her lies. I guess I kept hoping she would change. This from a woman, who pulled on a Salvation Army uniform at weekends, and became part of the very same congregation that had abused her boys for years and years. It defies belief, doesn't it?

She knew how to work people, and she had a super sweet side of her that I'll admit we didn't see much of. However, when we did, she could be charming and you would feel so happy! I remember those occasions and thinking to myself "Oh my God! She's changed!" It was a euphoric feeling of being wanted, loved and being 'seen', but each time it was short-lived and then you went back to feeling like her archenemy again, brushed aside so that she could continue living her dream.

I remember that my Aunty Fay, who didn't like her name so went by the name Rhonda, and June, my other aunty, never visited my mother in Australia. In fact, years later when I connected with them, they told me they didn't like my mother, and kept themselves estranged from her because of all her lies and deceit.

CHAPTER 39

Disclosure

Twelve years

Not long after being in my mother's care, I mentioned what I had gone through and what I had seen, while in the boys' home under the care of The Salvation Army to my mother. After building up the courage to speak to her, I went to Dale and talked to him about what I wanted to do and asked him to come with me to speak to her as well, but he simply said "No… I don't want any more hurt… leave it in New Zealand Darrell".

I was shocked. I had amped myself up to get our story out there and was mad. He was off hanging out with his older mates, in the street or the neighbourhood and I was home with Darren, so I guess I had a bit more time on my hands to sit, reflect, and get angrier about it. I had to go into this battle on my own.

I plucked up the courage and went into her bedroom one night to talk to her. She was lying in bed reading, when I walked in and asked her if I could speak to her. She said yes and I sat on the end of her bed and began. Here I was thinking that finally, the truth would come out, and our abusers would be brought to justice and would pay for their crimes against us. I told her what had happened over in NZ at Hodderville and that both Brian and Dale were also beaten and sexually assaulted.

I think she was shocked, initially, and unprepared as she probably thought it was a talk about what happened at school that day. However, nothing could prepare me for what happened next . . . she sat bolt upright and I could see straight away she was angry. She stiffened and threw her book down before scoffing at me. Then, she leaned in, swung her hand back, and hit me square across the face. She called me a liar, and said I was going to hell putting that on the church.

For reasons I didn't work out until later on, two days my mother announced, out of the blue, that she had arranged a visit to the Salvation Army in Geelong. I felt sick immediately that she was sending me back to the orphanage, which wasn't a stretch because she always threatened us with it if we misbehaved. I now know that it was my mother being her usual narcissistic, evil self and just wanting to prove a point while humiliating me.

The Salvation Army officer my mother took me to see just sat and listened to me as I poured out my story about how I had been treated. I explained the many times I had been sexually assaulted, beaten to near-death, and scared in every possible way. All the time my mother just nodded her head, interrupting and calling me a liar and saying that I would go to hell. The Salvation Army officer sat silent for the entire time I talked.

After I had finished recounting what I had seen, heard, and experienced, he looked at me and then got up and walked out of the room. My mother was in tears and started screaming and calling me a liar, and the devil of my father's reborn . . .whatever that meant. Shortly afterwards, the officer came back into the room and asked my mother to go with him. I really thought my problems would finally be seen and realised and that someone had not only listened but believed them. I was soon to learn otherwise.

They both came back into the room after a few minutes and sat looking at me. Then, my mother said, "Daryl, you need to listen to the Salvation Army officer". He started out by saying, "Daryl, kids have amazing dreams and imaginations and many times they don't see or hear things clearly". He went on to say, "It's hard to imagine any person doing the things you have mentioned, let alone a member of the Salvation Army". It was at that point, that I noticed that my mouth was open in disbelief and I felt my heart drop like a cannon ball to the floor. As he continued to speak, I felt as if he had kicked me right in the guts. A slow, deep feeling of wanting to be sick began flowing through my stomach.

He said my lies would get me into trouble, and that the only thing that would come from all of this was being returned to a boy's home for my remaining adolescent years. My mother then came back into the conversation saying she did not want me and my lies in her home, or around the other kids. How could she believe this officer over her own son? I thought I could at least trust her with this! I began to try to speak only to be shut down by my mother, who immediately said "You don't know what you're talking about and God will send you to hell for lying."

Afterwards, the Salvation Army officer asked me to come to church every Sunday and pray for forgiveness. I looked at him deeply, burning the truth into his soul without saying another word. It would be the last time I ever saw him, or ever walked into a Salvation Army service that was not a funeral, to this day.

They had both completely destroyed my trust in the system, and my hope that I would get justice and overcome the pain I had lived with in the boys' home. My belief that they would help me move on had been absolutely eroded.

Dale came back from his mates' place to see me sitting in my bedroom devastated and asked what happened. After telling him, he said very calmly, "I told you brother, let it go". Tears and more tears; anger and pain. Those were the only things I felt, as I realised he, my brother had given up and left me all alone. I was totally ripped apart, knowing my own brother had left me to get the truth out there all by myself.

At times I wished I had left it alone, I wished I could, but I've found out over the years that's not me. I just have to stand up and look for whatever hope I can find.

After that I spoke about the many bashings and assaults we faced many times, while at the home, and each time my mother would turn around and yell at me, "You're just like your father . . . lies and more lies!". I gave up trying to talk to her about the problems, I faced, and that I was struggling to cope with. If she had only believed me then, and reported it to the authorities, maybe—just maybe—many of the abusers would have been removed from the orphanages and hundreds more children might have been saved and a monumental complaint avoided.

Just for the record, and something I found out later in life. My mother was heavily involved with the Salvation Army and to this day is a registered officer with them in Australia. Maybe that's the reason she didn't believe me and is so dysfunctional. If they protected and covered up the abuse their officers carried out, then why wouldn't they filter that message through to their other officers?

All I know is, I suffered in the hands of that officer, and under the care of the Salvation Army, without reason, and they all had a hand in it.

CHAPTER 40

The Boxing Bag

Thirteen years

It didn't take us long to figure out Gerald didn't want anything to do with us. In fact, he mostly went out of his way to avoid us, unless he got drunk and decided to use me as a punching bag.

At times I wondered why it was only me and not Dale, as well? Maybe it was because Dale just kept as quiet as he could, or stayed away from the house with friends, knowing that in just months he would leave and escape the house forever.

He had been telling me about his secret plan of taking off with his mates- they planned to hit the road; travelling Australian, picking fruit and vegies, and working their way around the country on a year-long holiday. Finally, the day came, and he announced to my mother that he was moving on. She was far from happy and asked him why. Dale said that he just could not live there anymore. Who could blame him?

Dale was a blewer eh. He would ask questions first, but he did not back down when it came to hitting back and Gerald was scared stiff of him. He would laugh Gerald's threats off and say, 'Yeah ok, bring it on then!' Gerald never took him up on it. Dale was a lot taller. At almost six-foot, even at fifteen, so Gerald let him be and my mother did too, on that day. There was not a lot she could do to stop him from going.

What did surprise me before he left was that Dale decided to make and incredible gesture he proudly got a tattoo. He was underage, so how he did it was a mystery. All I remember was hearing our mother yelling at him for getting it. I think it was one of the few times he ever backed down. As crazy as it was, the tattoo read "MUM" and it was set into a background of a heart and roses. I'll never understand that one.

She was oblivious to his dedication to her, and all she could do was scream and tell him to get it removed. I think that was the final straw for him and he lost patience with her. In later years he had another piece of art applied over the reminder of that day and her selfish rant.

I guess that being small, I was the weak link and an easy target for Gerald. We had only been in Australia for a short time, maybe four months, when Gerald first hit me. I was in the back shed with Darren. We had found a lighter on the railing inside the shed. Darren said it belonged to Fairlie and that she would sneak out at night to have a smoke, because she was not allowed to smoke in front of her father.

Kids being kids, we started to flick the lighter for fun, but Gerald walked around and saw what we were doing. Darren was holding the lighter, as we looked up. Gerald looked at him, and then me and told Darren to go inside, as I stood there. I knew it was on and that I was about to get a beating.

Trying to explain that we found it on the shelf was a waste of time as he punched me clean in the face. The force was more than I expected, and I hit the back wall of the shed. He seethed, spraying words at me as he punched me until he had enough.

After just a few months, I was back to being beaten for no bloody reason at all! He left me lying there in pain and as he walked away you could tell he was still incredibly angry. I hobbled back to my room where Darren was sitting. He looked at me and started to cry. All he could do was say, over and over again, was "I am so sorry".

At the time, I could not understand why Gerald was so bitter and angry, but it wasn't long before the reason came to light—my Mother. I have no idea why Gerald married her, but his rage and ultimately the beltings I received from him, stemmed from the hurt, anger and frustration he felt at my Mother. Every weekend, she would do herself up, like a tart, dressed in short, revealing tops and a skirt and with long boots to her knees. Then she went out with her friends and other men leaving us, and often Gerald, at home.

In his own way, Gerald was a ticking time-bomb for sure, but he did not deserve the crap my mother handed out to him. We would be in bed and sound asleep when my mother returned home, drunk, most Friday and Saturday nights. Then she would throw one of her late-night parties, which were always loud, and rarely finished without arguments and fights.

Gerald just sat in his favourite chair, with a bottle of beer, cigs, and an ashtray, watching the party around him, and drinking himself numb to blur the sight, I guess, of my mother's male friends groping her, flirting with her and later on sleeping with her. They were all grubs. A group of total lost causes, who used our home and my mother, and showed a total disrespect for Gerald and us kids.

I hated realising, on Friday that the weekend was coming and knowing what would follow. As he always did, Graham would hide in his room, and Fairlie and Heather would stay out all night, while Teena just slept the night away. Dale would be with friends, and Darren and I would hang in our room. I played the guitar and he played with his cars; both of us waiting for the house to be safe enough to sleep, the people to leave at the end of the night, or just until we couldn't keep our eyes open anymore.

The parties would go on for hours, and not being a solid sleeper anyway because of my Hodderville horror nights, it was hard to get used to the sounds of a different kind. Eventually, it became a regular thing for us, and we all got used to it.

My mother was a very superficial person; it was all about looks and how others saw her. She did not care about anything, or anyone, other than who she was partying with at the time. As silent as he was, Gerald always seemed afraid of men his size and never had the courage to stand up to them. So he sat and got drunker and drunker to the point he would pass out.

One night, I sadly and stupidly went to look for my mother after the party was over. It was kind of my habit to look in after the party ended to see if she'd made it to bed safely, instead of lying, drunk on the floor, as she did all too often. Gerald was drunk and sleeping in his seat. My mother was naked on her bed with Rod Tilly, a loser she and the others spent time with on weekends. What they were doing is not hard to imagine, at least to me, and it was a bloody disgrace.

She didn't see me at the time, and to this day she never knew what I had witnessed. But, the image burned a hole in my brain, that's for sure. I wished I'd never seen it. It is not something a young boy wants to remember about his mother.

On weekends during the day, we kids would have to attend our mother's outings to her friends' houses, for a BBQ or get-togethers, which were boring no end, for us. Even Gerald did not like going to them, and the older kids made every excuse under the sun to get out of going. Teena and Dale became so creative with their reasons for not going, they virtually never went to any outings. It used to make me mad and I wished I could escape them, too. Instead, Darren and I put up with it and entertained ourselves.

Over time, I could see Gerald was becoming like a volcano about to erupt, with my Mother's excessive partying most weekends. He became a full-alcoholic and increasingly abusive; lashing out at me, the smallest and easiest target, because he could not get to my Mother. He was scared Dale would dob him back, and Darren was too young. My mother would have belted, Gerald if he had put his hands on her. He was fond of Teena, in all the wrong ways, and it was sickening to watch him get drunk at the parties and grope at her. As for Graham; well, he was a protected species. Then there was me; the human boxing bag for a weak adult man.

I realised that Gerald was scared of what the men, who came to our house, would do to him if they found out he had hit or bashed my mother, since most of them were sleeping with her or in love with her. Not taking it out on her, drove him mad to the point where he was constantly wound up with rage, anger, frustration and humiliation. He either drank himself to numb it or belted me. There did not seem to be any in-between.

It was a broken family. The parents left the kids to fend for themselves mostly, and there was no lunch for Dale or me any day (if we took any, we were called thieves). Weekends were a constant procession of drunk, mean, and nasty people, who took over our home. You never felt safe and you always felt anxious, hungry and on edge. I remember my mother telling Rod Tilly that I wanted to be a sports person, only to watch them both laugh after she said it. Any hope I had sunk deep into nowhere-land, as they kicked, stomped and squashed my dreams.

There was nothing healthy about living under the same roof as my mother and Gerald. Weekdays were chaotic, getting to school, and weekends were chaotic, with streams of drunken asses passing throughout our house. It was a real challenge living in a home that was half Brady Bunch and half nightclub. It was taxing, even though I had lived with thirty to forty other kids for ten years as well as suffered the abuse. Still, I battled with the lack of structure, routine and love. It was abuse, just a different kind.

In New Zealand, I accepted the abuse, knowing it would come to an end eventually. It was also shared amongst many and at times, not as painful. In Australia, I had no chance. The damage started and never stopped, with a constant barrage of physical abuse from Gerald and emotional and verbal abuse from my mother. There was little reprieve on any day.

I got belted for just being alive!

One day Darren and I found an old table knife in the back shed, the kind that had a pearl handle. It was rusty and dirty, but like anything, we found we could make a game out of it. We decided to play 'stretch', a game where you throw the knife into the ground, and the person you are playing with has to stretch out to the mark with their leg. If they fall over the game is over, and you win.

Gerald must have been dirty about something my mother had done, or who knows what, as he walked outside and saw us playing. He told Darren to go inside and wait for him, he then turned around and said to me, "You did this . . . taking cutlery from the kitchen to play with!". I tried to explain that we had found the knife in the back shed, and that it was old, but he was not having a bar of it. Before I even got the chance to finish, he had punched me in the head, and I went flying across the yard. He came after me where I had landed and began kicking into me, before he grabbed me around the throat and lifted me off the ground, yelling and calling me every name under the sun.

Darren came running out and started shouting at him to stop, yelling out that he had found the knife in the shed, but Gerald had already vented his rage at me and was done. He just looked at me and said, "That's a reminder of what will happen if you do the wrong thing". Darren sat down next to me, as my eye swelled up with another black eye on the way, together with sore and bruised ribs. Disgusted, he turned and told his father to go away. I was so sick of being a punching bag for grown men. I had had enough.

A few months later, Darren and I were playing in the yard. My Mother had been smoking out the back and had dropped her glow-mesh lighter on the ground as she went back inside. Its sequined gold and metal cover sparkled in the light and caught my eye. I picked it up, which was a mistake. I should have just left it where it lay, given the experiences I had already had, but I didn't, I picked it up and flicked it to see the flame, just as Gerald walked outside. I didn't have luck did I? He called me a little thief and punched me, sending me to the ground. The hit hurt like hell and cut my lip.

Darren was yelling blue murder, but it was all too late, Gerald was in full swing and way out of control, laying into me. I walked inside to clean myself up but I had arrived at the point of no return. I was done being hit. Still tiny at thirteen years of age, I mustered the strength of a man, and walked into the lounge where Gerald was sitting drinking his beer.

Positioning myself near the door, in case he came at me, I looked squarely at him and said, "You had better enjoy the times beating me up, because when I grow up, I am going to give it all back to you. One day I will be older, bigger, and someone you will be scared of. You are going to feel what it's like to be beaten without reason, and you are going to feel the pain I felt from you, and you will wish you had never hit me". I finished, turned, and walked away.

That was the last time he hit me. The truth was that until the day he told me to get out, he never spoke to me again. I think he realised I was done and had had enough.

CHAPTER 41

Blended and Broken

Thirteen years

It became a daily occurrence to have to explain to others how our family was.

Physically, the two families looked like chalk and cheese. My side was olive-skinned, with thick, dark hair, and we were lean, fit and good looking (I am sure someone had to think so ha ha). Gerald's side of the family had pale skin, freckles red and brown hair and body shapes in all directions.

The differences between the two families didn't stop on the physical side. Gerald's kids literally got everything including new clothes, pocket money at will and love. Yes . . . the weekly pocket money, that's another point. The kids from Gerald's side got weekly pocket money—normally on a Monday morning—so that they could enjoy the week. I could not say how much, but Darren and his allowance was another thing. He got pocket money and also a few bobs (about 20 cents) every morning as well. Gerald would always say the same thing, as he handed Darren the money, Don't forget to pay the school your fees". Really; did he think I was that silly at that age? What cracked me up was that Darren would walk out the door with me and say, "Daryl, see you at the shops after school" and he would buy me a lolly.

That was another reason we become so close. If Gerald had known that, he would have hit the roof and wouldn't have given Darren a cent more. For whatever reason, he didn't want us to have anything to do with each other, and limited our contact as much as possible, even going so far as to ensure Darren attended another school. Anything to keep Darren away from me, as if I was some kind of leper.

Teena—love her!—was boozy, sleazy Gerald's pet and he often gave her a little more to spend each week. Dale was just like me and even didn't bother asking. We had learned from the past that we wouldn't get it anyway, so gave up asking unless it was to pay for a school excursion. We still missed them in droves, as my mother said they couldn't afford to pay for them. The truth was that their party weekends took precedence, so we just had to miss out.

There were so many shitty horrible times and things I hated growing up. One handed me downs—from leftover lunches to second-hand clothes—we rarely had anything new at all. My mother would come home from time to time with a 'surprise'; a new piece of clothing straight from the Salvation Army bin; the smell was always a dead giveaway. I would know that smell anywhere!

As bad as some of them looked (and smelt), I still focused on how lucky I was to get anything at all, considering that I never got a thing at the boys' home. My local friends would say things, but also understood my circumstances, so didn't go too hard on me. I remember one year my mother brought me home a pair of pants and they truly looked like the Joker from Batman! I was forced to wear them, along with a brought home T-shirt that was twice my size.

When it came to Christmas and Easter, Dale and I both got the same things, always. Teena got her things and the other three kids got totally different things, again. Even though I hated the hand-me-downs, in many ways I was still grateful for them, as I had lived with nothing in the past. In the end, I gave up caring.

Upon entering our new home in Australia with our mother, Dale and I were told we would have chores to do which didn't worry us in the slightest since we were both very used to doing lots of chores each day. What did annoy us was that along with Teena, we got all of the chores. Not once did I see Gerald's kids do any of the house cleaning, mowing the lawn, or washing the car, yet they got the weekly pocket money and we never saw a dime.

It became evident, we were really only brought over from NZ to be their slaves, and of course, so they could get the government childcare awards that were paid to them weekly. There were many times I hoped to go out for the day with friends, only to be told… "Sorry, I have already given your brothers or sisters pocket money (meaning Graham, Darren, Fairlie, and Heather) and I can't afford to pay for everyone's fun". It really was appalling.

That was life under my mother's roof. It was a far cry from that of Mr. and Mrs. Lewis, in New Zealand. I didn't complain, even though it sometimes made me feel upset or annoyed, because I never got any of those things in the orphanage anyway. I was used to doing jobs without rewards.

Between my younger half-brother, Darren, who didn't ask for anything but who still got everything from Gerald, and my older step-brother, Graham, who seemed to get whatever he wanted from my mother, Dale and I lucked out. We did have the occasional outing to the movies, and once we went camping, but those special activities were done as a family. I didn't dwell on it though, because of all the things I had, which were few, I had my guitar and rugby ball. The two prized possessions that lit up my soul and gave me great peace of mind.

It was so cool, knowing I could close the bedroom door against that chaotic world outside, and pluck the strings on my guitar, making sweet music and songs to fill in the time. I would listen to the radio for hours and try to play the songs I'd heard by ear. I never learnt how to read music.

I'd strum away until I could replicate each and every one of those notes of my favourite songs. I could forget about my mother saying there was no leftover money, after they'd paid for Graham's sporting career—which never come about by the way—and Darren's toys, such as a dirt bike at ten years, of age.

Then there was my rugby ball! I would spend as much time as I could, running in the paddock across the road, practising ghost football tackles and drills, as I did playing my guitar. It served me well in the end. I still strum away at my guitar and play with songs at sixty-two years of age. Whereas all the training and money spent on Graham and Darren's sports did bugger all for them, me, who didn't have any sports money given by them, later went on to represent Australia twice; and both times self-funded.

The two families were poles apart. Gerald's kids came home clean with books tucked under their arms, while Dale and I would come home with scraped or bleeding knees, grass-stained, muddy, and wet. You name it! Did we get into trouble? Oh yeah, you bet we did! Were we in our element doing it? Always!

I felt so disrespectful asking for a little pocket money that I gave up asking, deciding instead to help a mate from school called Tony Rapper (Raps) who was mowing laws to earn some money. I would borrow his spare lawn mower to cut some lawns too, and make a few dollars on weekends and after school except for rugby days.

There were times when I needed a little help to pay for a school event and when I did ask, my mother would hit the roof! I would be told things such as, you are just like your father, un-grateful and selfish. We let you leave home chores to go push a lawn mower around to earn money, only for you to ask for more!

By the time I turned thirteen I was mostly paying my own way. I saved up enough to buy the mower I had been borrowing off Tony and started working for myself doing around 6 hours of work a week. My clients paid 15 cents for the front nature strip, and 25 cents for the front yard. I never did the backyards because the first and last one I did, a dog who was in the backyard jumped me and bit me. I always told everyone from then on, no backyards due to the number of vicious dogs wandering around in them. I used to combine the nature strip and front yard for a special of 30 cents. I had on average 10-12 clients a week which gave me about $3.80 a week or thereabouts to put into my own personal bank which I had begged my mother every other day to open up for me since I was under aged.

I didn't keep a lot of money on hand, I put most of it in the bank, but I always had enough on me to give to Dale when he hit me up for a bob or two on the few occasions.

I tried and actually did trust this lady time and time again only for it to be broken as many times as I trusted her. God that woman could lie sleeping. She was pathological.

It wasn't only the material things we got the short end of the stick—for me the hardest part was the lack of affection.

Growing up, I always wondered what my mother was like. As with any child, you read story books where the mother and father are loving, showering their kids with kisses and cuddles, and in some way even knowing our mother didn't want us, I still hoped I too would experience a mother's love.

It never came.

I gave her every chance in the hope she had changed and also in the hope that finally I would be accepted by her, loved by her and every time I did it ended badly.

Such a bad move on my part still brings tears to my eyes even now. So sad.

CHAPTER 42

Unravelled

Thirteen years

The year I turned thirteen, all hell broke loose, and the family unravelled even more than it already had, as the separation in the family began. Lying in bed one night it hit me how messed up and damaged my mother really was. The older I got, the clearer it became; she was a train wreck and she destroyed everything in her path.

Some things just didn't make sense, at times, when I was younger. It was consistently challenging, trying to fit into such a dysfunctional family, who didn't know you or what you had been through (and didn't want to) because of your own issues.

Our mother would walk into our bedroom to say good night to Dale, Darren and myself, and would then walk outside to the bungalow to say goodnight to Graham, who was around sixteen or seventeen years of age, at the time. It always seemed strange to me that my mother spent more time with Graham than her husband or any of the other kids. Gerald would sit in the lounge watching TV, and fall into a drunken slumber, and when my mother was not entertaining her grubby friends, she would be out in the bungalow in her stepson's room.

One night, after about six months of hearing her and Graham talking and giggling most nights, it got the better of me. I pretended I needed to go to the toilet, which was also out the back next to the bungalow. I slipped out of the room, as Dale and Darren were falling asleep and snuck out the back door, as if I was heading for the toilet. I changed course at the last minute and edged toward the bungalow door instead. I could hear my mother talking and giggling, again, and it was very clear to me that she was building a relationship with her husband's son, a boy. It wasn't long after that Graham was the first of the kids to leave. He joined the army and I didn't see him again, until many years later, after I decided to let my children visit their grandmother.

Teena left home to be with her boyfriend Neil; an incredible, loyal, and supportive guy, who idolised her, was kind, and looked after her. Our mother hated him because he was kind and treated Teena so well. Jealousy is blind, and while our mother never saw it, we all did. Teena flourished, and I was proudly her greatest fan. Her stunning looks saw her win the local beauty pageant at sixteen years of age, and then go onto come second in the State beauty pageant for girls under eighteen years of age.

It was an excellent year for her, and I enjoyed the fun of seeing her do all her raffles, social events, and functions to raise money as part of the pageant requirements. As her brother, I was so proud, knowing my big sister had gained such recognition.

She had left school and taken a job at Crosby shoes in North Shore, a suburb of Geelong, and soon afterwards, she built a strong network of friends up around her and decided to leave home to begin her adult life with her love, Neil.

Our mother went right off when Teena tried to leave. The police were called as she raged and argued with Teena out the front of the house, where Neil was waiting. Finally, Teena won and I was happy for her and wished her joy in life. My mother was ropable at losing yet another meal ticket.

About two months later, Fairlie also decided to leave home to go and live with her partner, Peter, who later also became her husband and fathered their two children. He was also an amazing man and showered her with the love she deserved. Mother was annoyed to no end. She hated the fact that another source of income was gone and she hated the fact Peter treated Fairlie so beautifully.

To this day I still admire Peter. He went through hell and back. He was one of four employees at the Shell Refinery in Geelong, who suffered horrendous burns and injury when part of the refinery blew up. The physical scars he carried, after months of being in the hospital, were absolutely diabolical, and he carries those same scars today, as a reminder of how easy things can go from good to bad. Unfortunately, it really affected Fairlie badly, and she was so scared of the way he looked she just couldn't live with Peter afterwards and they separated.

Dale was at the age when boys wandered the streets getting into trouble. He wasn't in the best of company and got caught up in it and led astray, way too many times.

I lost contact with Heather, after she moved out to pursue her life with her now-husband, Allan, in Canberra but I did hear that they had two children, girls, if I am correct. I never had much to do with Heather. Like Graham, she was reserved and stuck to her values in life. She had a great heart, which is what I would like to remember her for.

CHAPTER 43

Kicked to the Curb

Fourteen years

Life was life, and nothing much changed on the home front. I kept myself busy enough. My mother worked later on a Tuesday and Thursday, so I was allowed to head over to Tony's after school to collect my lawnmower and do some lawns before rugby training. They were big days for me, and I often didn't finish and get home until after 8:00 pm. We'd also have training on Sunday mornings if we lost our game on Saturday.

Every other day on a Monday, Wednesday and Friday I would hang out with my mates for a bit, before having to be home by 4.30, to look after Darren, until Gerald got home at 5:00 pm. Then I would do the household chores and head down to the shop for my mother, to get the milk, bread and cigarettes with the regular permission note.

Even though my mother was home on those days, it was up to me to look after Darren. She wasn't a maternal woman, and she didn't do any of the motherly kind of things. She just kind of co-existed with us in the house. I had no idea why she even had kids, in truth, since she did everything she could to not be a mother. Gerald was more maternally-minded than she was with his kids, doing the lunches etc.

I didn't mind these days, though, because it was always fun hanging out with Darren in the short time we had before Gerald came home. Our mother would be in the kitchen drinking and smoking with her girlfriend, Joan Porter, while Darren and I played before I began the chores.

The end of life, as I knew it, happened when I arrived home one Monday after school.

I'd just been to Tony's house to hang for a bit and walked in at 4:30 pm, ready to spend time with Darren. I dropped my bag into my room and headed to his room to see if he was home yet. As the older kids all moved on, I had a room all to myself, now, and Darren had moved his bed and things to the front bedroom, which had been Heather, Fairlie, and Teena's room. The bungalow that Graham had lived in had become more of a storeroom, where all the kids, who had moved out, stored their things until they eventually collected them.

Walking past Darren's room, I noticed he wasn't home yet, so I went in search of my mother, fully expecting to see her sitting in the kitchen as she usually was, having a coffee and a smoke, or a drink with Joan, but she wasn't in there.

I went into her bedroom thinking she may have been lying down and saw that all her drawers were wide open and all her things were gone. Shocked, I immediately panicked and I checked the wardrobe. All her hanging clothes were also gone¬. The room was completely empty; bare to the bone. Fear began to rise in me, as I searched the house from room to room. I even went out to Graham's old bungalow in the hope she was there, but there was nothing. I looked out to the side driveway, where she usually parked the car. No car; it was missing too.

I raced back into the house and noticed pieces of furniture were also missing. It was then I saw an envelope sitting on the mantelpiece in the lounge addressed to Gerald. I bounced back and forward, thinking "Do I open it? Do I not?" I couldn't help it; I had to know what she had written. I was hoping like hell it was just a note to say she'd be home soon. Risking the consequences of what I would no doubt receive for opening it, I did just that. I carefully opened the envelope and began to read the letter . . . after which I felt sick, and stood there crying, and shaking all over with the overwhelming fear of the unknown.

My mother had written Gerald a "Dear John" letter. The start of the message was destroying enough, let alone the rest of the letter. I could barely read through the tears welling up in my eyes.

"Gerald, I can't live like this anymore. My feelings and love are with another man, and I need time to search deep. I know what I am doing is wrong and that you will feel hurt…"

The remaining words blurred as my tears fell along with any hope of having a mother in my future. Taking deep breaths and lifting my head, I tried to read on but I was numb to her words, until I got to the last line, when started to shake and felt sick from the uncertainty of my future. Her parting line was a request of Gerald to "Please take care of Daryl". With that, she had left our home and our life.

I went to my bedroom and sat there, waiting for the impending explosion from the lounge. Darren arrived home and I took him into my bedroom and explained what I had just read in the letter. Poor Darren lay down on my bed, face-first into the mattress, and cried his heart out, which just gutted me. Through shattered eyes, he raised his head and asked me "What are you going to do?" I stood there lost. I didn't know.

There was no doubt my mother was a horrible person, but one thing she did right was to stand between Gerald and me, to stop him from beating me after Dale had left. With her gone, so too was my protection. About fifteen minutes later, I heard Gerald ride up the driveway on his 500cc Suzuki motorbike. All was silent at first, as I imagined him reading the "Dear John" letter. Minutes passed and nothing. Then, without a single sound of warning, my bedroom door burst open. Gerald glared at me, his fists clenched, and yelled, "Well, your mother has done it again!".

I was terrified of the repercussions I would now have to face as a result of my mother's actions. I stood by my bed and had put my guitar down beside the bed out of sight by my side, in case he grabbed it and broke it, and I waited . . . for anything. I wasn't sure what, but I braced myself for it, regardless.

Darren who had been standing by my tallboy, was shaking and scared of Gerald too, Gerald told him to go to his room, and he carefully, but quickly, walked behind his father and slipped into his bedroom, to safety.

Gerald threw a plastic bag at me and said "Pack your things, I don't want you. You're not my son, and you're not staying here!" I didn't even have a bag! The bag I used to own had been stolen by my mother, that day, to pack her own stuff, along with my bank book and I later learned she had emptied my account, the week before.

So, here I was packing all I had left into a shitty plastic bag; my clothes, my shoes, my rugby gear and anything else that was mine and that I could stuff into it. I couldn't think and just grabbed things randomly, as quickly as I could, terrified Gerald was going to lose control at any minute and kill me. I couldn't fit my school uniform or some other belongings, so I left them. Holding the full plastic bag with one hand, I grabbed my beloved guitar with the other and hesitantly walked out of my bedroom.

Gerald had been standing there, watching me the whole time. He turned and opened the front door, pointed to the wet road, as the rain came down, and said, 'Get out!' I walked out of that door for the last time in my life, angry at my mother for once again destroying any kind of stability I had, and for leaving me alone again once more.

I recall Darren running out and yelling at his father, but his words seemed to mean nothing- He grabbed me and said "NO" please don't leave me, but the decision was not mine. I knew that if I tried to stay, I would not only be physically thrown out, but also beaten. Gerald walked over, grabbed Darren, took him inside, and slammed the door.

To this day, I still feel shaky reliving those moments, and the tears, fears, loneliness, and sadness having been tossed. I had been thrown around from one home and country to another, and had had to rebuild my world using whatever means I had. I had made connections with people and then lost them over and over again, at the hand of my mother. These people now included a little brother I had grown to love.

With my whole life in my hands and not one red cent to my name, I walked out the door of 23 Warrawee Avenue, Norlane Geelong for the last time in my life. I was angry at my mother in a way I cannot describe. She had destroyed any kind of stability I had and had left me alone, once more.

Feeling lost, hurt and scared, I had no idea where I would go or what I would do. I was just fourteen years old. I was a child with no home, no father, no mother, no food, and no money, walking along a road to nowhere with a plastic bag filled with the remains of my life. I didn't even know where my brothers or sister lived, so I couldn't walk to their homes and look for refuge.

For the first time in years, I would have to survive with my wits, somehow. I stood on the street as the rain began to drench me looking up and down, with no clue really of which direction to head in. Call it intuition or a gut feeling but whatever it was it had me favour the left direction. As I walked away from my house and towards the corner, the rain pelted down and I took shelter under the next-door neighbour's front yard bushes trying to keep dry and warm.

I sat in his bushes, as the rain kept coming, mixing with my tears of sadness. The fear I felt was overwhelming, as the immensity of the situation I was in slapped me into a steely and surreal reality. I never really had a fear for the dark; it was more what came out of it. This was something that I had lived with in the boys' home, so an adjustment in a new life would be easy or so I thought, as I started to imagine everything terrible.

Being alone in the dark was scaring me, tough. I was lucky that there had always been two streetlights out the front of my once- home. One was to the right and the other a little way up the path, on the left, so the light did give me some vision and help remove the imaginary ghost. I started to feel ANGRY. I seethed with hate and it was directed fully at my mother. Hate is a powerful word I know. I found myself hoping she would die. It seemed something only the evilest of people would wish on another, but that's what I was thinking, as I huddled in the rain under the bush. I wanted her to die. Sadly, I also wanted to die that night.

What I knew of life was how I had lived it till then seemed a total waste. As was all the hard work I had done to adjust to a new life, and to accept a culture I was not born into. I felt that, even though I was looking for new ways to move forward, all of a sudden, a big "STOP" sign had been thrown in front of it. Hundreds of thoughts raced around my mind, not allowing me to control them or even take the time to think.

Aside from O1, O2 and the other Salvation Army officers who abused us, I have never hated anyone, before or since, as much as I did my own mother at that moment. If tossing us into an orphanage wasn't bad enough, she had completely disregarded her responsibilities, by betraying and neglecting me again. It is beyond me, how any mother could just walk away and leave her children to an abusive man, so she could live a single, responsibility-free life. The damage this woman had done in my fourteen years of life, threatened to eclipse every good thing I knew I had inside of me.

It was just after 6:00 pm, when the neighbour's dog started barking and pushed me on, into a future I truly didn't believe I'd see let alone survive. I extracted myself from the bush where I had taken refuge to begin looking for a place to stay, eat, and sleep. I could barely breathe, feeling the full weight of what I had just been through that afternoon. My body started to burn in rage and I could feel every bit of anger I had tried to bottle up, coming out, and I screamed out loud with the gut-wrenching soul hurt I was feeling . . .

CHAPTER 44

The Longest Night

Fourteen years

People talk about the longest walk in their life, that mile with no real ending. That night, I soon began to understand what they meant. As night fell, and still with no idea of what I was going to do, I had to hurry up and think of something. I can't tell you how frightened I felt. Everything was heightened; my emotions, my mind, and my body, yet at the same time I felt dazed.

Somehow, I ended up behind the local shops in Alkira Avenue, Norlane. I found some cardboard that I grabbed as I thought I could use it as a bed, but the rain was relentless, and soon my cardboard bed and I were a wet mess. Hunger set in, and with no money or food, I had to think about how I would get some food. I couldn't go to any of my friend's places, I felt humiliated, and a great sense of shame that my family had done this. I hated the thought of what my friends would think of me. So, I waited in my soaked hiding spot, until the total darkness of the night before I crept out.

My 2nd home at 14 years of age, living behind the local shops on dirt while using cardboard as blankets to stay warm and dry. The local garbage bins became my food providers for meals.

I knew the area well, so I also knew which homes had fruit trees that I could go to pick some fruit. Under the blanket of the rainy night, I crept out of my hiding area and went to one home and took a handful of apples and then another home to get some oranges to fill my empty belly. Sitting eating, the reality kept coming at me like waves. So many things to think about all; they all came flooding in like a tsunami. What about school the next day? What about my friends? What about me?

So many thoughts, it became unbearable. I eventually fell asleep, my mind exhausted from all the things I now had to think about, and emotionally drained from all the crying I had done, and that my body had spent, shivering with cold and fear.

I did wake up a few times over the night, but I think more in fear at the sounds I could hear that I wasn't used to hearing and the discomfort of being on a hard floor as well as the stinging under my eyes, from the constant wiping away my tears. The next day came too soon. I was soon up walking the streets, with my plastic bag over my shoulder, looking for a place to be during the day, instead of behind the shops where I would be easily spotted.

Heading up the street, I made my way towards the local football ground which seemed to be the best choice. I knew it had freshwater to drink, toilets and an undercover shed that could protect me from the elements. Along the back boundary was a row of pine trees that would also give me a good hiding spot, if needed.

I played my guitar and ran around on the oval with my rugby ball, to busy myself and escape the constant worrying, I was doing. If someone came, I'd run to the back boundary, under the trees, to hide and then I spent more time thinking about what I would do.

A few boys from school saw me and asked what I was doing. Embarrassed, I walked off without saying a thing. Where would I begin? How do you tell others what took place the night before and how do I try to explain that I was now living on the streets? I felt so ashamed. They knew what my life was like, before coming to Australia, and they, (like me), thought this was my new beginning. I couldn't let them see that it wasn't, or what a disgrace my mother really was. I didn't want them to know that what she had done was all too much for me. I just couldn't bear to face them.

I hadn't had any food for the day, having eaten all the fruit the night before, and my stomach began to gnaw at me. I didn't know a lot at that moment, sitting under the shed at the footy grounds, but I knew one thing, and that was I wasn't going to sleep on the streets or beg, borrow or steal food for the rest of my life. Somehow I would find a way. I had to move on from the shed, in the late afternoon, as the area soon became filled with other kids and adults. It was football training day. I dragged myself to the back fence and sat watching between the trees until it was my training time. The fun and good times the other kids were having, only reminded me of the days before all this happened.

I sat and thought. I worried about my future. I reflected on my past. Minutes turned into an hour. My starving mind and body tried to reach for memories of better days, when life wasn't what it was now. I recalled how, at the age of thirteen and looking for a new challenge in life, Darren had suggested I play AFL.

I'd laughed at first, and then I thought, maybe it's not a bad idea. That was the only thing my mother brought me; AFL footy boots, as we weren't allowed to wear the rugby ones in games. Our sprigs, tags, or stoppers, as they are often called, were too long and made of alloy back then, so they were deemed too dangerous on the AFL field with all the jumping in the air that they did.

So, my mother bought the game-standard boots which had short stops and were made of rubber. I was even allowed to play in the same AFL club as Darren, the mighty Norlane Bulldogs, who wore the same colours as the big league. After a few training nights and direction from our coach, I was ready for my first on-field game. It was different and also challenging. At the time, I had to wonder why you would spend all your time chasing a ball that was being kicked from end to end. I had been given the position of winger inter-change rover, because of my speed and agility. The weeks passed, and I slipped right into the game. At times the coach took me off the field for rough play, but that was just my rugby days coming out.

We got close to the end of the season and were sitting 3rd on the ladder. We ended up staying in that position for the rest of the year. Somehow, and I can tell you it amazed me, I was selected to play a curtain-raiser at the senior AFL game in the city, along with Darren. I got to wear the Geelong colours, which was such an honour for me, and to represent my home city in a fun game in front of thousands. It was terrific! We played Charlton and won . . . well kicked the most points, because back then there wasn't a winner. It was all about fun and learning.

Four-thirty finally came, which meant it was my rugby training time. I didn't have my full rugby uniform, having left most of my clothes and also my school uniforms, at home, but I did my best to train in what I had. I just couldn't perform, which made me even more upset. It might have been from the lack of sleep, and maybe my red and rubbed eyes from crying or the lethargy of not eating, I don't know. Derek Costello, our coach, came up to me and said 'Daryl, are you ok? Is everything alright at home?" I said "Yes, I just have to go" and left before I couldn't hold back the tears any longer. I was totally gutted, walking off that field. Now I really had lost everything that was important to me.

Years later I would play once more and was even offered a game salary of $30.00. Not much but it helped to pay the bills.

Hunger can make you think of silly things, and I was having an avalanche of crazy thoughts, that night, as darkness fell. I set up a new bed behind the shops again and went off on my nightly walk, jumping people's fences to get food, to clear my head.

I felt so bad having to take the fruit and to be stealing to survive. One night, I stole a jumper from someone's backyard and a towel, so that I could have a tap shower in the mornings, at the football fields. It makes me feel bloody awful saying it out loud and writing it even now. I never took anything that wasn't essential to keep me alive or in reasonable health.

I began wondering what else I could do to get by and what I could eat. I started to look for and collect empty coke bottles, which I would take to the shops the next day to collect the 5 cents refund. When I had collected and refunded four, I would take the 20 cents and buy some warm food.

This went on for days, as I desperately tried to figure out how to fend for myself. Each day and night, I took the risk of being spotted and dobbed in for taking fruit off trees to feed my hunger. I knew, in some way, that sooner or later someone was going to see me and ring the police, which they did.

CHAPTER 45

Surviving

Fourteen years

Five days of being homeless ended, as a car pulled up beside where I lay on my makeshift bed of cardboard, behind the shop A big bright light was shone right at me and then I heard a voice, before seeing two men emerge from the light and stand over the top of me, just looking down at me. One asked me my name, and how old I was. I told him I was fourteen. He asked me to get up and hop in the car out of the rain. More questions followed as we drove up to the house I had once called home in the suburb of Norlane.

The policemen got out of the car and walked up to the front door and knocked on it. Gerald opened the door and the policemen began talking to him. I could see Darren looking out at the street from his bedroom window. The street-light lit up the police car I was sitting on and Darren saw me and waved. I waved back and at that moment I knew it was a "Goodbye Brother, see you again one day" wave, at least I hoped I would.

Soon I could see Gerald waving his arms around in the air, as he talked and after a while, the policemen turned and came back to the car. They said I would be driving back to the police station with them, to wait for a ward of state officer to come from the city to arrange home support. I just nodded, I knew what that meant. It was hard, knowing I had spent eleven years of my life in a boy's home, and then had lived alone as a street kid at the age of fourteen years of age, with no home or food. I had had to drop out of school because I no longer had a school uniform to wear and I wasn't able to answer the personal question teachers and friends put to me.

Being a ward of the state only meant that things could get far worse, as the likelihood of going back to an orphanage was the general course of action back in those days.

We arrived at the Norlane Police Station, where I was asked to wait in the car, while the driver went into the station to grab something. He returned and said I would be taken to the Central Station in the city.

I was glad to be in the car. It was warm and safe. The policeman asked if I had eaten any food and I said I had. I had been eating fruit and hot chips. Then he asked me if I had stolen it and I told him I had. It was my only way to survive. He seemed to understand and left the questioning there.

The city police station was ancient and looked more like a detention centre. As I was escorted in, I could feel all eyes on me as I entered a room that had a dirty-looking vinyl floor and wooden walls. There was an Australian flag and a picture of the Queen hanging above the main table, which was strewn with scattered files and other stuff.

I sat down in a chair, while the two officers, who had escorted me in, left me in the hands of a female officer, who had been standing at the door. The police had all been really kind and had got me some hot chips and a warm drink. My first meal in a few days. It went down so fast it didn't even touch the sides.

After some time, a tall man walked into the room and introduced himself as Robert, a local part-time ward of state officer. He must have been an ambulance officer also, as he was wearing the uniform. We sat and talked, mainly about my life to start with, and then about the events that had seen me living on the streets. As he spoke and told me things about what might happen that night, he mentioned being taken to a boys' home, and I just cried, I didn't know what to do. Being told I was going to have to go back to an orphanage was the last thing I wanted to hear. I was desperate not to have to go, but it looked as if there was nothing I could do about it.

Robert left the room, leaving me with the female officer. Not too long afterwards he came back to the room and told me he had made a few phone calls, and that I was going to a foster care home, until the state could decide on what to do with me. I felt some comfort knowing that I wouldn't be going to a boys' home, that night, and was looking forward to being somewhere warm and clean. The clothes I had on were dirty and smelt, the plastic bag I had was torn, and everything inside was wet, including my beloved guitar which I was still carrying. As I was led away, Robert looked down at me and said, "Things will be ok. These people are very friendly, and will take care of you for a while".

We drove about 20 minutes to Newcomb, a suburb at the end of the city limits, before arriving at a lovely white cottage house with a pebble stone driveway and white picket fences running down the sides. There were trees everywhere. It was amazing and, like the boys' home, it was well-maintained. The people of the house came out and introduced themselves to me as a state foster care family and then they led me inside.

Once inside, I was taken to a bedroom, which I soon learnt had been their son's room. He had passed away a few years earlier, from a medical condition associated with asthma, just like Darren, my younger brother. I'll admit to feeling a little weird and creeped out at being in there and sleeping in their deceased son's room. Their daughter, who was about twenty years old, came into the room and chatted to me, doing her best to make me feel welcome, which was a lovely gesture and it relaxed me. She was a teacher, so she was used to dealing with younger kids.

The first night went fast, with a shower and then straight to bed as it was late. The days to follow were filled with trips to an office in the city, as talks took place about my future, as well as shopping, and helping around the yard. Things at the foster home were very relaxing. They were lovely people and made me feel so at home and comfortable. Their daughter spent hours teaching me the piano and I must admit I enjoyed hanging out with her. She was a bit of a looker, with a brilliant smile of pearly white teeth. They had two little Scottish dogs, so twice daily walks also became part of my routine.

A little over two weeks went by, and still, there was no word on what was going to be done to settle me back into my life. Was I going to the orphanage or not? The question kept ticking over in my mind. It was hard to get used to all the peace, after going from a crazy life of eleven years with the boys at Hodderville, and a further three years with a family of six kids at my mother and Gerald's house. I wasn't back at school and I was beginning to feel really lonely, with no friends to see or play with. I was going a little stir crazy, just sitting around each day with two retired adults. I began to struggle.

I know I should have been grateful, and I honestly was; this was a golden opportunity for me to turn my life around. But, with the upbringing I had had, I found I couldn't process everything I was dealing with at the time. I wasn't coping well, and they could see it. I would go for walks and think, wow I could just take off right now, and they wouldn't know. Or I could wait until the dark of night and make a break for it. What we do and think at times just to fill the void in our minds.

Looking back, I know now that in the middle of all the chaos, I was missing my new Australian and foreign friends, both those on the streets and at school. I would sneak to the back of the yard and have my daily cry, thinking they never knew, but I was wrong. One night they sat down with me and said they had watched me sit against the back fence, crying, which made them sad too. They asked me "What do you want to do, Daryl?"

My answer completely shocked them. Their daughter moved across and cuddled me as I had never honestly been held before. She was crying, and after a short while, I realised why. My answer to their question of what do you want to do was . . . die. For them having lost someone special not too long ago, it was crushing. Later on, after I had gone over everything, I realised that the best thing for me to do would be to leave so that they didn't feel upset about how I was feeling.

That night I packed what was mine in a clean plastic bag. I sat and wrote a note to the family thanking them for all they had done for me, and explaining why I needed to leave. I left the letter in the kitchen, on the sink, next to the kettle; knowing that was the first thing they did on waking up, turn the kettle on to make the pot of tea. I left their home while they were asleep.

That would be the last time I saw the foster family, as I walked down the drive to leave what was special, but special for another child. I had decided on my future, and it wasn't with foster families or in an orphanage. Somehow I found my way back the 10+ kilometres to Norlane. It was a long and lonely walk, but one I had done many times. My rugby field for training and playing was only up the road from the foster family's house, and around 10 km from Norlane and I had walked, run, biked, and bussed this route, many times.

So many times I have asked myself ﹃" Why not just jump in front of a car or truck? Would I be better off finding a tall building and leaping off? I did think about the ocean bay, but drowning was not going to work as I was an excellent swimmer. Anyway, I found my way back to the same shops, set up a bed and collapsed from the long walk. It would be another four days before I would come into contact with anyone again.

CHAPTER 46

Gaz

Fourteen years

During my school days, I met many wonderful people and made great many friends as well. There was the odd one or two who saw me as a "black wog" as they put it back then, and the same few who would try to beat on me. It never worried me much, I would cop it on the chin and move on. Those few words had nothing on the abuse I experienced at the boys' home. In a way, I was a tough little kid and already had a good understanding that only the weak themselves preyed upon others for personal satisfaction.

I missed my school mates greatly, but I found new friends on the street, such as Gaz, a kid who was a couple of years older than me. He was the older brother of a classmate and another fella, called Trevor, who was in the same school year as me but in a different class. I connected with Gaz right away. He just seemed to get me, and I got him too. He became my best friend and the first person to really see who I was behind the mask I had on. The dirty street kid—the wet, hungry, tired, and homeless orphan.

At sixteen Gaz had a lot of worldly wisdom. He had been on a terrible path, himself, after losing his father to suicide some years earlier. They say, "like attracts like", and I am thankful it does, because I will treasure always his simple words and the understanding we both had of each other's worlds.

A group of boys I had started hanging out with, before my departure from home, had heard I was living on the streets and that my mother had left me, to live in another place with another man. Incredibly, they decided to look for me. As I lay wondering what to do, I heard voices. Unsure, I hid under the cardboard, hoping not to be seen, but there is only so much you can do to hide. Without warning, the cardboard was lifted and above me stood Gaz, brothers Dale and Trevor Gundry, Stephen Houwit, Raymond Milligan, and Keith Cripps. Like good mates, they asked me what was going on. As I talked, they sat with me, listened, and heard my story. Gaz sat down next to me and said, "You'll never forget the past mate, but you'll get through this, come with us mate".

At first, I went back to Trevor's house, where his mum Shirley took me in. She, along with the others, made me feel so welcome and the truth was I felt at peace again. Sadly, that peace didn't last long, in fact only four days, before I was told to leave. Dale, Trevor's older brother and I were getting ready to go bowling. Dale grabbed his father, Fred's, aftershave and slapped some on him before turning around and slapping some of it on me also, and off we went bowling.

Returning happy from a fantastic night out, we bounded into the house, excited to tell Shirley and Fred all about our night and how we had won the game. When Shirley heard us, she called me into the lounge and asked me if I had used Fred's aftershave? I dropped my head, as I said no. She then asked, "Are you sure Daryl?" I had never had to cover up before, but I also knew I had the aftershave on because Dale splashed it on me. I replied 'yes' trying to explain how I happened to have Fred's aftershave on and why I smelt like his aftershave, but was asked to stop.

Shirley looked at me and said, "Daryl, the two things we don't like in our house are liars and thieves". I had nowhere to look other than at her and knew that if I tried to tell the truth, her son Dale would be punished. As much as it hurt, I took the blame that night. Shirley asked me to leave their home that night, which broke my heart. My only crime was to protect a friend and look after him. What was more upsetting was that Dale just stood there as I took it. Dale took weeks to apologise to me, and even longer to tell his mother the truth at which point it was far too late. The damage had been done, and my integrity was destroyed.

Twiggy, their younger sister, also apologised to me years later, telling me she always knew it was Dale, but she loved him too much to see him get in trouble, and that I was just another kid off the street, so she didn't really care at the time. Nearly three years later, before my eighteenth birthday, Trevor asked me to come over to his house At first I said "NO" but he insisted. I had avoided going there since the day in question, but I did it out of respect. Shirley and Fred asked me to come inside and have a seat. I thought she was going to ask me to stay away from her boys but instead, she looked at me and said, "We are so sorry Daryl."

Shirley said Dale had come home, drunk the night before and a few words were exchanged, before Dale told them the truth about that night. I have no idea why he decided to confess then, but I never mentioned a word Shirley and Fred had said to me. However, Shirley did ask me why I took the blame? I replied "It's simple Shirley, a mate's a mate, and over the years, I have lived through great hardship. To me, it was better that one person was punished that day, not two."

Fred just looked at me and said that Dale was fortunate to have such a good friend. Shirley said, all these years you kept Dale's secret and his dishonesty, but still stayed his friend. I looked at her and smiled, before leaving, saying, "That's what mates do Shirley".

I lost contact with this family down the track, but did learn that Fred HAD passed away FROM cancer and that Trevor HAD followed down his dad's health path and also passed away from cancer at a young age, leaving a wife and two children.

After Shirley had asked me to leave, I walked to Gary's and told him what happened and the result of Dale's little bit of fun. He looked at me and said, come with me. Gaz took me into his home and asked his mother if I could stay. It is funny, but her name was also Shirley. I was given a bed in Gary and Keith's room. Somehow through talks with people on the streets, the police found out where I was.

After many days of the police coming around, and the legal issues that saw me in offices daily, I was told I could stay at Shirley's. I was over the moon and so happy to be allowed to live with Gaz and his family. It was kind of like adoption in one-way (foster) care until all the legal jargon was finalised. I reached the age of fifteen and was still under the control of the state, but living in a foster arrangement. I was offered an apprenticeship. Being so tiny and weighing around 40 kg I followed my dream and my love of horses, by starting an apprenticeship as a Jockey.

My apprentice sponsor was Bart Cummings and over the next eighteen months, I worked for him. He treated me very well, providing the best training and schooling, as well as sleeping quarters, food and a small wage of $10.00 a week. I was able to earn even more funds, working as a strapper on the weekend at the tracks for owners of the horses we stabled. I would help the owners prepare the horse for its run and would walk the horse to the mounting yard, where the jockey would meet me. A win would see me collect between $20.00 and 30.00 dollars, and with a place, I got up to $15.00 from the horse owner, as a thank you reward. On a good weekend, I could make between $60.00 and $90.00. In those days that was a serious pay packet and it was tax-free, too!

After it was clear my weight and height would keep on increasing like any normal teenager, it was decided I would move and sign off from my apprenticeship through the Victorian apprenticeship board. I moved out of Bart's stables and back in with Gaz and his family and continued to live there for a short period. I had connected back with my sister Teena, who asked if I would come and live with her as she had moved to the country with her husband. They had rented a big property, so that they had land for their horses to run freely.

Neil shared Teena's passion for horses and had a couple of his own as well, which he had on other properties and which was costing him a fair bit each month. When the property came up for rent, they jumped at the chance to grab it. The only problem was Teena felt uncomfortable out there by herself, with their two girls. Neil worked the afternoon shift at Ford's casting plant, so the nights were lonely for her.

I moved in with her and helped out on the farm for around six months, to give her a hand. The problem was it restricted my ability to get to work, as it meant I would have to walk approximately 2.8 km to get the bus to and from work. It became too much in the end, so I arranged for a friend to board with Teena rent-free, to help her, which was a great arrangement for both of them. I moved back to live with Gary once more, and to continue my everyday life. During this time I saved as much as I could, to buy my first car.

It was tough because I was still only seventeen years old and working hard to cover all my own costs such as board, food, travel and entertainment. Gaz and I would always be up to something. He loved parties, so we went to heaps of those at night and we would also go to the movies or head off on great ocean road trips on weekends or just hang out. There was always plenty of fun to be had and we were never bored or stuck for things to do.

One long weekend, we all had a four-day break, along with the weekend, so four of us drove from Geelong to Perth and back, in time for work on Tuesday morning. We set off on Wednesday, after work, and took turns driving the long hours, so we could spend two nights in another state, and another fantastic Australian city.

Over the next few months, we spoke about our hopes and dreams, and made plans to continue our journey after we had grown up. That big day came not long after Gaz turned nineteen. He decided to go it alone, and move out to rent a small unit in Cario, Geelong. Not too far from his mum's but far enough to have a private life.

I can still remember the day he told me he was moving out. He had made the arrangements the week before but didn't tell anyone. I was happy for him in every way, but I was going to miss him too, and wondered if I would still be allowed to stay with his Mum? We were yacking away, talking about how cool the unit was going to be, when I asked Gaz if there was a bus stop close. Gaz just looked at me and asked, "Why Daryl?" I said, "Well I'd love to come and visit you, mate". Gaz sat back in his chair, pulled his shoulders back, and said "Why are you saying that, mate? You're coming to live with me too!"

"Holy shit! . . .are you for real?" I asked. He just stood up and said, "Mate, pack your clothes, grab your things and let's go home!" I was beyond thrilled! I was packed and in the Combi before he even knew what was going on.

For close to two years, Gaz and I lived, worked, and shared an incredible journey together. God we had some fantastic times! The best! He not only saved me from a life on the streets but he showed me how to live well, too. He was my mentor; a brother and he filled an empty and desperate space in my life. He pretty much showed me how to be a man.

Our unit was small but suited us fine in every way. It was built of standard brick, with a small courtyard. The building accommodated three units in total, so the privacy was excellent. It only had one bedroom, so privacy on visits from female friends had to be shared. Later, over the next 12 months, we had two friends move into the units next door.

I worked both at KFC and Fords' casting plant and Gaz was an assistant manager at KFC where he stayed for fifteen years. I met and made many friends over this time, never realising, until later in life, how hard they had to work to befriend me. For the longest time, I believed people just felt sorry for me and that's why they invited me to places and to hang out. As the years went on, I learned differently. I found out I had great friends and I was a great friend.

Sadly, many of the boys from those days have since passed away, but the fond memories, of the fun we used to have, remain. I have caught up with Gaz over the years though, and he is happily married and a proud dad and incredible provider to his three children and beautiful wife.

The only thing Gaz and I didn't have in common was my love for bikes. Gaz was a Combi man through and through. Our road trips in his 1969 Beetle were fantastic. I later, followed suit and bought a 1969 Combi and a 1974 VW beetle. Mind you, for some reason, he later converted to Mini, get that! A Combi to a Mini!

Sadly, our last catch up was at the funeral of my niece. We took the time to catch up and the talk was and will always be special, with Gaz.

Even now, his guidance steers me strong.

CHAPTER 47

Sixteen

Sixteen years

You could say I was looking for an answer for why I went through all the things I did, and why I was still alive at sixteen years of age.

I did some things I wasn't proud of, such as hurting a very close friend; someone I had built a trusting relationship with. Not to justify it in any way, I know I was wrong, but I hurt people. It was a lesson I learned and have taken with me through to this present year. Just for the record, it wasn't a physical hurt, but more a personal one that affected him emotionally.

How it happened still gives me the shivers, just thinking about it. The one thing I have always been proud of was my integrity and respect for others. Keith was the younger brother of Gaz, and truth was he was the reason I met Gaz. The night started off harmlessly enough at a small birthday party for a friend of ours, Peter Corstin, at his house. They had a swimming pool, so it was not long before we were splashing around in it. Peter's mum called out that the food was ready, so we got out to get dressed.

At the same time, a young girl turned up. She was my age and her name was Cathy. She was Polish but spoke very good English. Her parents had migrated to Australia many years earlier to escape the wars and hardships. She was an attractive girl with blue eyes, long blond hair, and quiet nature.

In fact, she said little but had always shown me amazing respect and friendship. Keith had taken a liking for Cathy; in fact, he had become a little obsessed, which we had all noticed. Cathy had also noticed and avoided him, just to stay friends, but sadly Keith didn't see it that way. He morphed into a control freak when she was around. He would become very jealous if we talked to her, or if she sat down next to us. It was very awkward.

I waited for Peter, Gaz, Allan, and Steven to dry and dress in the rear bungalow while talking to Cathy and a few others. At that point, Keith was working, so the night had been relaxing up until then. The boys came out dressed, so I went into the room to do the same. I had just undressed and was drying myself when without warning Cathy walked in and closed the door. I looked up and said, "Cathy I am getting dressed". She smiled and said "I know", and then without missing a beat, she walked over to me and kissed me.

Why or for whatever reason, I only know I didn't stop her. I had always found Cathy attractive too, but had stayed away from her, because of my friendship with Keith. As she moved to kiss me again, I let my defences down, thinking how nice the moment, but suddenly all hell broke loss. Keith had finished work early and had turned up at the party. I am assuming he was told Cathy was in the bungalow with me. The door opened and without warning "BANG" he punched me.

Keith ran out screaming. I asked Cathy to leave and got dressed. I ran to Keith's place which was only a few streets away. After many sorry words he let me in and sat in sadness telling me that of all the people, I was not the one who he thought would do this to him. I talked and explained how Cathy felt about him, as a friend only, which broke his heart. It had to be done. He had lived for too long thinking she was his.

I am glad he learned the truth, but sad about the way it happened. The next day I went to Cathy's home and sat with her, talking about the crazy night before and how Keith felt. She understood and said she would also talk with Keith. She also asked me if we had any chance of more than a friendship, I hesitated. It was clear as she looked at me that I was going to say "No" and she said "Please don't say it Daryl", but I did. She looked at me, and her eyes welled up. I gave her a hug and left the house. I only saw her one more time after that, as we avoided each other afterwards.

Keith played it down, but it took months to be accepted back into my mate's life and I learned a valuable lesson. Never take a friendship for granted, it will hold together even when you do the worst possible thing to a friend.

Keith eventually got married and had two girls. I am happy for him and the life he built.

Like other kids, I tried smoking recreational drugs, but Gaz put the brakes on that together with the fact that I lasted all of a few puffs before I vomited. I tried to be one of the boys and have a beer, but that also made me vomit. I guess I was never cut out for the partying lifestyle. It was not meant for me and was the reason why I didn't drink until I was much older. I was twenty-eight before I tried a few different drinks and finally settled as a Scotch man.

Gaz's strong guidance and his being sports and fitness mad helped me keep mostly on the straight and narrow, which was a good thing. One thing Gaz loved to do was dance! He thought he was John Travolta. He could dance for the record! As for me, I was more like a broken-down helicopter on the floor. It was a case of stay back when Daryl's on the floor, people.

I was still sports-mad at sixteen. I had gone back to playing rugby and had taken up boxing for the extra fitness, as well as Tae Kwon Do. Throughout the years, I hid my past, so people did not see me as strange or different. I desperately tried to fit into the partying scene, but it just was not my thing, and I would fall asleep. When people invited me out, I would make up excuses, telling them I was working late, every Tuesday and Thursday, going to rugby training instead. On the weekends I would tell them I needed to sleep in after a hard week at work and would go and play with the team, around the local area and in Melbourne.

It worked for a while, but they soon found out. The true measure of these mates was that instead of being annoyed or casting me out, they supported and cheered me on at doing my own thing.

I worked hard to save for my first car, and when I finally did buy it, I did the stupidest thing ever. I showed off like an idiot and ended up crashing it, which cost me thousands to fix. Another lesson learned, one I know I am not alone in, but it does not lessen how silly I still felt doing it.

My love for bikes became an early passion; from buying my first bike, a 78 XR Honda, to slowly building up through the years. I went through: a 250 Suzuki, a 375 Montesa, a 750 four Honda, a 400 Honda supersport, a 360 Yamaha DT, a 650 Triumph, six Harley Davidsons and another Triumph 1100. Over the years, my garage has been a revolving workshop, feeding my passion for them.

I also had a love of horses and had two when I was fifteen years old; Patches and Red. Patches was my everyday ride on weekends, and Red was my super horse, standing 21 hands high. He was a retired pacer and had a heart as big as they came. I worked on weekends for a man by the name of Gerald Duke. He had about thirty horses and I would lead trail rides for him, on the weekend, for holidaymakers to earn pocket money.

Having that small income also helped me with my endeavours and my goal to save enough to buy a block of dirt, one day. There is no question that I had my fair share of fun, toys, and treats in the years that followed. I sometimes think I was trying to fill that missing void of what most kids had over many years, into just ten years.

During those years, living with Gaz, I reunited with my brother, Dale. My brother truly was a man who cared for everyone, and thought the best of everyone, which ultimately had him running headlong down a track of self-destruction. Drawn by a need to belong and be accepted, he clung to his group of mates, no matter the consequences. Dale's travel around Australia ended sadly on his return, after he decided to catch up with his old mates; the same mates who had lead him to break into the local shops up the road.

During the shop break-in, a local noticed what was going on and called the police. On their arrival, and with the lights flashing and sirens sounding, the boys climbed up into the roof. Dale followed them, but it was unlucky for him, as he fell and landed on the floor in the shop where the police were waiting. The other boys got away and to Dale's credit, good, or bad, he would not tell the police who they were.

Dale was charged and faced the courts. It had been two-plus years since I had seen him. Somehow, he was able to track me down and called to tell me what he had done and he asked me to go to court with him. Dale was around eighteen years of age, so this meant that, if he was charged, it would be as an adult, and he was worried. I went to his trial, with high hopes of him not being locked up. The judge was a fair man, and after hearing all of the information, and about Dale's past life in the orphanage, he took into consideration that it was his first offence, and gave Dale the option of jail for six months, or three years in the army.

Dale crossed his fingers as he stood and apologised to the courts for his actions. In a clear voice, he said "Sir, I will join the Army". I was so happy he made that choice. I had a smile from side to side knowing that.

Dale joined the Army and ended up serving for six years as a member of the infantry corps.

CHAPTER 48

Teenage Days

Seventeen years

Girls had come into my life and like drugs and alcohol, I had flings with them, all the while trying to fit in with everyone else's expectations, of thinking I should make time to have a special someone in my life. Most of my friends had girlfriends, or were in relationships that gave them someone to be with on weekends and that left me alone, or feeling like the outcast of the group in some ways.

Try as I did, my background, and life just did not initially lend itself to having a girlfriend. I was still young and found them too much work, to be honest, ha ha ha. I just did not have the emotional capacity for them. I felt they needed too much of what I couldn't give at the time, I didn't want to be asked a thousand questions about my past, and I didn't want to sacrifice the time that I needed for sports and training. I also didn't want to go to the all-night parties, which reminded me of my mother. It just seemed easier for me to be alone.

There was never any shortage of attention though, girls always wanted to spend time with me, I just didn't feel the same way back. In the shadows of my mind, I would ask "Why me?" There were so many other guys out there who could give them so much more than I could, and who could spend time with them and understand them. I was happy with friendships. Some evolved to be a bit more than that, from time to time, but they quickly fizzled back to being friends.

I was private, protective, and happy not to need a girlfriend, or so I thought. I recall thinking, one day I will find my girl when it is meant to be. Turned out, it was not that far down the track, when I met a girl who did not expect anything from me other than great companionship. Every time I saw her, she would put a smile on my face. I enjoyed her company. She was an incredible friend, and over time we built a great bond. Although shy, I did my best. I had just turned seventeen years of age when I met Debbie Lee Nichole, who was younger than I was but who showed a maturity far beyond her age.

Debbie's family were amazing, and I adored her older siblings and her incredible parents. We spent a lot of time hanging out at the KFC, where we both worked part-time, which was almost a family affair as her mum also worked there as the store manager. Debbie was a sincere and friendly girl, and over the years, she became a big part of my life.

Between sports, working and spending time with the boys, I would find time to visit her a few times a week and on the weekends.

I found it hard to understand the female gender and even harder to grasp what to do when in a relationship, growing up as I had restricted by life as an orphaned child, and raised with poor parenting support and mostly boys around. I faced a real learning curve as I looked to my other friends, as role models, to guide me, asking them questions, watching their interactions with their girlfriends, and slowly introducing those into my life.

In some ways, Debbie's father, Cliff, was an eccentric character, but he was also a man with an honourable heart who worked hard for his family. Nothing seemed too much for his children. Her mother, Heather, had a heart of gold; nothing was too much trouble and she bestowed the same love on me as she did her children. I was fortunate to have her as a mother-in-law. Any man would be proud of what I was gifted.

It was hard to imagine any family openly giving so much to a total stranger, let alone one that had built a relationship with their youngest daughter and sister, but this is how they accepted and treated me. Her brother, Stephen, and her two sisters, Rayleen and Tammy, all made me feel at ease and welcomed me in as one of their own. They continued to do so as we eventually got engaged and then married.

PART 3

Survival of the Fittest

CHAPTER 49

Kapooka

Nineteen years

At nineteen years of age, I realised I was never going to fit into mainstream life. My background and awkwardness in social groups left me feeling lost and confused.

As a child, I had always wanted to be part of a selective service, be it the Scouts, while still a child; or the air force, navy or army as a man. I would often imagine myself proudly wearing a uniform, one day. So, I joined the military, hoping this would help me find the place I belonged. I figured the "Yes Sir! No Sir!" style of discipline would do me good and be the foundation I was looking for, to build a new identity and to allow me to safely hide from the past.

Military life fitted me like a glove, and the ease with which I got into the service, in the beginning, seemed to be either a piece of sheer luck, or a confirmation that I had finally found the right place. What a life change it was! I could write an entire book about my time in the service; the many friends I made, the thousands of things I learned, how it helped me to become the man I am today, and the great times I had: all of which I'll never forget.

The opportunity to join the army arrived on a winter's morning in May 1978, in the most unexpected way. I had reconnected with my step-sister, Fairlie, out of the blue the day before. She called me up to ask if I would go with her husband, Peter, to Melbourne the next day to support him in his enlistment test to join the service. At that point, he hadn't made his mind which service (Army, Navy, or Air Force) he wanted to join. He decided he would choose if he passed the first initial tests. I jumped at the chance. I wanted to encourage him and it was also a great way for me to check it all out as well. I didn't know what to expect from the day.

We set off early and along the way, Peter told me that he would be required to do a number of assessments; some general enlistment tests, which would involve English Maths, Science and Engineering, as well as a psychiatric evaluation and a medical. He must have been starting to get nervous, because after we had just passed the Werribee turnoff Peter lost control of his car, through constant talking and lack of focus, and we headed straight for an open paddock. The car slid and jumped a few mounds before coming to rest just short of a cattle fence, about 200 metres from the edge of the highway. I don't mind saying that I said a few choice words. I thought we were buggered!

Call it lucky, or maybe it was thanks to a well-built road and easement, but we survived along with Peter's treasure; his 1971 Ford Falcon GTHO Phase III XY. It was a beast! Racing-red with the 351 GT badge. Apart from his kids, this car was his life. Fortunately, a kind man with a FWD was passing and stopped to pull us out. Peter was pretty quiet for the rest of the trip; maybe he was a little shaken up, or maybe he was thanking his lucky stars we'd survived (and his car too), or maybe he was contemplating life with his near miss? I don't know.

On arrival at the army office in Melbourne, which I later learned was called Victoria Barracks; we were quickly assembled and divided into three groups. I stepped out and went to walk away when a guy in a green outfit asked what I was doing. I explained I was only there to support my brother-in-law.

He asked, "Why don't you do the entry test also?"

I looked at Peter and he said, "Why not?" so, I thought "Oh well, why not!" and I stepped back in with the others.

Peter was in another group, so I didn't see him for another thirty to forty minutes. I was directed to do the physical test first, where I had to do push-ups, sit-ups, a hang test from a beam, and end-to-end sprints for one minute as fast as I could. This was followed by the one-minute step and pulse recovery test.

Next came the psychiatric test. Two officers, a male and a female, asked me four questions; 1) What was your relationship like with your parents?, to which I replied that I had been orphaned and then left to fend for myself on the streets at fourteen; 2) Are you in a relationship that could be affected if you were to join the army? Of course I wasn't; 3) Where do you see yourself going in the service? I said I wanted an education; 4) Why do you want to join the Army? I replied that I needed a stable pathway to living a structured life, so I could grow as a man and learn.

The educational test was next up, and lastly, I did the medical test, which was a heart and pulse check; the duck waddle, where you have to squat and walk like a duck, to see if your hips are in alignment; a check flat-footedness; and lastly, a health questionnaire and allergy check. I put down that I had eczema as a child, but over the years I had managed to control my skin issues. I was advised I would have to do a further medical test, a day later, which I passed because my eczema only presents after I eat starchy and highly sugared foods.

Between the education and psychiatric tests, we were given a 30-minute break. During this time I went looking for Peter. I found him sitting in the hallway looking a little lost. I asked him what was happening. He said he'd just finished his first and only test, which was the psychiatric evaluation and smiled and said casually that he had failed it because of his strong family connection.

Those who hadn't failed any of the tests straight away were taken to the main room, and were told to wait until the officer came in and he told us we had passed our first initial test. "OMG!" was all I could think at the time.

They presented me with some paperwork to complete and hand back to my local recruitment office in Geelong. They said that if we still wanted to join the Army, we would have to do a further two assessments. First was a criminal history check, and from that point, you were accepted but on the condition that you passed another medical with a recreational drug and alcohol test. If you passed that, you would be allowed to board the bus to head off for the army.

Fairlie was, to say the least, pissed off with Peter for not trying harder: As for me, I completed the paperwork and handed it to the recruitment office in Geelong the next day. Not even seven days later and three days before my nineteenth birthday I was prepping dinner, after work, when I heard "KNOCK-KNOCK-KNOCK" on the door. I opened it to see a guy standing there in an army uniform.

He asked if I was Daryl Lewis, to which I replied yes.

Now before we go any further, it must be remembered that, from the time I arrived in Australia, until I signed up to join the service, I was known by the last name, "Lewis", because my mother had told me that Gerald had adopted me. I later learned this was yet another lie and that he had never done any such thing.

The army guy asked me if I was still interested in joining the army. Apparently, there were several other people who had pulled out of the mid-year recruitment process, and so I had been offered one of the available positions. It was a bit of a shock, to be honest. When I took my paperwork to the recruitment office, I was told it would be at least three months before I could be considered for the summer intake of 1979, so it was a surprise to be offered a position so quickly.

I said a big yes after which he handed me more paperwork, and asked me to complete it and return it to the recruitment office the following day. I did as I was instructed to do and within fourteen days was scheduled to report for training.

Gaz was beside himself, as were all of my friends, after I told them that I had enlisted for Wednesday the 21st of June 1978. This was ten days after my birthday, so the boys decided to throw me a party. That day came and went with many of the boys and girls waking up to hang-overs. As for me, the day was fresh, as I was not a drinker in the full sense and only managed a few heavily watered-down drinks over the entire night.

The day came, and it was time for me to head off to the recruitment office in Melbourne, where we would be met by service personnel and then taken to our destination, the First Recruit Training Battalion in Kapooka, Wagga Wagga, and NSW, commonly known as 1TRB. Gaz decided to drive me to the recruiting office, which was kind of him. Our parting that day caused a few hidden tears, as he walked away from the curb and hopped into his car. I took a deep breath and walked over to join many other guys, waiting to start a new life as a soldier, just as I was.

This moment reminded me of another time Gaz went out of his way to help me. I was eighteen years of age at the time and had just woken up after a hard night of physical training. Normally I would bounce out of bed, but on this day, things were far from normal. As I attempted to get out of bed for work, I found I could not open my eyes. After a few minutes and struggling to gain composure I called out to Gaz for help.

When he came into the bedroom, I told him I could not see. He apparently looked at me, to say in return, "fuck your eyes and face are swollen!". This would explain the fact I could not see. Gaz drove me to the emergency department. There, I learned that I had suffered a reaction to the infection of a nerve in my face which had caused my face to swell, forcing my eyes closed.

From there, Gaz drove me to Melbourne Medical and Dental Hospital, where they admitted me. I underwent day surgery to have a tube inserted up into my gum to release the poison that had built up, from the infection. After a penicillin needle in the 'BUTT' and a lot of pain, I was released to go home. What a great mate he was.

Gaz went on to live his life, with visits from me on my recreational leave once or twice a year, but he never shared his unit with another person, opting instead to live solo.

I had to produce my birth certificate at enlistment and it was noted that my birth certificate said Te'Nadii even though all the paperwork I had filled out said Lewis. However, after a few minutes of discussion, they realised what had happened within my family and arranged for the rest of my paperwork to be updated, so I was able to proudly return to the name Te'Nadii.

As I stood in the group of other men, I sensed many were in two minds. Their conversations seemed to be more about, what if I can't do it, what if I don't like it and I did it because my dad said it would make me a man. As for me, I stood in silent anticipation, ready to do whatever it took to be a soldier and to move on in life. True, I had thought "Shit, what have I bloody done?" I wasn't frightened, but I was concerned because I was so tiny, and I thought about all of those orders I would have to follow. But then, I thought if Gomer Pyle can get through it, I can get through it ha ha.

Two men, both in army uniforms, walked out of the doors of an old-looking green building. One was short in stature with a face that looked as if he had been in the sun too long. He seemed to have a redden blush, when he spoke but seemed kind and gentle. The other was taller with a distinct look of command on his face. Like me, many of the guys were trying to avoid eye contact, but that was a waste of time as the shorter of the two asked us to stand in two lines and lookup.

He then proceeded to call out our names, one by one. Each person would say "Here" or "Yes". I stood thinking they had forgotten to put my name on the list as the line dwindled. I had been used to being called Lewis, but now had to wait until the T's were called, with my recovered surname of Te'Nadii. It was something I had to get used to; I would be towards the end of the line for everything, which included pay, medicals and supplies forevermore.

Then it was on the bus! One by one, we placed our bags under the carriage baggage compartment and climbed on board. As we took our seats, not too much was said. I sat in an aisle seat next to a guy who introduced himself as Adam. Heads turned, and we exchanged smiles between each other as the bus pulled away from the curb. Finally, I was on my way!

Maybe ten to fifteen minutes had passed before the nice army guy, Corporal Stone, stood up from behind the driver's seat. He opened his mouth and out came this powerful, deep voice and a look that made it clear that playtime was over, and it was down to some serious business! He had transformed from this nice passive gentleman into something that resembled the incredible hulk!

The look on the other guys' faces showed they were as startled as I was. Corporal Stone said, in his authoritative voice, "Ok girls. Your life as you knew it is over now, and your time is ours! Quiet and look to the front!" All in a moment, I was thrust back into the past, to the years in the orphanage, and in an odd way, I felt comfortable. I was no stranger to men yelling at me, after all, this is what I had lived with day in day out for over eleven years. So this guy's yelling may have freaked the other guys out, but it seemed normal to me.

We stopped along the way, for lunch which was handed to us from a green container, together with a juice and an apple. Many of the guys sat in silence in the park, while others murmured in quiet conversation. I took it all in and kept my distance from everyone. I didn't really want to have much to do with anyone else at that point. After eating, we were herded back on to the bus and told to sit.

On second thoughts, there was something else. It was at this point that the return mini-bus was pointed out to us it sat at the edge of the car park. We were given the choice to continue to the army base or to return home. This was an option all recruits got before stepping off the enlistment bus on arrival to 1 RTB.

The next order came from the taller army guy, who introduced himself as Corporal Slone, (not to be confused with Corporal Stone), and that was all we needed to know. "If any of you want, you can get off the bus now and go over to that van to be returned to your Mumma" he said and smiled. There were no takers and we were on our way again.

As we arrived at 1RTB, we approached the sentry gates, where a military guard was standing at his post. We pulled up and he came on board the bus and talked to the NCO (Non-Commissioned Officer, Corporal Stone) and checked the paperwork. We then proceeded through the gates and up a winding road off to the left. We turned right and stopped in a carpark outside the First Recruitment Training Battalion Headquarters. The building was flanked by other buildings; medical centres, training blocks, accommodation facilities, mess halls, amenities, and so forth.

We were ushered off the bus and onto a grassed area where we received the next order, "Form up on the two lines; not a sound, not a move!" after which they took a general roll call. We carried our bags, four men per group, and were escorted to a big three-story building, which was to be our home for the next thirteen weeks, if all went well. You could smell the fear radiating from the other men and you could see it all over their faces!

I was on the lower level of the building, in what we soon knew to be Charlie Company. I was in the second room on the left, down the hall. My bed space was under a window and my name was displayed inside a shiny brass frame.

Another loud commanding yell came, and we all ran to the hall and stood against the wall as instructed. We were told the procedure for the remaining part of that day and night. As night fell, we were once more told to come to the hall, which was the assembly point for roll call. The command for our assemblies was known as Hallway 29. At this call, all recruits would have to repeat the same command and then assemble, as ordered against the wall.

It was dinner time and the first of what would be our meals—army-style. The entire recruitment establishment was built on a hill, and covered about two to three hundred acres. The barracks for Charlie Company were at the bottom of the hill and the mess hall, where we ate, was halfway up it; a five-minute march for our platoon. As we walked, tripped and slogged our way up that hill, for the first time, the size of the environment, we would soon become part of, became clear. In the mess (or dining room as it is called in the civilian world), we saw a huge number of other new recruits. The mess hall had room for one-thousand-three-hundred people, although only half the room was ever used.

We were allocated a table and seat which would be ours for the remaining time at Kapooka. Table by table we formed up and walked over to a long bench, which had containers of food from one end to the other. Around the room were other benches with juice, fruit, and dessert. It was like being in a hotel, or so I thought at the time. After the first six weeks, after we returned from our first recreational leave of five days, we were placed on ration packs for the last seven weeks of training, and which consisted of processed foods that were dried or dehydrated and which had little if any taste. We discovered that, because the government had cut its funding to the defence forces, so we would receive one pack of either A-B-C-D or E each day. In fact, the government had blown their budget and were in the red. They were drawing money from wherever they could, to get the country back on track, and as a result, we were put on rations. They also cut our pay and, in some cases, soldiers weren't paid for weeks during this time.

After dinner, we had showers and then it was "not a sound" until the next morning.

I soon understood why they built this place in the country, as far away as possible from ordinary life. For some time there was not a noise, and then—from nowhere—the earth seemed to open up with the thundering sound of army men yelling and trying to outdo each other for the loudest voice. "Hallway 29!" was commanded; "Hallway 29!" we repeated, then not another sound was heard.

Day one was upon us, and orders come from every direction, as we tried to remember what, when, why and how. A beam had been mounted from room to room, between every second room, and the penalties for doing the wrong thing were quickly addressed by chin-ups at the nearest beam. The orders were relentless, and delivered in loud and commanding voices: shit!', "shower", "shave", "get dressed" and "make your bed", along with "shut up", "not a sound", "just do it", and "now".

I could see many new recruits were starting to be frustrated by the commands and the pace at which they were set. You could hear heaps of recruits sobbing and groaning at night. There was no emotional support. The only thing they did when the going got tough was direct us to pick up the bible that they had issued us in the barracks and read it.

Weary and stressed recruits ran around, getting in each other's way, and the pressure began to mount. It was quite a way to start each day for them, and this was only week one! It was nothing new for me though; discipline, orders and hurry up and wait had already been a way of life for me in the orphanage.

A lot of guys buckled under the constant pressure and we lost a heap of them in week two, and even more after our rec break which was six weeks after training started. Even I was dreading going back after my first five days off and I remember thinking, "Oh, God no!"

Week seven was excruciating and more guys threw in the towel, and in week eight we all felt like walking pin cushions. In a single week, I got fourteen needles for all of the mandatory vaccinations we had to have. I still remember walking down the hallway of the medical centre at the barracks, which was lined with rooms, each one of which contained a nurse, armed with single needles and one had a sort of gun with five needles in it. As you walked past all you could hear was the sound of the gun as the medical NCO injected each recruit with his vaccinations. Strangely, we soldiers, who had Islanders' complexions, mostly handled them ok, but the recruits with red hair and freckles suffered or collapsed. They said it was due to our having a stronger immune system, apparently.

There were two other guys in my room, strangely, both named Adam. One was thirty-eight years of age and the other was only eighteen years of age. I felt for him; he only lasted three weeks before calling it quits. He was very young and homesickness got to him, so he headed home. After young Adam left, we had a spare bed in the room for a while, and then a guy called Moe came along and filled the empty bed space. He had failed his first initial six weeks on weapons and navigation assessment, and as such go to 13th Platoon (where you spent, at least, one week before starting the training all over again). This was known as being back-squatted. He was a good guy and we paired up during training quite a bit, as he was short like me, so we were a good match for physical activities.

Like all recruits, we underwent thirteen weeks of basic military training which included: weapons, marching, map reading, fitness, and general enlistment training. The mornings were always the same until after breakfast when we underwent service training on a variety of subjects. Some I loved, such as the PT sessions and sports days, and the weapon training was cool too, although I had to work hard to keep on my feet. Being small, I took the full brunt (kickback) of my 7.62 SLR (self-loading rifle), as every discharge slammed the weapon into my shoulder with no mercy. Then we'd have lunch, more training and get ready for the night-time training.

Army life was not a nine to five daily event; it was 24/7, and we quickly learned this. Corporal Slone, who was an ex-SAS soldier, just loved to push us to new limits, with night training until crazy hours, fire drills at will, early morning runs and combat training. There was never a dull moment, and medicals, dental, and physical assessments added to our lack of sleep. It was one thing after the other, with no stopping and no time to rest or relax. As Corporal Ken Mohngan, my section corporal, said, "The war waits for no man, remember that".

After our thirteen weeks of training, the rest of the Charlie Company and I, or those who had finished the training, made our honorary march out. There were approximately seventy-five soldiers on parade, not including the junior NCO's, sergeant, and platoon commander. It was a very moving moment, but one that I had to celebrate alone. Everyone had parents, family members, and friends who turned up to watch their historical event except for me. I was the only one standing alone.

Weapons training at the first Recruits Training Battalion, Kapooka NSW. The rifle was a 7.62 SLR (Self Loading Rifle).

Intense training done—we were ready for bigger things! I was still excited by the opportunity for a new life. After completing my Initial Employment (IET) Training, I was posted to Brisbane, as essential personnel in the 1st & 9th Military Police Unit, in Indooroopilly. This unit would become my service base for the next two years.

Over the initial training days, Corporal Mohngan had cottoned on to the fact that I was Dale's brother. Dale had been posted with him in 8/9 RAR in Brisbane three years earlier, and in the same platoon and had also been deployed overseas with him. Towards the end of my training, he welcomed me into the service and said, "I never expected you to make it through, let alone be awarded the most outstanding recruit for this enlistment!" That gave me more confidence that I could do this and start a new life.

CHAPTER 50

Puckapunyal

Nineteen years

IET (Initial Employment Training) saw me sent to Puckapunyal in Victoria in the later weeks of September 1978. Puckapunyal was a huge military area, which provided training and on-site employment for over 3000 service personnel from the transport corps, the catering corps, armour corps, and general enlistment posting.

Within the base surrounds were schools, grocery stores, doctors and dental services, local shops, and a service station which also had a pizza/café attached as part of the business. Businesses in Seymour, the nearby town, thrived with the financial input and it was clear that without the military in the area, Seymour would have slowly faded as many small towns did over time.

Some of the soldiers were married personnel and they lived in service homes, with their families, either on base or in the local town of Seymour. The families had the use of two religious nominations' churches, as well as an aquatic centre, a sports fields and a theatre. In an effort to build a relationship with all ages, the area also provided a BMX track both for training and competition riding. Later, this track became the (Victorian) state's number one track for major events because of the financial support offered by the service.

I would spend the next six months there, undergoing intense training and studies in cookery alongside assessments, trades' tests, and food functions for varying dinners. Alongside this, we were still required to continue with military training and ongoing tests. One bonus that we got here, and that we hadn't had at Kapooka, was downtime. We got time to ourselves, after trade training and studies each day and on weekends. This allowed us to go into town and buy things and was the first free time we had been given, apart from one Saturday morning in Wagga Wagga, back in August of the same year.

Seymour became my local town for my next six months and would provide me with many options, one which was the luxury of pizza, which the other guys in my barracks also enjoyed on weekends. Another was that I was also able to drive down to Melbourne with a few other guys, who had family down there, and then catch a train to Geelong to see my friends.

During my training posting to Puckapunyal, I undertook extra educational studies, knowing that I would need these skills in the future for further promotions. This was also a time to get to know a little more about the PTI (Physical Training) requirements. Gary Asher was our PTI sergeant at Puckapunyal, and he became a valuable resource of information for me and provided me with extra training formats.

I didn't know it at the time but four years later we would both be posted together in the same training area, and would also tour together as part of the (Australian) army gymnastic service team. Who would have guessed that? I also got to play many sports on Wednesdays, but this time I decided to participate in as many different codes as possible so that I could learn more about each.

During my time at Puckapunyal, I built a wonderful friendship with two other guys, who also did their recruit training at 1RTB with me. Tragically the friendship was cut short when they were returning to the barracks from Ballarat on a weekend pass and were killed in a motor vehicle accident, only 2000 meters from the barrack's main entrance.

It was devastating for the whole base, and we honoured them by spending the next week preparing both soldiers for their military funeral, before their bodies were flown home to their families.

Another person I became close friends with was a private by the name of Craig King or Kingie as I called him. Kingie was not your normal recruit. He had already done four years in the service, in the infantry corps, and had been posted to 6 RAR. Like many others, Craig had been drafted directly into the infantry corps after enlisting in 1974. This was not by choice, as at that time the system required more Infantry soldiers. They were given the option later on to request a corps transfer which is what Craig had done.

We talked a lot about the days he had spent as a foot soldier in the infantry and the things he wanted to do in the future. In truth, he didn't have a clear and colourful image of what he had done or what he was expected to do in the future, within the Infantry regiment, which was why Kingie applied for a service transfer. After around six months of submitting his application for a transfer, he was granted the change and landed at Puckapunyal the same time as I did.

I had a mere thirteen-weeks in the service, whereas Kingie had over forty-eight months under his belt. Lucky him and even luckier me, as having him in the same barracks allowed me to pick his brains on the many options available to a soldier. Later on, as fate would have it, I would later be posted back to Puckapunyal as an instructor; the very same position as those who were currently training me.

Days passed first, followed by weeks, and then four-weeks of R&R at Christmas came, followed by the final four weeks of my trade qualifications. After completing my trade studies, in 1979, I was sent to my first service posting. I packed up my belongings in the barracks and handed them over to the unit transport and movements division, who would arrange for my personal belongings to be transported to Brisbane.

I had seven days to travel to Brisbane, so, I headed for Geelong where I would spend a single night before finally say goodbye to friends and departing for that 1900 km trip to Brisbane, Queensland.

CHAPTER 51

My First Posting

Twenty years

Arriving in Brisbane at the start of 1979, on my first service posting, was exciting. I had purchased a car before joining the army—a white 1976 Charger—which I had left in Geelong at Gaz's place, until my recruitment and IET training were over. I spent the night hanging out at Gaz's and in the morning packed up and headed off to Brisbane. On arrival to take up my first posting,

I pulled up in front of the main entryway, which symbolised that at one point or another the property had been one of importance. I sat and stared in awe at the two large gates attached to stone pillars on each side of the driveway, which led up to a sealed road between grand palm trees. I looked around and to the right, I saw there was a train station, which I would later learn was the train station of a suburb in Brisbane called Indooroopilly.

My second posting was to Fort Queenscliff in Victoria. This was an amazing unit housing an abundance of wartime memorabilia and museums.

Looking up the drive I could see the military unit I was soon to become a part of in the distance. Standing proudly like the White House, it held command atop the property on a massive parcel of land overlooking the Brisbane River. Positioned behind, and to the left, was the original Governor General's living accommodation; it was huge and had its own driveway leading off to the left of the main road's entrance.

The unit itself was built as part of the type of military garrison you'd see in movies, which looked like a protective fortress from many years ago. This one had been converted into a detention centre, for soldiers and prisoners who had been charged and placed under guard in military confinement cells (prison), for anything up to fourteen days. In my time, it comprised part of the barracks that I would call home.

The unit was incredible. I loved it and my roommate was a military transport NCO (Non-Commissioned Officer) by the name of Tony Bell—whom we all called Dinga. Dinga was the commanding general in Queensland's personal driver, so he was on call 24/7, which had him working some strange hours at any part of the day. He and I got along great and soon became mates.

He introduced me to his local AFL team, South Brisbane, and wouldn't give up asking me to come along and play. During my second year of posting, Dinga finally talked me around and I went down for a training run. The coach asked me if I would fill in for someone who was out that coming Saturday, which I enjoyed and I played three more games with them while posted there.

During my time in Brisbane, I really amped up my fitness and when I wasn't working at the barracks, I had a book full of all kinds of fitness activities, and I loved it. I started running daily, around the local streets, either during my lunch hour or after work. At first, it was to familiarise myself with the area, but later I did it to improve on my fitness. I also swam at the local pool up the road, in St Lucia, doing around 2—3 km, twice a week.

Still passionate about Rugby, I hunted around for a local team to join, and began training and playing with a team in Annerley in South Brisbane. However, I had to stop after seven games because of service commitments and field training.

I had unknowingly followed in my brother, Dale's, footsteps to Queensland. He had moved to Brisbane a couple of years before my service posting, so it was great to be able to spend some of my weekends at his place. Dale hadn't really found his roots in life yet and he had not really changed. He still always wanted to go out and party, or go to concerts, and loved a good beer or few.

He was also a mad AFL fan and wouldn't miss the opportunity to watch it on TV, live at the games in Brisbane, or go to the ones in Melbourne, after he returned to live there three years later. It always surprised me how passionate he was about the game, especially considering his culture and love for rugby as a child. He still loved his music, too, which became his favourite pastime during his years in the military, and after discharge.

Unlike me, Dale hadn't entered the army of his own accord, but had selected the option to enlist for three years, to avoid a prison sentence. He did his service training at 1RTB and went into the infantry corps 8/9 RAR, where he spent the remaining three years under his court order and a further three years of his own accord. However, Dale just seemed to find trouble in many places, and while he was on deployment overseas, the company he was part of received 48 hours on shore leave. A few mates and he got drunk, and decided to get a few tattoos . . . well, EIGHT tattoos later, he returned to his post only to wake up bleeding the next morning.

He attended the RAP (regimental aid post) where he was treated for the bleeding and, as if that didn't hurt enough, he also got a military charge. It was a chargeable offence, in the service, to self-inflict wounds, which was what they said his were. Dale had a nice little rest, to cure his hangover and to heal, as he spent the next twelve days in detention.

By the time I arrived up in Brisbane he was already out of the army and working as a truck driver and was still as loose as ever! He was always borrowing my car and crashing it—the bugger! Every time he had a good story and an excuse for how it happened! I recall one time I took annual leave and flew to Geelong for four weeks to see Debbie and her family and friends. Dale asked to borrow my Charger for a week— he loved it! Wrong move on my part, because by the time I got back it looked more like a crushed can than a car! Apparently, he had lost control on a wet road and hit a tree. Because he wasn't on my insurance policy, I had to wear the cost!

Another time, silly me trusted him again. I flew to Melbourne on leave again, only to return to see the backend of my car compacted by half. This time he wasn't in the wrong, though, which made it a little easier to take. Another driver had rear-ended him at a set of lights.

It wasn't all Dale, though. I had a few accidents myself. The mechanic had said it would be a long two months before my car would be fixed from Dale's last accident, so I decided to buy a motorbike—a new 1979 XS 650 Midnight Special. It was an early twenty-first birthday present for me to get around on. I spent the morning of my birthday with Dale, before my arrangements to fly to Geelong for my two-week R&R, to see Debbie. On my way to drop my bike off at the barracks, a driver ran a red light and hit me head-on. That was some accident.

All I remember at the time was the emergency crew cutting me out of the other guy's windscreen. Three days in the hospital and a cancelled holiday wasn't my favourite memory that's for sure! On top of that, the other driver had, unbelievably, taken out a law-suit for the damages I had inflicted upon him. OMG! What the hell? He ran a red light and hit me, yet he was suing me?!!!!

I handed all the documentation over to the service lawyer, who handled the case. I ended up going to court with a member of the army's legal department, who looked after the summary hearing. The driver of the vehicle turned up in a neck brace and on crutches, along with his legal team, which consisted of a lawyer and interpreter.

The judge listened intently to our back and forth discussion and it was soon evident that the driver was going to be found at fault, with no claim entitlement. He was also formally charged and had to pay the overtime and legal costs incurred by the commonwealth, which included the replacement of my bike, medical support, and surgery. Thank goodness the judge saw right through his little con.

Following my little hospital stint, I went under the knife again, a little later, to have part of my major pectoral muscle removed, as it had been crushed and just wouldn't re-attach. It was slowly dying, so the only option was to remove it. This did place a lot of restrictions on my physical abilities, because of the pain and my strength limitations, but over time I built more muscle support and learned to manage what I could and could not do.

From that day on, I amped up my training again, this time knowing what direction I wanted to take in my service training. I had not yet worked out how to get there, but at the time I felt I was doing something that would build a solid base for what I wanted to achieve in the service.

CHAPTER 52

Fatherhood

Twenty-two years

During my first service posting in Brisbane, from March 1979 until early 1980, my partner, Debbie, visited me several times and stayed with me at Dale's place; a few suburbs away from my army unit. As I was a service personnel with fewer than twelve months of duty, and unmarried, I was not permitted to seek private accommodation, and had to live in the barracks.

Debbie and I had been together, officially, for about two years, when one day I received a phone call from her, letting me know she was pregnant and I was about to become a dad! I was beyond shocked and remember thinking that we had talked about this and had decided it was too early. It was obvious we would eventually get married, have children, raise them, and spend our retirement years on the back porch reminiscing as we grew old. Debbie's falling pregnant so early just brought the timeline a whole lot closer and a whole lot earlier.

I felt I was still too young to be raising a child at twenty-two years of age, but I had to put on a smile and get used to the idea, because, in a matter of months, I was going to be a father. I still had that great wall of protection built up around me and the enormity of the responsibilities I had to face overwhelmed me. I still had so much to do, before settling down into family life. I did care for Debbie, but I wished this had happened later in my life, so that I could have focused and concentrated on the path I had planned out and set for myself and my family.

All that aside, we started to make arrangements. I said we needed to get married, because I did not want my son born into a relationship that wasn't formalised. So preparations began, with Debbie making many trips between Queensland and Geelong until all was ready for the big day. I had flown Debbie up to Queensland to live with me so that we could manage things from one end. Because we were going to get married and have a child, the army approved my move into service accommodation, outside the barracks. This allowed Debbie to live with me in a de-facto relationship until we married.

As the date drew close, Debbie flew back down to Geelong, two weeks before the big day to enjoy her bridal shower and to spend her last weeks as a single woman with her friends. I took early holidays, also two weeks out from the wedding, to spend time with friends. Gaz, Allan, and Peter flew up to Brisbane and stayed with me for a week, enjoying relaxing bucks, before flying down from Queensland to Geelong to complete the wedding preparations.

Debbie was around seven months pregnant on the day of our wedding. Gaz was my best man and, as expected, Allan Dennett was alongside him. I'd met him with Gaz and he lived across the road from the unit we had shared in Geelong. Peter Corstin was my other groomsman. Amongst the many things I had hoped for, was to have all three brothers and my sister at my wedding. I had no idea where my older brother Brian was. I had heard that he had returned from his band tour of England and was now travelling around NZ, making music as he had always wanted to do. It was the same with Darren, I had heard on the grapevine that he'd moved to the Gold Coast to live with his father, Gerald, but wasn't really sure where he was, or what he was doing.

Teena and Dale were easy to invite as I was still in contact with both of them. My mother was a different story, though. I hadn't kept in contact with her at all and the last time I saw her was when I was seventeen and working casually at KFC. I had serious concerns about inviting her to the wedding, but Debbie wanted me to invite her. I succumbed and thought that, at the very least, she would know where Brian and Darren were at the time, so I invited her to the wedding and held my breath.

Brian and Darren did not RSVP to my invitation, and I don't know if my mother even told them. Teena and Dale did RSVP and both came, which gave me so much joy on the day. My mother came along with a tribe of people whom I'd never met and didn't even know were coming! An Aunty; Aunty Fay, nephews and a niece, none of whom I knew! However, for some reason, I felt closer to her than my own mother and I still do today. It was frustrating having my mother there; she was as annoying and disruptive as always, and she did her best to make the day all about her. I kept my distance, but she was nice to Debbie, which was the most important thing at the time.

After the wedding we moved back to Queensland as a married couple, taking up residency in another service accommodation. Our first service property was a small unit over-looking the Brisbane river, just up the road from the barracks, but on the second level.

Debbie's mother and nanna came up, the week before the birth, to give Debbie support. On the day of the birth, Debbie began having pains, so we rang the hospital and they said to bring her in. I was there for about an hour and the doctor said it was going to be quite a while, maybe even the next day, before the baby would be born. I drove home with the intention of going back that night. I had just driven into the driveway when Debbie's mum yelled out to me from the house "You've got to go back! She's in labour!"

I flew back to the hospital and, with six minutes spare, made it back in time to be in the room when our son was born. It seemed that I transitioned from a boy to a man overnight, with the birth of my son, Damien Travis Te'Nadii, on the 1st of May 1980. The responsibility I felt for someone so tiny was incredulous. That day and how I felt seems like yesterday—standing there in the hospital room, looking at him. If only to have that time again . . .

It is so easy to forget times like this; when you hold a child, your child, in your arms for the first time. Between the shaking of the sheer nerves and the intensity of the moment of looking into his face and warming with the joy I felt that nothing in my life had meant more to me. He was a beautiful boy. My firstborn and the first of my children to call me Dad. How can you forget that moment? I was overjoyed.

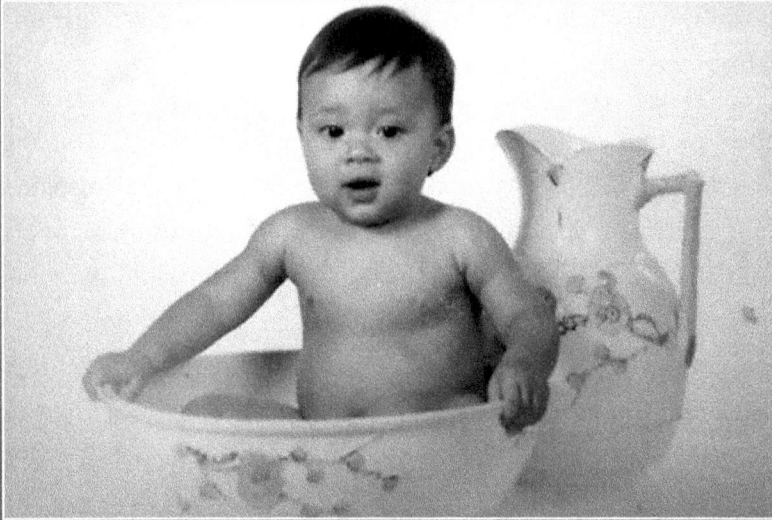

My prized picture of my son Damien Travis Te'Nadii.

Love has so many meanings, in so many different ways and cultures, but when you hold your child in your arms on the day he or she is born, your mind explodes filling you with a thousand thoughts. Looking at him for the first time, I felt warmth come across me, and a tear slid down my cheek. Is this how love feels? I thought it was.

For the first time in my life, I felt a really peaceful feeling and like any parent, I also thought about the many ways I would protect him. I wanted to see the world through his eyes, and to feel and reach for all the possibilities to come his way, and have him know I would always be there for him. His hopes were my hopes, his dreams my dreams. I wanted him to know he could trust in me and my love and support for him on his journey. As his father, I would do my best for him, and I would ensure he never felt alone or hurt as I had.

On that day—his birthday—I made it my intention to wholeheartedly take up the responsibility of being his father, guardian and protector. I held him and loved him more than I ever thought possible. All I wanted to do was take him home and lay him down next to me. It had taken the birth of my first child to bring an understanding, into my life, of what pure joy was. It had taken my firstborn to break the wall I had built up around myself and he did it in a matter of seconds. When he reached his tiny hand out, as if trying to stretch to reach out and softly touch my face, I completely caved and opened up my heart as I had never done before—our bond set.

He was an incredible baby, in fact, the nurse at the hospital had concerns about him initially because he was so unlike the other newborns in the hospital, Damien never really cried. He was content to sleep, feed, and repeat. At home, he slept well and was one of those dream babies every parent hopes to have. As a toddler, he was a quiet little lad, who never stopped smiling and watching everyone intently. He showed strong learning capabilities early on, in his own quiet way.

The only negative thing, and something I felt awful about, was that he inherited eczema from my side of the family. Like me, it used to irritate him if we didn't keep the moisture upon his skin and he would scratch until he bled. Thankfully, we were able to control the worst of it through medication, a reduction in sugar and a healthy diet.

He loved to be outside and he'd be outside playing at every opportunity, with his ball or toys, in the fresh air and sunshine. He loved tinkering with things, pulling things apart and trying to put them back together. He was my little shadow, holding on to my legs, and whenever I sat down, he'd sit on my lap. When I cooked, he'd sit on the bench, helping me or chatting away while I prepped the food.

My first picture with my son Damien on arriving home from the hospital.

He loved watching cartoons and sports with me on TV. Like father, like son. He loved rugby and he couldn't wait to begin playing the game. Being a father like all fathers, you think only the best for your children and that was no different from how I saw my life with Damien. I would find any reason to talk to him, walk with him, or just look at him, thinking "Look what I have brought into this world".

Through the years we had our ups and downs, growing up, but that is to be expected as they grow, learn, and develop self needs. In addition to all this, and to this day, I will always be so proud of and love my son.

CHAPTER 53

Service Training

Twenty-three to twenty-four years

Fitness and the knowledge of the human body absolutely fascinated me—I couldn't get enough of it. During my years at the college in Victoria, I completed lots of activities, wanting to learn as much as possible. In 1982, at the age of twenty-four, I was invited to attend the 1/82 Subunit PT Course. This course was designed to assess future instructors in physical training and upon passing would provide minor units with a base instructor in exercise specifics.

Attending the course was the easy part; the contents and physical requirements were something else. This was a whole new level of required physical condition, to anything I'd experienced before, and without question the hardest physical fitness I'd ever put my body through up until that point. "What was I thinking?!" went through my mind a lot. I will never forget the pain and strain I went through. There were many times I wished I had never started. I was sure they were tearing every muscle in my body out, and almost breaking every bone more than twice, as well as starving me of sleep nightly, just because they could. It was tough!

The physical toll was hard, but the emotional side was even harder. I was away from my new son at such an early age and for a whole nine weeks. It was the worst! I thought I had readied myself for it, but I was very wrong. It was really hard to adjust to not seeing his smile, smelling him, or hearing him. I knew many of the other members on the course were also married with children and they struggled too, not seeing them. We were able to make calls home each night and talk about our children during the day, which made things a little more bearable, but the lonely nights were a killer, though.

The Physical Education School was based within the Artillery Unit at the top of North Heads in Manly, Sydney. The base was situated at the top of the headland before looping along the most eastern edge. What a sight it was, looking over the cliffs in the early mornings on our routine 5 km run with our instructors in tow. Originally, a hospital and quarantine garrison sat on the land in the 1920s and 1930s, for new arrivals into Australia with possible diseases. To this day, it is believed that the area is still walked by those who died there.

The training was demanding, with 5—10 km runs daily, along with a weekly 26 km run. At the instructor's discretion, we could also do extra distance training, if we chose to. I did this many times, to help break down the fatigue I carried, and on the days when studies took up the greater part of the day. Sitting around always built up chemicals in my legs that I needed to remove and what better way than a few kilometres to clear the head and body.

Every Wednesday we would bus to Frenchs Forest Aquatic Centre. Here we would do three hours of intense water skills. Through this, I obtained my teacher's qualifications in swimming and life-saving. At the end of the swimming training, we would get dressed into running clothes and head of on a 13.7 KM run back to the barracks at North Head.

Along the way we would stop and, on the instruction of a senior PTI, we would meet up with a service truck that would have training equipment stored in the back. We then did extra training, such as:

- Carrying exercises with each other as weights, and always while heading uphill
- Beach sprints of between 300—600 and 800 meters
- Ocean water sprints up to 50 meters out and back
- Log carry exercises along the beach
- Tyre pushing and pulling exercises along the beach

On one occasion we were taken to a park where four army service trailers sat. We had to load our personal gear and backpacks into a trailer with eight members to each one. From there, we had to push or pull the trailers back to the barracks, some five km away with 2000 meters of uphill.

There were times we would be required to swim up to 3 km, from Manly Beach across to Shelly Beach as part of the extra training, in the ocean, in full kit and dragging a log, which was a bonus in a way, knowing that the log floated. This used to petrify me as everyone knew Manly Beach was very "sharkie". Along with this training, we would have to take our service backpacks with us. We used black garbage bags to place them in, to keep them waterproof.

On arrival back to the barracks, we would find yet more physical training set up. This included the elements of training that broke the best of the toughest men I had trained within my life.

We would take a short 500-meter jog up the heads of Manly, to find 105 Artillery guns waiting in the sand. We would be divided into teams of fourteen and told to push, drag, or do whatever it took to returns the 105 Artillery guns back to their holding bays at the barracks. Yes, all well and good, except the return to barracks came with two options.

1. Pull and push the guns to the road about 120, meters and then continue along a hard surface up to the top of the heads, around the return loop and back down to the barracks. A distance of about 4.5 km give or take. The road was hilly and windy, but also had downhill periods which would make the control of the guns difficult.

2. The second option was to push the guns across the sand for 500 meters onto the road and across to the 105 Artillery Gun holding bays. This seemed the best option and would take a lot less time, but it also meant about 200% harder work required by each soldier, grunting, swearing and just becoming physically destroyed.

I was not one for walking away from hard work, so I would always chose option two. It just made sense to do it, and get it out of the way so we could look back on another victory. There were team members who never saw it this way and I am sure many times they held back, of leaving a lot of the physical yakka to the few who didn't give up.

Another running exercise we often did was stretcher runs with a person lying on it as if injured. Here we shared the load, by rotating around the stretcher from handle to handle to rest our arms. We also got to lie back for around 500 meters, as we had to change the patient being carried every 500 meters. Crazy, but I loved this training.

Another favourite of mine was log exercises. We would collect them from the gym and take them for a sunny hot or raining and cold run around the heads of Manly or down to the beach and back. Along the way, the instructors would stop us and give us formation exercises such as:

- Team squats with the log held above the head or across the chest
- Log chest presses
- Log throws between teams
- Log pulling and pushing events
- Single man log drag relays

My favourite was the log sprint and climb. We would run 100 meters with a log, and then stop and raise the log so that one end was pointed to the sky. The only thing here was that we also had to have a team member lying across the top like a starfish with arms and legs extended. Being the smallest I was always the one on top of the log....woo-hoo. If I fell, it was straight to the ground some 6.2 meters below.

Gymnastics was a must, and as part of our training, we had to reach a level of competence, demonstrate it, and show we could also teach it. This specific requirement saw the demise of many as injuries were prevalent.

We would run to the water police training facilities down the road and complete beach and water obstacles. Any spare moment was spent in the gym going over lesson plans to learn how to demonstrate, explain and then have the student practise all of the physical training aspects of what was being taught. This would include conducting and being assessed on each by the instructors. Every move was scrutinised.

Combat and self-defence classes, minor team games, and more running made the day complete, but only up to a point. Just as you thought the day was done, it was time to sit half asleep and exhausted, for one hour in studies, such as anatomy, physiology, exercise performance, as well as human movements, functional training, aerobic, and anaerobic movements.

At the end of all this, we had a shower and a solid meal followed by a phone call home. Every night's class studies required work plans to be presented the following morning on the application of exercise, and the format and how to conduct all of the group classes we had taken each day. That was together with our medical studies and assessments. I would generally have another night shower to cool down around 11:00 pm, followed by five fantastic hours of sleep.

I watched as grown men walked up and rang the bell, as an acknowledgement that they could not go on. In truth, I had thought of it a few times myself, but only because I missed Damien so much. Every night, on the phone, I would be reminded why I wanted to do this and how I would be recompensed later.

The PT course was only conducted every second year, and when we had started we had been told that 3,600 service personnel had applied to attend the 1/82 Sub-unit PT course, but only 60 had been selected. in addition to those selected for the course, there were also three invited members of the Papua New Guinea Defence Force: two soldiers from the army and one from the navy. They found the course extremely hard and far beyond their physical abilities but, because of the international exchange and diplomatic relations, they would be required to complete the full duration of the course and pass, even though they did well to complete the course facing moments that would greatly challenge them.

We had to give them credit, they did every requirement daily, as best they could and at the same intensity as us, and always with a smile. To us, they were part of our team and deserved the right to go back home with their heads held high. They achieved every right to be called instructors back home.

I was amongst the few lucky men and women who were assessed and seen as having the highest chance of passing the course and being placed into a posting as a Physical Training Instructor.

Of those 60 highly fit service personnel who started the course, only nineteen elite soldiers made it through, I was one of them. Six of us were to be offered the opportunity to become Physical Training Instructors within the service. I was the first to be posted as an instructor from my course followed by John Miles, who placed second and Mark Charles Jones who was third. It was quite an achievement for me, considering the training course started off with so many applicants. Not only was I accepted into the course but I came out on top of my class.

The proudest moment on the course was being asked to stand front and centre before the class, to receive the Most Outstanding Attendee Award. My report said, "Private Daryl Te'Nadii attended the 1st of 82 sub-unit PTI course. He showed high levels of physical fitness with a 10/10 result in all aspects of testing."

In later years I would return, to complete further studies and my senior training requirements before my promotion to sergeant. Today the school has been re-located. If you're a fan of YouTube and want to check out our training, I've added a link to our session, at the back of this book. To get an idea of the training I undertook, there is a short promotional film on the training that the Physical Training Instructors did at the school of Artillery, North Heads, Sydney.

Today, that same building has been used by Channel 9 for TV shows, such as The Biggest Loser. What a building, and what a location! It sits up high on the headland of Manly in Sydney. When we were there, the gym had a heavy musty smell from the gallons of human sweat that had been shed in it, as we pushed ourselves through pain to glory. It excited me and drove me on.

One of many reasons I never gave up was the thought of all of those people with me, and before me, exerting themselves, and leaving nothing on the table and everything on that gym floor. It was immensely motivating.

Looking back, I wonder what possesses any man or women to do what I did, to break through the pain threshold only to endure it again a second, third and fourth time. Yet, I did even more while I was on the course. I swam, ran, jumped, lifted, and ran some more, on weekends, outside of studies, and the homework assignments. I just loved the feeling of it. I lived for the excitement of it and of going beyond my physical capacity, as I had known it.

Those, who know me, know I don't do anything half-hearted and will never say I can't do it. If anything, this has been my strength in the fantastic health and fitness industry I loved back then and still do, to this day.

I have done many physical things in my life since then. Still, none were as spirit breaking, physically demanding, and mentally draining as what I went through at the Army School of Physical Training Academy. It took eighty days to qualify as an elite Instructor in the service, and I would duplicate this four years later, by attending the senior Physical Training Instructors course for the rank of sergeant.

After the course, I went back to the life of a regular soldier at the Queensland Cliff Training College for officers in Victoria. I waited for information about where I would be posted, only to hear it would be around two years before a vacancy would become available. That shattered me and left me thinking about my next training opportunity so that I could stay prepared for my posting. With so long to wait, I decided to set my sights higher and requested permission to do the Special Air Service (SAS) selection course. This is a training format, for elite soldiers to do as stage one of the SAS—Special Air Services Regiment entry criteria.

After around one month, I received a message notifying me that my application "Stage One" had been accepted.

Through my unit, I learned I would be required to undergo a physical fitness test which my CSM—company sergeant major—thought ridiculous. After all, I was the units PTI, and I had just completed the mother of all the physical tests the army could throw at anyone. But, to keep the selectors happy, we started the test. It had to be completed within four weeks and returned, for any potential move forward, which was to the medical assessments and psychological evaluations.

A little shy of two weeks after requesting to enter the Special Air Service (SAS) Selection course training program, I received word, out of the blue, that a promotion and posting for a Physical Training Instructor had become available if I wanted it. My thoughts of becoming part of the SAS were soon forgotten, and I left Fort Queens Cliff, with my family, to begin a new exciting employment adventure in Puckapunyal Victoria.

I also had the chance to visit Teena, and Dale, before I left. Dale had relocated to Box Hill, in Melbourne, and had married an amazing woman called Robin. We talked and along the way I answered many questions on the new posting. Dale knew a lot about PTI's, being a past serving member, but to Teena, it was all new.

I was in a good place (as were both Dale and Teena). We parted and I felt happier than I had ever felt and was excited about my future as an instructor. I was excited to be looking after the wellbeing of so many and within all ranks. Driving along I smiled. Debbie could see the happiness in my eyes, as I looked back at Damien, who was fast asleep.

CHAPTER 54

Casie J Te'Nadii

Twenty-four years

It was during my posting to Command and Staff Collage that my second child was born. For any man, having your first daughter is a moment you never want to lose or forget, and that was just how it felt for me.

My second child, Casie J Te'Nadii, was born with a sparkle in her blue eyes, and she stole my heart the minute I saw her. Falling in love was an understatement. The love you have for your son is as immense as you have for your daughter, yet both are different in many ways.

Casie was born Tuesday the 22nd of March 1983. She was a fair-skinned princess, with the odd freckle, a genetic inherited from her mum's side I am sure, along with her soft golden-blonde hair. From my side, she got her mouth, eyes, and cheeky smile.

Casie J.

As she grew, more of the Te'Nadii genetic traits became apparent. She spoke her mind, just like me; she made friends everywhere she went, just like her uncle Dale; and she just had that smile and crazy way of bringing people towards her wanting to know more about her, just like my older sister Teena.

I watched in amazement as Casie grew, day-to-day and over the years, all the while realizing just how blessed I was. I watched her discover her talents and carve out her path, with her strong mind. I knew that in her learning, she would not be told. She learned her way and, being the leader that she was, she then taught others when the time was right.

This incredible girl opened my eyes and heart every time she smiled. To me, she was like an angel, who had been sent to me, to help me move on and come to terms with my past while helping make a difference in my own and other people's lives. I felt a bond with Casie that nothing or no one could break. How could I not be so proud of this beautiful girl who gave me even more reasons to want to live?

Casie grew into an even more amazing young lady, as she entered adulthood, which is something I, and probably most fathers, didn't look forward to. Knowing I would have to pass her hand over to another, one day, was something I could not come to grips with back then. How could any man look out for his daughter, support her, and love her as deeply as I had; only to watch her walk away with another man, and trust him to give her what only a father can.

Casie became a mother and over the years gave birth to three beautiful children. She has two daughters and a son, who—like her—show incredible traits of leadership, trust, and friendship.

Life with my two amazing children held so many good moments, however, life with my wife was not all I was hoping for. In a way, I felt I needed a friend who could dig deeper within me; a friend who would help me to escape the demons I had allowed into my life. A friend who could understand I was hurt and carrying the scars from the pain, no matter the outcome of each chapter in my life. I needed help, but I could not open up. Debbie was many things, besides a mother and a wife, but she was not the person who was going to help me along that road to recovery, and that was what I needed at such a young age.

One of the many things I had to learn quickly about Casie J, was her many complexities, as she grew through the years. Along with this I also had to learn to tolerate them to the point where I could guide her. Even as a small child, I soon learned she had girl-secrets, some of which I had to respect and understand were hers alone. But from this, and the ones she did speak about, came the great gift we shared, which is the bond and love we had for each other.

Today Casie is my closet friend, alongside her little sister Baila Rae, and Janet, my wife. We will randomly message and call just to say hi. As Casie grew older, she also became a very mature woman and one I could and can talk to openly. Casie is an amazing beauty therapist and loves using her talents. Her girls grow year by year; both in beauty and height, and her son had evolved into an incredible young man with amazing skills in sports.

One of the many moments I look forward to each year is catching up with Casie and the kids. Being a grandfather has made me more aware of the love I have for my children.

CHAPTER 55

Becoming an instructor

Twenty-four years

These times in the service were some of the best times of my life; playing rugby again and putting new soldiers through their physical training. I loved challenging them to bring them up to the level they needed, as a fit and strong field soldier in both combat and non-combat roles.

On my arrival at Puckapunyal, I was welcomed by the staff of the admin department; some of whom were military personal and others, who were civilians. This combination of personnel had become more apparent in the past years, as the government realised the need for civil support in some areas. I was directed to the housing section, where my accommodation had been pre-booked in a local hotel. We would stay here for just over a week until my furniture arrived.

The house I was allocated was nice, with an open backyard and spacious rooms. I took my wife, Damien and Casie J to the hotel and left them to rest until I had completed my full march in process, as required for all incoming service personnel.

Part of this process was to attend the gym I had been attached too. There, I met Quinten Carlos, a junior NCO at my level, and Sergeant Ray Mawhinney. Ray was softly spoken with signs of hard work that showed on his face. As for Quinten, he was a lot taller, skinnier than I had expected and over time he demonstrated above-average traits of power and control. Over time we built an incredible friendship and bond between us. PTI's weren't the most liked people on base, but that came with the role, and I learned to accept it.

Another person I met a little later was Gary Asher, the sergeant of the Puckapunyal Transport training unit. Gary was a lot stockier than the other two men and liked to have fun with his classes, but when it came to hard work with the soldiers, he was always the man. I had spent time with Gary in the past, during my IET training back in 1979. After talking to him, I learnt he had been posted to a new unit in 1980, but on request took on a second posting to Puckapunyal. I always wondered why; after all, it was an average posting with little potential for promotion and miles from any major city. The answer came as I soon realised a female soldier he liked had been posted there and he wanted to be in the same area.

I spent a further two-plus year here, undergoing in-field supervision and assessments, and later doing my Subject 2 for sergeant. It was full on from day one! The first unit that I took for PT was 21 Construction Company. I soon learned they were a tough group and I had to gain their trust and respect. After a few sessions with them, I decided I needed to up the volume and intensity, which risked pushing them in the wrong direction. Something I had learned from a past instructor came back to me then; if I expected my soldiers to do it, make sure I was prepared to do it too. I took this on board as I introduced Murderball into their PT session on the day, and the pool.

This game is a bit like water polo but played side to side in the shallow after I had decided to play, I picked a side, and it wasn't long before I went under the water only to come up with blood running from my nose. I got a few looks from others and it was play on, as I matched the more significantly sized guys with my skills and strength. Twenty minutes later, I had their trust in a red-soaked pool where their heads were bowed in respect. It was a hard way to learn, but worth every moment. I spent many hours later with the same guys training them and also three weeks fighting the Ash Wednesday Fires with them.

Soldiers were always ready to support state emergencies, if and as required. As 21 Construction were engineers, they had the manpower and equipment to set blaze tracks around the fire's edge and to build up embankments to help fight the fires. Apart from this unit, I was also responsible for several other units; some small in numbers and others with up to 120 personnel.

I lived and loved every moment of my posting to Puckapunyal, learning from Ray and Quinten in readiness for the advanced courses. I played rugby, tennis, and badminton as sports. The agility from each helped me in many ways. As I become more aware of the community, I also started teaching gymnastics for a local club at night, which was fun as well. As I was new to PT, my role also meant that I would have to do extra duties at the pool. We had one indoor 25 m pool, a 50 m outdoor pool, and a junior pool for ages six and under.

The weekends saw many road trips back and forth to Geelong, as Debbie' parents lived there and always wanted to see and catch up with her and the kids. On the weekends I drove down, we would venture out doing things and exploring the outer regions.

I kept my mind ticking over with various study courses; such as Subject 1 for corporal, Subject 3 education, Subject 4 PT, and open survival training. I loved the learning in that one and retained the information about bush skills. I was hungry for more. I pushed on and enthusiastically took advantage of any learning I could get.

Further promotions meant more education, about which I was not overly excited, but I knew that's what it would take. I hit the books again and returned to school to complete my HSC (High School Certificate), which I had never done when I was younger, because I was too busy trying to make cardboard beds to sleep on and find food—to eat just to stay alive before being rescued by Gaz. As soon as I finished my HSC, I attended the advanced Physical Training Instructor course, as well. In later years, after a posting to the Army Apprentice School, I was rewarded with another promotion: to SGT (Sergeant) and I took on a newly created role, as part of the 4th Military Hospital and two field Ambulance unit. This was a pre-training service unit, specifically for field operations, just like the TV show MASH.

This job had me Townsville bound! As it happened this new journey in my life created many good memories and also, it would turn out, one very bad one.

CHAPTER 56

Darren

Twenty-five years

The day I found out, in 1969, that I had a little brother, meant I was no longer the youngest in the family. Although Darren was just two years younger, and my half-brother, we became amazing friends. We were both sports-mad and joined athletics together; finding we both had terrific levels of endurance. We would train together, go over tactics together, and talk sport every moment. We both enjoyed sprints; Darren loved the shorter distances, and I the longer ones.

Darren introduced me to Australian Rules football, which I had a crack at playing one season, but I was often benched for being too rough, so I went back to rugby. Darren stayed with it and did ok.

I introduced Darren to my other passion—motorbikes, and later the world of Harley Davidson. It was not too long before he brought his first bike; a 1972 HD Soft Tail. What a beauty she was, with chrome from end to end, a raked front end, and ½ ape bars. For those who don't know, ape bars are your handlebars and come in three lengths, ¼ - ½ and full. Darren was completely in his glory when he was on the bike and I got it completely. It was the amazing feeling only a biker knows of that freedom as you cruise the roads, as if you are the only one there. There was also the thumping power of a V-twin motor vibrating through the bike frame as the thunder and glory travels through your body.

Then there is the Harley sound. It is so distinctive, and like no other bike. Just the thought and sound of one passing was enough to have me stop and pay respect for what I call the GOD BIKE of the road with the Devil's rage.

Like a true brother, Darren had my back not only on the streets but also at home, as much as he could. Gerald just never saw Darren for who he really was until after our mother left. It wasn't until afterwards that Gerald realised what an awesome boy he had, and stepped up and became the parent he should have been: protecting him, building a bond with him, and spoiling him. Gerald's cheque book was always open for anything Darren—his only remaining child at home— wanted.

Darren went from being my "little" brother to my younger big brother, as he towered above me and grew taller each year, as we grew up. Darren was built like his father, in many ways and, initially, he had that same stringy look. When he got a job as a lumberjack in Tasmania, he had his head shaved to a crew cut style and became really solid. When I first caught up with him, on his return from Tassie, he had gone from a boy to a mammoth of a man.

He had arms like guns, wide and broad shoulders, and a fully muscular back and chest. The hard labouring work and lifting heavy timber had helped him build an amazing physique and body, with muscle upon body muscle.

Darren.

Darren did join the service also, but came head-to-head with what happens to many young lads on joining the army, Injuries. During his recruit training, Darren had a fall during physical training. He hit his head and left ear so severely, on the edge of the pool, that he was medically discharged, only six weeks into his service career.

It really knocked him for a six mentally as well, and left him feeling a bit aimless. We had our fair share of arguments, as brothers do, mostly over me trying to teach him values that I hoped he would adopt as his overtime. He took many of them on board but shrugged others off as well. In many ways, I was his real big brother, as he didn't get along well with Graham or his sisters from Gerald's side. Graham and Darren were like chalk and cheese, you couldn't find two different people if you tried.

Over the years to follow, Darren grew up and became an independent man, which is what I had expected, given his upbringing. He travelled around a bit, finally ending up on the Gold Coast and it looked as if he had settled. He met a lovely girl, and was looking at the possibility of getting married and having kids.

But unfortunately, his love for bikes led him astray in all the worst ways. He hooked up with a bikie gang there and was soon living a life of an outlaw. On the many occasions I caught up with him and talked to him about it, I also met some of the other guys, who were in the gang, and it really worried me.

Drugs became a way of life for Darren, as well. It was devastating to watch the brilliant boy, I had known and grown up with, evolve into a man and a user of many drugs. His drug use threatened our bond and relationship a couple of times, as I tried to direct him away from it.

We lost touch for a while and by the time I next caught up with him, he had almost become a different person. He had a lot of ink, and not the most tasteful I'll admit, but as he once told me he did it to escape the hurt he had felt at being abandoned by our mother at such a young age. Clearly, the pain of her up and leaving that day had scarred him for life.

Darren turned up for Teena's birthday in 1977 as a surprise, the year before my service enlistment. It was an incredible surprise for Teena and she held him like her baby brother just as she always did. It was so beautiful. They were very close, and Darren saw her as the big sister he had never had. Disappointingly, he had also brought a black cloud with him and one that I wish I'd never seen, one to this day—his addiction to drugs. He was off his head on some kind of drug when he arrived. The carefree, biker culture he found himself in didn't agree with him and it introduced him to another side of life that wasn't healthy. I had no qualms about telling him just that.

During the night, I lost sight of Darren only to find him out the front away from the party smoking drugs. He knew how I felt about drugs, and for him to do this in a family environment made me wild. Little brother or not, I dragged him away and gave him a bloody serve, letting him know how we all felt about his drunken and drugged-out behaviour. After a few choice words to him, and him back at me with more of the same, it was on. All the anger I had felt and been subjected to, living with my mother was released. He didn't take it well. I had clearly hit a nerve. He lashed out with an off-balanced punch at me that went wide. Mine didn't however and connected with sending him to the ground faster than a lead ball.

He looked up at me with a look that I had never seen before. It was one of sheer disgust. He got up and I was beside myself that I had swung at him. I broke up trying to comfort him. What I had done? I was ashamed and felt so bad for hitting him knowing who he was, and what he meant to me. I went over to him, knelt, gave him a hug, and told him how sorry I was for hurting him. He stood up, looked at me for a moment and he said, "Sorry brother; that will never happen again". That one moment, that single action, made me see he wanted to say so much more, so we sat and talked about events in his life. There were many he felt ashamed of, but admitted it was a cult thing and he had to follow to fit in.

This wasn't him but as he knew, once a member, always a member. You can't run or hide from what has been started. This was the club's way, and must be respected and honoured, and Darren knew that.

He also carried a deep regret about never telling our mother how he felt or asking her why she had left him at such a young age. I said to him "Oh well mate, at least it will only happen to you once in your lifetime, from the same person." My little half-brother may have been the big tough bikie, but he also had a giant heart and would never walk away from anyone in need. He was always lending a hand and was loved by many. He never faltered in his love for his family.

He told me he wanted to move on in life, the way I had. Mind you he never really knew who I was and how I felt about life. That was something I hid from him and many other people. I had concern's knowing he really wanted to stay connected to the bike gang. I knew that once he had lived the life, he could never walk away from how that freedom felt.

I mentioned how I was confused; on one hand, he wanted to make a change in his life and on the other he still wanted to keep his ties with the bike gang. I told him it would not work and to stick to what was now his bread and butter. I was so proud of him. We chatted for ages, and he told me that his passion for riding bikes and, in particular, Harley Davidsons was alive and well, which I loved hearing. He loved them as much as I did, and you could hear it in his conversation. Everything seemed as if it was going great for him. His life was on track, and he sounded happy.

After that night we parted, and it would be many years before we would bond again. The time apart never stopped me from thinking about my little brother and how he was. My biggest fear was receiving a phone call to tell me Darren had passed away because of a bike accident or from drugs. That fear was something I lived with for a long time and one that I never let go of.

After I was posted to Puckapunyal, as a PT instructor, he called to tell me he was coming down from Queensland to Victoria for a bike ride and a rock concert. I didn't think much of it at the time. He'd called before, saying he was coming to see me and then not shown up, so I took the call with a grain of salt. It was a quiet weekend in the neighbourhood, I had just finished mowing the lawn and had gone inside when I heard what sounded like military tanks rolling up the road. The roar was so crazy the families from the adjoining homes came out to see what all the noise was about.

I walked outside onto the front porch to see six Harley Davidsons parked in my front yard. All at once, the huge roar was silenced as each of the bikes was turned off to rest. The first rider got off his bike, followed by the others. Straight away I spotted Darren and he smiled and said, "Hello brother". I ran out and gave him a big hug. God, it was good to see him.

He was on his way back to Queensland from their ride and had made sure he came to see me, his nephew, and niece. After many hours of talking, the boys from the club dropped a few tinnies, as they called them, and four of the bikies left as they wanted to get home as soon as possible. Darren and one of his mates stayed the night and left the next morning. It was bloody awesome catching up with him; I didn't want him to go!

He talked about his beautiful lady, called Amanda, and said they had moved in together, got engaged, and were to be married in 1986. He spoke about all their plans for the future.

I asked him to stay for the week with us, but he said he needed to get back to Queensland, and to his father Gerald, with whom he lived with. I was disappointed but very glad for the time we had.

We spent an incredible day together in Seymour, Victoria, where I was based. On leaving, I told him I would see him soon. With a thumbs-up he rode off with the other member of the gang. I felt sad, as I watched him ride away.

Two days later, I was back at the barracks instructing a class, when out of the blue, Brian, my older brother, called to tell me of some bad news. The message was taken by headquarters as Brian didn't have my direct line. Through respect and service protocol, this was passed on to the army chaplain, who came to the gym and took me aside. The news I received that day is still imbedded in me; I learnt my little brother had passed away.

I asked Ray to finish the class I was taking, and made a painful phone call. It didn't feel real, and I just couldn't process it at the time. When I called back to the Gold Coast, it was Gerald who answered the phone. He told me that Brian, Teena, and our mother were there with him and that yes, Darren had passed away. As I listened to nothing, I realised that not even 48 hours ago he had been with me. I just couldn't believe it.

Shattered, speechless, and incredibly sad, I soon became angry, when Gerald told me Darren had died from a drug overdose. Apparently, he had tried a new drug that he hadn't used before and within minutes he had slipped away. His life was stolen away from us from some bloody drug. Such a waste of life! I felt completely gutted knowing such a young man, who had everything to live for, had thrown it all away.

I doubt he ever knew the great impact taking those drugs had on him, and every one of his family and friends. It was devastating to feel it myself and to see it on the faces of those that loved him.

The army and, in particular, my commanding officer were fantastic; they organised my flights and transport and I flew to the Gold Coast to bury my brother. I sat in silence on the plane with Dale, who I had arranged to meet at the airport. My mind played back hundreds of memories to me like a movie, of us as young boys sitting on our beds planning out our day, right through to those last hours we had spent together.

When we arrived at Coolangatta Airport we were met by Brian and Teena who were both as drunk as skunks. I was so angry and embarrassed by their behaviour, but Dale just looked at me with a "Not now Daryl" look. We walked outside to get a taxi because my family were in no condition to drive. Brian offered to let me drive in a drunken manner, but at that point, the last thing I wanted was drunken people around me.

On our arrival at the caravan park where Gerald lived in Carrara, and as expected, my mother took control looking for all the attention she could get. I was beyond disgusted as she carried on about losing Darren; her youngest son—the same boy she had abandoned long ago, together with me. Once again, Dale knew me only too well and pulled me aside, asking me to back off in respect. Please remember Darren the way he was to you.

The day was emotionally taxing. I struggled with my grief, while dealing with my mother and fighting to stay in control and not lash out at Gerald I wanted to demand answers about why he let my brother live a drug-infested life right under his own roof! Gerald knew, he could tell I was livid, as he glanced at me a few times with a look that said he had no idea about the extent of Darren's drug problem.

I was consumed with grief and seeing Gerald just brought up feelings of the old days; of not being accepted, of being an outcast and being thrown out and discarded like rubbish. All this was compounded with my mother's antics and my rage at her as well. I simmered, barely able to contain it.

Then, there was Gerald's older son Graham, who was with my mother. When I say with my mother, that's literally what I mean. Graham and my mother had started a relationship many years earlier after he completed his basic training. This was clearly her reason for leaving us, back when I was fourteen-years-old and I was forced to live on the streets. She had married Graham, her stepson, some two or three years earlier. It disgusted the hell out of me.

I felt for Gerald, in many ways, even after all the shit he had put me through. That action alone from my mother had been a low blow. Gerald and Graham hardly spoke and had nothing to do with each other. That must have been even harder for Gerald. He had lost the only son he felt he had left; knowing that his first born son had had an affair with his own wife, and would later marry her.

Darren fiancée, Amanda, was beyond devastated. The poor woman was a complete mess and inconsolable as she battled to come to grips with what had happened. For whatever reason, we connected through our shared grief. I am not sure why, but I think it was because I was the only one, besides Dale, not drinking and carrying on.

Dale could see what I was about to do and stood back, so as not to get tangled up at the moment. I was standing in front of Gerald looking at him. I couldn't keep quiet any longer and said to him "Really, you sat out the front drinking every night, while your son was doing drugs, and you never knew what was going on?"

I was mad and had every right to be. Brian walked over and said not now and not this way brother. I was in another world by that point and told him very plainly to stay out of what he knew nothing about. This was my fight and don't get between me and those who have destroyed my life and my brother's life. My breath caught in my throat, as Gerald's eyes filled with tears. He knew what I was saying and how I felt.

This man had hurt me in so many ways and left me lying in physical pain, with cuts, and bleeding and fat lips. He had left me to die on the streets and now he had felt the pain of death, just as I had. I think that at that moment the world stopped, as his eyes connected with mine and he heard my words. I was hurt. I was mad. I was disgusted at what this family had done and I was not pulling back on the words I used.

I was shaking, crying and looking for hope, which I knew would never come, but I had to do it as both my mother, Gerald and other family members hung their heads. I had just lost my brother and they were sitting around drinking, feeling sorry for their loss, and talking about moments that Darren never wanted to remember.

I stood there as time stopped. I looked at what should have been a family and I wondered how on this earth I was part of them. I could taste the anger in me and was even more scared and ashamed of what I had just done.

Then, I looked at Gerald and realised he had also lost someone very special. The pain of all that he had done to me, and the words I had spoken in my head a million times to pay him back for his appalling treatment, faded as empathy replaced rage. I took his hand and told him I am so sorry for your loss Gerald. I guess I had finally had my say and not in a physical way but through words of love for Darren.

For the first time, Gerald stood to face me man-to-man. He said, "Daryl, please forgive me, I am not that man today", I will never be able to take back all the hurtful moments I put you through. For the first time, I saw the man I had hoped I would respect, teach, and care for me as a father should. I closed my eyes, with a soft head tilt, and walked away.

I had my moment, after twelve years of sadness and anger. Did it feel good? No, but I did it and today have no regrets.

One hour passed in silence, well to a point, then round two threatened to begin with my mother trying to grab the limelight over everyone. She started to say something—I just looked at her and said, "Don't say a word!" I wasn't that pushover kid that she could dominate, anymore. She shut up.

I told Brian and Teena to leave, sober up, and show some respect for our brother. Tony, one of Darren's riding mates, who I had met before, realised how mad I was and took Brian and Teena to his tent.

I went back inside to Gerald, wanting to have my questions answered—what happened to my brother?

He told me Darren had suffocated from lack of oxygen. A cocaine overdose laced with an upper, and it was all over. Darren was a chronic asthmatic and injecting such a lethal dose affected his breathing and he suffocated to death. My medical knowledge set in. I knew he would have been alive, sitting there, struggling and trying to breathe but also knowing he was failing to which point he was going to die. He was alone, he was lost, and he was looking for help that would not come I was mad in every way, at that point, knowing this and that I could not help him, hold him or give him life.

I was a grown man and had been through hell and back as a child, teenager and into my adult years, yet this moment overtook all of my emotions. I was hurt and struggling to understand. I was looking for answers and in ways hoping for what would never come back, my little brother. He was gone—dead and from that day would never walk back into my life.

That protective wall in my life started to rebuild itself that day and with it, later on, my own destructive road. The next day came too soon and so did many other things. My mother did what she did best, and made the whole event about her. Even though Darren had lost any respect for her many years prior and hadn't had anything to do with her, she put on a performance worthy of any Golden Globe award.

In her eyes, no one else's pain meant anything—hers was the greatest pain, her loss the most tragic. She carried on so much that the real reason we were all there was perilously close to selfishly being cast aside.

It was embarrassing. As I walked into the church, I spotted Gerald, who was sitting alone. I realised he was in pain in a way many never see and decided to sit next to him. He looked at me, placed his hand on my knee, and nodded his head with a tear of thanks. Wow, that was all I could think. For the first time in his life, he recognised me which made me feel so much better. Truth was it was better than sitting next to my mother, listening to her bullshit.

After the ceremony finished, I got up and spoke to Gerald, asking where the cremation was to be held and would Darren's ashes be settled into the Wall of Remembrance. My mother came up to me, from across the room and told me, right there in the funeral parlour, that I was a nasty person and had showed no respect for her loss because I hadn't sat with her during the service. I said, "I'm not here to pick sides, I'm here for my little brother".

I could have predicted her saying something inappropriate and selfish, but really that was the one thing on her mind at her son's funeral? I just stood in amazement trying to hold back with all my might from letting her know how I really felt, and finally telling her how I, Darren, Dale, Brian, and Teena felt about her, her affair, and her sickening marriage to her step-son.

Not to mention all the shit in NZ. her abandoning me as a baby, leaving me in the hands of molesters, and not even bothering to make contact with us and then abandoning me yet again to live on the streets, after she had.

I was through, but I had promised my sister I would stay calm, and that is what I did. Without a word to her, I walked away and went to the clubhouse where Darren was a member. They were about to have a member ritual there. We cremated him with full honours, surrounded by members of his club. Out of respect for Darren, the club had arranged the gathering. It was not my thing, but I attended for a short time, more for Amanda, as she had asked me to be with her to support her. We placed his helmet and jacket on his bike, back at the clubhouse wake and burnt them all never to be touched again.

As much as I was, and should have been, angry with the club and the members who allowed the use of drugs, I also had to except Darren that decided to live the life he did. On that night I would learn that Darren did not get the drug he used from any of the club's members but through another friend on the street.

Teena asked me to sing our song; a song in memory of my brother which meant so much to me. The clubhouse had a guitar, which they handed to me. Over a drink, they listened as I shared the music of our song. It was a ballad written by Bobby Scott and Bob Russell and originally recorded by Kelly Gordon in 1969, called "He Ain't Heavy He's My Brother". The title came from the motto for Boys Town, a community formed in 1917, by a Catholic priest named Father Edward Flanagan. It is located in Omaha, Nebraska, and was a place where troubled or homeless boys could come for help.

What was ironic was that this song was the very song we had both listened to in 1969, a few months after I arrived in Australia. If it was on the radio, as we sat in the lounge, I would grab my guitar and try and learn the music as Darren watched me. I ended up learning it and we called it our song and would sing it many times over together, brother to brother.

The remaining days spent on the Gold Coast were a total waste of time, as disagreements and crosswords flew between family members, mostly stemming from my mother's lies. When she was caught out she would pour on her victim tears.

Gerald was deeply affected by the loss of Darren's death, and this was only compounded by the loss of his wife to his own son. He had lost the last part of his life and the only child from it, who he ever really loved. He tried to get by for a while, but the devastation was too great. Gerald passed away, a few years later, from alcoholism and loneliness.

CHAPTER 57

Army Apprentice School

Twenty-six years

My second posting as an instructor was to the army school of apprentices in Bonegilla—a remote area about 13 km east of Wodonga on the north Victorian border. This unit was a shared training facility, for both the army service apprenticeship scheme, which also worked in conjunction with TAFE, and the Australian Survey Corp. There were also logistical units that provided daily support in administration and supplies.

The size of the unit was amazing. It had barracks for the apprentices that resembled hotel rooms, with a common room in the centre and four sleeping quarters attached. Each apprentice had their own room. There were also the main headquarters where all the administrative work was handled, a hospital, training rooms, transport services, kitchens and two mess halls. One hall was for the apprentices and could seat up to 600, and the other was a smaller mess for staff.

The physical training facilities were the best I had seen, to date, with offices for all eleven PT staff; one commissioned officer with the rank of lieutenant, a second class warrant officer, three sergeants and six bombardiers, which is a rank equivalent to corporal.

The gymnasium had a full indoor basketball stadium with upper balconies. Off to the side were four indoor squash courts, and located at the end of our offices was an indoor Olympic-sized swimming pool, with a cargo net hanging from the roof at the deep end for rope training. Below the building were two weight rooms, each equipped with the best of training gear, a yoga room, and a storeroom which held every type of sports equipment.

Outside we had a man-made dam we used for water obstacle skills, and above this, two fully-set out ground obstacle courses were laid. Further down the road were a full athletic track and field provisions, an AFL field, two rugby fields and a soccer field. I can say this ... the government had not stinted on the cost to build and provide the best facilities for the apprentices.

Along with all of this, we also had 30 Tri-Athlete road bikes, 12 mountain bikes, snow skiing equipment, a ski-boat with all the equipment, canoes and kayaks, at our disposal.

While I was posted here, I underwent further studies to complete my Subject 2 for sergeant in medical support studies, field triage, field ambulance, and hospital procedures. I also realised I would be required to return to the Army Academy of Physical Training to complete my Subject 4 for sergeant, once more. It was at this point that I decided to up the level of my fitness. Following this decision my week went a little like this:

Monday morning	*run to work, 13 km*
Monday afternoon	*ride home*
Tuesday morning	*ride to work*
Tuesday afternoon	*run home*
Wednesday morning	*drive to the unit, swim 5 km swim in the pool, followed by a weight session*
Thursday morning	*run to work, 13 km*
Thursday afternoon	*ride home*
Friday morning	*ride to work*
Friday afternoon	*drive home after a weight session*

This training schedule was in addition to my daily PT workload, of between six and eight classes, my personal life, and a part-time job as a personal trainer in a local Health Club where I worked six hours a week. These eight weeks took the very last drops of energy from my tiring body, but the outcome was worth every bit of effort.

8-week Pre-course training resume			
Day	Allocation period	Training	Duration/ Time
Monday	Morning	13km run to the barracks	1 hour
Monday	Afternoon	13km Bike ride home	30 min
Tuesday	Morning	13km bike ride to the barracks	30 min
Tuesday	Afternoon	13km run home	1 hour
Wednesday	Morning	Dive to the barracks, swim 5km	1 hour
Wednesday	Morning	Functional Weight session	40 min
Thursday	Morning	13km run to the barracks	1 hour
Thursday	Afternoon	13km Bike ride home	30 min
Monday	Morning	13km run to the barracks	1 hour
Monday	Afternoon	13km Bike ride home	30 min
Friday	Morning	13km bike ride to the barracks	30 min
Friday	Afternoon	Power/Strength Weight session	90 min
Saturday		Recovery	
Sunday		Recovery	

I also worked part-time, two nights a week, in a health club in Albury, just 14 km from home, to improve my instructional skills. The classes back at the barracks were full on with up to a minimum of six, daily and always up to 30 km in group training weekly. I was lucky to have four senior PTIs, which all had an incredible experience, and this was something I tapped into as much as possible. This help also included personal instruction from them, in readiness for my promotional courses.

During my posting at the Army Apprentice School, I set my sights on more challenges. Powerlifting was something I had always wanted to try. As I had both the time and the training facilities available, I embarked on this new venture. Several months into my training, I suffered an extreme injury, playing rugby union for the service, and realised that returning to my favourite sport was going to be an impossible task.

The injury was too simply great to allow me to continue. This meant months of rehabilitation, to avoid a service discharge for medical reasons which would end my role as a Physical Training Instructor. After four months of sitting at the desk, as a paper junky, and hours in the pool, on the floor in the gym and weight training, I started to show signs of getting better. I had six months to prove my fitness and justify staying in the service and I was not going to let a simple knee reconstruction put a stop to all my hard work.

There is a saying and one I started to use often… SOLDIER ON. I did soldier on and passed the physical assessment that allowed me to stay in the service as an instructor. This accident also gave me a new direction towards what would later be an incredible journey.

Twelve months later, and still powerlifting, I was talked into competing in a bodybuilding show, to be held in Melbourne. Not knowing too much about this sort of thing, I relied on a friend in the service. He had not competed, but knew a lot about the preparation and training that was required for the show. I had four weeks and a lot to learn, when I started that crazy journey.

I committed to extra training and more training, accompanied by eating fewer carbs, no fats, or sugar and filling up on protein. At times, this adventure had me wondering why I had even begun. I loved my food and I knew I also needed the calories to do my daily duties. I had to sacrifice for my vision; so, I put a smile on my face and worked even harder.

The day came. We arrived in Melbourne, and went to the registration area, out the back of the stage. OMG . . . and I will say that once more . . .OMG, the other guys were built like tanks. Plus-sized, all over and then there was me, all 69.2 kg. I was lean, cut, shredded, and hard with veins running in all directions. But every time I looked at the other guys, my heartbeat 20 to 1.

Was I nervous…yes definitely. That was, until a guy called Chris, from Ballart, came up to me, and said "Total package dude! Did you just come from the butchers to be so cut?" he smiled and added, "Man I hope I am not standing next to you on stage" as he walked by.

That made me feel so much more comfortable and I showed it on stage. I won my first competition and my division against eight others and also placed second overall, against a guy that was 96 kg. What gave me a thrill was that I received my trophy from the one and only Mr. Olympia, Lee Haney. In addition to that incredible moment, a guy came up to me, from out of the crowd, and said, "Keep training man. You are a natural and one day will own the stage." I later learned that person was the one and only, Australian champion Sony Smit.

I thought the day could not get any better, when suddenly I felt a tap on my shoulder and I was asked for a photo to go in Physique Magazine. This was the biggest magazine on health and fitness in Australia, and to be asked to be featured in it just blew me away.

I have the trophy and the magazine to this day and I am proud of that one moment. After that I was elated to be employed, as one of Australia's best athletes, by Men's Body Building, for six months, to give my direction and support for future shows. That one move set the wheels in motion and opened up a whole new world of competitive bodybuilding, in which I would continue for a further twelve years.

On top of all of this, I juggled being a husband and father, enjoying the next two years in Victoria, before my next orders came. It was time for this old soldier to move on and take up another posting. This time I had my promotion to sergeant and was based in a four camp hospital in Townsville; as the senior instructor in physical education and as the coordinator in remedial exercise, working alongside the service physiotherapist and rehabilitation officers.

This posting and the education I received here later played a significant role in my future employment and development process. The promotion also meant a higher level of respect and, most importantly, a pay rise which helped a lot, as I was the sole provider of our home's income.

With a final farewell to my work friends and the friendships that had been built along the way in Bonegilla, we hit the road, on a 2400 km journey—destination Townsville, North Queensland.

CHAPTER 58

Heartbreak

Twenty-eight to thirty years

Army life was exciting for any soldier in Townsville and always filled with a full day's work and then some fun with the family. PT sessions were done early morning to avoid the heat, which was brutal up there in the northern end of Queensland!

PT sessions consisted of swimming skills and techniques, water rescue, and water obstacle crossing, as well as endurance running, strength and power sessions. Together with this, all of the soldiers underwent training that was specifically related to their employment and tasks therein; e.g., weapons exercises, indoor and outdoor obstacles, circuit training, weight training, self-defence and combat, minor team games, games sports, gymnastics, general exercises and pushing-pulling activities. Pushing and pulling normally consisted of moving trucks, jeeps, and trailers or what-ever could be moved—even up to Artillery 105 guns—through the sand, bush and by road.

For me, being a physical training instructor simply meant I took the soldiers for PE. However, like all soldiers, I also had to meet the basics in field-craft, weapons, and general enlistment requirements. My days started, early in the morning, in Townsville, preparing lessons for the first PT session, and ended with a final check on all the rehabilitation patients before heading home in the early afternoon. Then I changed the army hat for the family one and the day started again, but this time with Debbie, Damien and Casie J and home duties.

Being part of the Medical Corp, I also had to complete a number of senior studies, such as medical subject 2 for SGT training element and subject 1 for SGT, which all soldiers were required to do. My medical understanding and training would prove to be highly valuable, after the army and increased my diversity which later became a great help in my chosen future career, sports and hobbies.

One thing I was concerned about, but never discussed, was the low wages. Given the work performed, the duties, and extra regimental duties, soldiers were at a disadvantage to their civilian colleagues. All of this placed considerable stress on their everyday lives, particularly if they were away from their families, which is hard enough for a soldier on Australian soil, let alone those soldiers who were deployed—many of whom I worked with.

For me getting home at around 2:30 pm and having the weekends at home was a luxury, certainly compared to the deployed soldiers. Debbie handled things beautifully at home though, and I would help in the evenings and on the weekends.

During my posting in Townsville, I found out that my mother was also living there. Graham, my mother's stepson from her second marriage, and now her third husband, was also posted to the same military area and at the service base in Townsville. I suppose it was inevitable that we would run into each other sooner or later, during my posting.

Sure enough, it wasn't long before I received a call at work, from my mother, asking if I would put things aside so that she could meet her grandchildren. Like any parent, I believed a child had a right to know and meet their family members. This included grand-parents, but my mother—well you could just never trust her to do the right thing and she was always making trouble, so I was hesitant to allow her in.

I spoke with Debbie about it and ended up agreeing to her taking Damien and Casie J over to my mother's house. Every visit had me on edge, but Debbie got along well with my mother, and Damien and Casie J enjoyed going. I felt as if I just had to live with it, for the sake of my wife and children and respect the fact that it was their choice if they wanted to see her.

During my time in Townsville, I was also required to attend several promotional training courses. These were the pathway to higher ranks in the service and increased wages. However, when I was sent to Sydney, to attend nine weeks of training to complete my Subject 1 (Subj 1) for sergeant, I began having more terrible flashbacks from my childhood. The distance and time away from my family had a real effect on me and I felt deep emptiness, sadness, and intense loneliness.

Even though I loved Debbie, and had immense respect for the mother she was to our children, I felt the love we had for each other had become almost platonic. I had yearned for her to understand who I was, and to support me in overcoming my past but for some reason, I just couldn't open up to her. She only knew me as Daryl, the boy she met some twelve years earlier. I had never really opened up about my life from the past—I just didn't feel comfortable doing so. I suppose I was also too ashamed, and scared she might judge me poorly. It seemed easier to hide the truth and deflect question rather than recount the stories of my life back in the boys' home.

At the same time, I longed for someone to see how I was struggling and help me find a way through it. I wanted to talk about it, heal from it, and stop it from governing my life. I knew there was no way I could do it on my own. I wasn't in a good place with all this going on, and during my time away at the course, I met a female soldier, whom I connected with. She seemed to be like me and was unable to find her balance and happiness. We spent time talking about each other's struggles and one thing lead to another and the connection progressed to being intimate.

Regardless of where my relationship was with Debbie, I knew it was wrong of me to have this interaction with her. Debbie didn't deserve it. She had done nothing wrong and I shouldn't have done it. Regretful, I returned to Townsville and told Debbie what I had done. Understandably, she was very upset. We decided she needed to get away and have some time to think. We talked about it and both decided that it was best for her to go to her mother's, with the kids the next day, so she could have the space.

I clearly remember walking into my children's rooms, that night before they left, and hugging them and kissing them goodnight. It was the worst feeling. I felt sick and scared of what the future held. The next day came too fast. At the time, we didn't tell the kids the truth about why they were going to Nanny's. All they knew was they were going on a holiday. As we drove to Townsville airport, I wanted to turn around so many times, but Debbie held strong and said, "This has to be done, Daryl". The kids were in the back of the car singing and telling me what they would do on their holiday and that they would call me every night. God it hurt, I fought to hold back the tears.

We pulled up at the airport and as I helped unload all the bags, I told Debbie I just couldn't go in. She understood and I told the kids I had to go back to the army base and that I would call them later. They gave me the most beautiful cuddles and kisses all the time telling me they loved me. I looked at Debbie and said, "I am so sorry for what I have done".

She was totally devastated, and knowing how much I had hurt her, killed me inside. This was the girl I had met in my younger years, and the woman I had married, and who had given me the most beautiful kids. I had repaid her by abusing her trust and insulting her with my actions. I had to hold on just a few more minutes, after they had walked away to catch the plane to Geelong, before I got in the car. I waited until I had seen their plane leave, before I lost it and cried my eyes out until I had nothing left—I felt like a shattered man in every sense.

On arrival home, I contacted the unit company sergeant major (CSM) and explained the situation. He was understanding, and told me to take a week's leave immediately to work things out and to seek advice from the service padre. That night I sat in a home that should have been filled with laughter, but which was deathly quiet, and so empty. Every room resembled nothing more than an empty shell devoid of life. I didn't eat, and I barely moved for days, grieving the loss of my family.

Then it hit me, I had become a person I had never wanted to be. Hurting others was not in my nature, yet I had done just that. The stark reality hit me like a ton of bricks. I could not even reach out to friends for help, or talk about it—the shame of what I had done was too great. I couldn't bear to look into their faces and know I had disappointed them, too.

I'd made my bed and now I had to lie in it—alone.

CHAPTER 59

Change of Life

Thirty years

After talking with Debbie, night after night, we agreed we had to separate, but finding a way to tell the kids was the hardest thing of all. Each night I called the kids, and each night it broke my heart. The time came, however, and I told Damien his mother and I would not be living together anymore, but that we would always be in his life. My son cried—he was devastated, which tore at my heart, as I desperately tried to calm him down. How do you hold your son and take away the pain, when he is thousands of miles away?

Casie J. was so young at just four years old. She didn't really understand at the time, but I did, and that was enough to weigh on me, knowing I would not be there to tuck her in bed that night and the many after it.

I realised how cruel life can be. We are burdened with pain and suffering that others inflict on us, only to subject ourselves to more from our own hand. I battled being separated from someone special, whom I had spent many years with and struggled as I, seemingly, watched all of my dreams and hard work being flushed away. As the weeks passed, I questioned everything, including my career in the army.

I tried to find positives at work, and attended a heap of sporting events, in the hope of filling in the gaps in the loneliness and emptiness I felt. Focusing on my passion for fitness, I took on part-time work at a local Health Club, as a master coach, to get a foothold on happiness again, but it was all in vain. I missed my kids terribly. I missed our adventures, and cuddling them, talking to them, and being in their lives. The distance was great but my love for them greater. I held on to the hope that things would get better.

I knew that, in many ways, they would not understand the separation, because they were so young, but I hoped that one day they would forgive me. One of the greatest things I learned, from the separation from my wife, was that ultimately I discovered who I really am—i.e. the real Daryl Te'Nadii. I did not want to be seen as a failure in life. I decided it was time to leave the army; however, in accordance with my service commitments, I had to stay enlisted for the next six months.

About four months after my separation, and while I was still in the service, I met Carol. I was out enjoying dinner and a few drinks with a few buddies when a stranger walked past our table. He was drunk and unbalanced, which led to his falling onto the table and wiping out our drinks and light snacks. He just got up and took off laughing.

I still can't say why I did it. All I remember is getting up and chasing him with another person, only to run smack into a car that was coming out of a carpark. My instinct kicked in as I jumped and slid across the bonnet, kind of like a scene out of James Bond. I stopped to say sorry to the young female driver, only to be abused by her. I saw I had scratched the hood with my boots, but at the time I sensed any apology would not work or calm her down.

It must have been a few days later, and after 6:00 pm, when the receptionist of the gym, where I was working out, came to let me know that a woman was at the front desk asking to see me. I walked out to find Carol, the young girl whose car I had scratched, standing in the reception area.

I apologised for the damage again and was about to wish her well and go back to my gym workout when, out of the blue, Carol handed me a bunch of flowers and asked me out for dinner! Another surprise! I thought, why not, and accepted her invitation.

Over the following months, our relationship grew into something even more special. However, thoughts of the boys' home, my kids, the army, and my new relationship all overwhelmed me. so I decided to take some long service to clear my head.

The time with Carol was incredible, I felt I had met my match and she was someone I could easily fall in love with. Only months into the relationship and we were living together and enjoying some crazy times, fun times and a few down moments. These down times were due to my insecurity knowing I had in the past lost so much and could face the same issues again. Carol was younger than me and that also played on my mind. Did I have a right to someone so thoughtful, honest, and caring?

What I did know, was that my feelings were growing every day for her and with this came judgement on my part and by me. I would sit and look at her so many times, wake up to see her next to me and welcome her home. I guess I had to ask my-self, did I have this right, and would I fill the missing void in my life?

Being away from the army, helped me clarify what was important to me. As fond as I was of Carol, I couldn't stop thinking about my children and didn't want anything to come between them and me.

After some deep soul searching, I knew what I had to do and that was to leave the army and fly back to Geelong, to and be with my kids. I put in my request for a discharge from the service and prepared myself to tell Carol about my decision. I phoned Carol's parents, who were really lovely people, and asked if I could come over to see them. I needed to explain to them how much I missed my kids, and why I would be leaving Townsville and Carol, to be with them. I wanted her to be ok and have support when I told her later that night.

Her parents were amazing and completely understood my thinking. They actually thanked me for being so caring and looking out for their daughter, and for showing them respect by discussing it with them, so things could be put in place to ease the hurt for Carol.

I packed the personal belongings that Carol had left in my unit and waited for her to return from work, at her mum and dad's place. I gave her a hug when she walked in and let her know I needed to talk to her.

The next five minutes, of sharing what I had decided to do with her, seemed like an hour. I felt every bit of hurt she was feeling as she listened to me talking. She sat across from me with her head in her hands, tears streaming down her face, and asked why and I explained it the best way I could.

It's never easy saying goodbye to good people. I hated that I would be hurting yet another person. Carol was an amazing person, who helped me more than she will ever know. I'll always be thankful to her for that. I needed a friend in my life, at that really hard point and it was really important finding that one person, Carol had definitely become that person and more.

Carol's parents arranged a holiday the next week, for her to visit a close friend in Brisbane, while I packed the unit up and got ready to move back to Victoria. The army went through its processes, making a thorough check of my records and service entitlements and discovered that during my posting to Puckapunyal, where I had been required to work late two nights a week, I shouldn't have been doing any extra regimental duties or guards.

Their investigation meant that I had 186 days owing, which had been accumulated over three years. Together with this, I had ten weeks R&R left and eight weeks long-service remaining. In total, I had 24 weeks that I could take on full pay. It was a great windfall, which ultimately allowed me some more breathing space. I took twelve months' leave at half-pay, to cover me until I could find work back in Geelong.

I did make contact with Carol some years later, and if I recall correctly, it was back in the first half of the 90s, on a return trip to Townsville to visit a very close friend. I had promised him I would take a holiday and come visit him, when the time was right.

Over the years, since I last spent time with Carol, I had lived a busy life, working and growing older with my children close by, but I missed the connection that I had with Carol. Knowing I might be able to catch up with her did give me something more to look forward too.

My friend arranged for a catch-up and dinner with Carol, as friends. We enjoyed dinner together and talked for many hours. I think in many ways I had returned as an older person with wisdom and smart. My children had grown up and I felt ready to move on.

As the night passed, I could not stop looking at her. She had grown in years and beauty, and matured in many ways, and she showed signs of a very confidant person. I felt we still had feelings for each other, be they personal or hidden. But I also felt a weakness in our relationship during that night. It felt as if I had moments only to be reminded of what I had done to her back in the past.

I may have been hoping for too much, or even failed to realise or think that Carol might have moved on in her life. I guess the old saying 'Love can be blind or misleading' has substance.

Not really sure what I was doing or thinking and if I even had a right. I was hoping for the impossible, only to learn I was too late. The old saying strikes again 'The ship has sailed' reminded me of that. I left Townsville a few days later without the hope that I had been looking for and shattered by knowing what I had done.

I would later learn, through friends, that Carol did meet someone (after I left Townsville), as I did, and settled having found love and had children. When I learnt this, I was happy for her and the women she had become.

It would be nice to sit down with her one day and talk about the past times over a coffee. What we both have achieved and how we have travelled over the years. Maybe one day?

CHAPTER 60

Discharged

Thirty years

Having those extra weeks holidays helped so much. On arrival back in Geelong, I gained employment as a Health Club Manager in a local gym. The fact I had taken long service and extra leave meant I had to wait until the completion of these holidays to get a service discharge from full-time duty.

I had missed Damien and Casie terribly—being back with them or at least in the same town so that I could have them on weekends, meant so much.

After all of my training in the service, I had a wealth of fitness knowledge and a hunger to do something with it. My role as a remedial trainer and physical training instructor in the army opened the gates to the community, I became part of. The opportunity to build a fitness-based business also appealed to me. Building a career around fitness in the same town as Damien and Casie was wonderful, because I could be more involved in their lives which sealed the deal on my decision.

Water, gas obstacle and mine field training.

As I was a senior-level sergeant, and employed full-time, I didn't have to stay in the barracks while awaiting discharge, however, I was still required to attend the Watsonia Barracks every Monday, for the four weeks leading up to my final discharge date. During the waiting period, I took up a position with the army reserve. It was with Deakin University, as a senior instructor, and it was a great way for me to stay connected to the service but in a less committed role. It also gave me the flexibility to do a lot more for the kids than I ever had, which was also terrific.

As the time drew close to the final days of my time in the service, many emotions overflowed. I soon realised why my service time had meant so much, as I thought and looked back on the many years of training, comradeship, and times enjoyed. Over the last weeks, I contacted all of my service buddies, to pass on my thanks for their friendship and collected their personal contact details.

My day of discharge was like any other day At 7:00 I was at the HQ discharge cells, in Watsonia Barracks in Melbourne. This took around two hours of do this, do that, I had to return all of the field stores and sign the required documents. This was followed by a last medical and dental check. Then I was ready for my move forward into civilian life.

Just completed my Subject 2 in Medical and triage for Sergeant. I am on the far right, second row from the back.

It was all over; I was no longer service personnel. I was, however, informed that if Australia ever got into a conflict, the Australian Government had the right to reenlist me on notice, within the next ten years.

Driving back to Geelong, I reflected on the past years, but every time I thought about what I had given up, I was reminded that my children were waiting at the end of the road, which only endorsed and validated my reasons.

Geelong and my children became my life, for many years to follow. Watching, listening and spending time with those two beautiful kids meant I began every day of my life with a smile. We may not have been living under the same roof, but they were only a few kilometres away from me, which was as good as it got.

Over the years both Damien and Casie J grew, from little kids to mostly well-adjusted teenagers, with many friends: they went from toys and dolls, to playing rugby for Damien and makeup for Casie J. Damien had been dating for a while and then Casie started, as well. I knew the day would come, soon enough, when I would have to share my little girl's time with a significant other, but the thought still bothered me.

I loved watching Damien play rugby; he was good at it too—a natural sportsman! Casie's love for makeup and fashion led her into the field of beauty and, ultimately, her chosen career as a beautician, which she still does and loves to this day.

Thankfully, they never blamed me for all the hardship I placed on them in their younger years, and I enjoyed every moment of being wrapped in their unconditional love, as well as the time I was able to spend with them.

PART 4

Rebuilding

CHAPTER 61

Geelong

Having settled, after re-locating back in Geelong, I established a good connection with my kids, and wanted to ensure I never broke or jeopardised that connection again. Since the separation from the children's mum, I had spent a lot of time thinking about how I could be a better father to them, as a single person. Although it was hard at times and frustrating, I knew I had to stay focused and move forward. I will admit, I was too young and had lacked the essential maturity and skills to take on the responsibilities of a husband and father when the kids were younger. My upbringing was rare and dysfunctional. I had never had a proper father figure in my life, and had no mentors to draw upon in this area, to learn from or to model myself on.

In many ways lacking these qualities, I had left it up to Debbie to manage the day-to-day things, such as school and home affairs. She did one amazing job raising our kids on her own—something I had never intended or wanted, but at the time I just didn't have what it took.

During the times I had the children, we would go to parks to play, sit and talk and go down to Eastern Beach if it was a nice day. Having restricted time was hard, but it was something I adjusted to and I gave it my all to make the most of it.

I had taken on a part-time job so that I could have more financial freedom, but that time took away hours I could have spent with the children. Along with finding time here, I also wanted to re-connect with my brother, Dale, and sister, Teena. This I would do on the weekends I didn't have the kids, or during the week. Every week felt like my time was taken from me, which placed many restrictions on my aim to move forward, but somehow I got through.

My background in sports was vast, and I loved the challenge it offered—I guess in some shape or form it was my way of getting away from and forgetting the past.

I decided to take more of a role in my training and to commit to it seriously. This would be a second move towards returning to competitive events in sports. I would sustain this lifestyle for some time, knowing the outcome would benefit me.

Suffering, home life, the kids, work, and training became my life.

CHAPTER 62

Competition Life

Thirty-four years

Over the years, one of the many things I enjoyed was weight training. It was something I had started many years earlier and continued with. I'd recently split from a relationship, where we had purchased a house, and I had renovated it. The relationship did not continue as she did not want my kids staying at the house, so now I had more free time on my hands. I decided to return to competitive bodybuilding and to get back on track with my passion for fitness.

I realised the journey was not going to be easy. I was not in peak physical form, after a few years of only a basic fitness regime. I had dropped a massive fourteen kilograms, most of it muscle, from spending more time renovating than working on my fitness. I had a lot of work to do!

All of that aside, I wrote up my plan, adjusted my schedule, and prepared for what would be for many physically taxing times. I knew that if I put my mind to it, I could do it, and with passion. It was intensity time and a new lease in life for me in 1991!

I had my children, my health, and an even bigger reason to challenge myself again. With every training session came more demands, along with more learning. So much had changed in competition over the years, and the physique of yesterday no longer stood up to the new era. Pounding the mat and lifting weights far beyond my past abilities became my focus with every training session.

As in my past years, I was not going to allow weakness to become part of my life—I would not accept failure. I became that man from before; the strong soldier I was. I drew strength and motivation from those memories and focused, reinventing myself and pushing forward. By attending competitions, and watching the latest videos on training and national competitions, I found myself moving forward in leaps and bounds, and much faster and sooner than I had expected at first.

I took on a training partner in Geelong, to help with the extra loading of weights in my training. His name, funnily enough, was also Daryl—I must attract them! We would spend many hours training, adapting, and preparing for competitions. After months of hard training, the first competition arrived, and we were both ready, Daryl, my training partner, decided to compete in the middle-class height division while I decided to enter the short class.

Looking around at the competitors I would soon stand next to on stage, I felt very small. Most of the other competitors were around 85 kg to 95 kg; my weight on the day was 76 kg.

I felt good and ready though, along with a body that I felt had been chiselled to perfection. I was lean, separated and cut to the bone, with excellent mass for my height.

Over the months leading up to the comp, I had taken time out to study two international competitors who were close to my height and had a similar build.

The first man was an icon in his time and, to this day, showcases what has been recognised as the most refined and symmetrical physique of all time—his name was Frank Zane. He, along with many other top athletes, graced the stage in the 70s, 80s and 90s; but, it was he who went on to win the title of Mr. Olympia.

The second man was Lee Librada who, even today, is still highly regarded for his ability to destroy some of the biggest men ever to walk on stage. A highlight in my life was to meet Lee and his wife in Melbourne, Australia and to spend some time with them.

I knew that having these two as my personal (but silent) mentors would make such a difference, both in my stage presence and my showmanship. When the final calls were made, I was called out to stand on stage with two other competitors. Like all sports, there can only be one winner and to my delight, it was me that was announced as the Australasian champion.

Winning that one event changed my competitive life, from that day onwards. One of the rewards was a fully-paid trip to New Zealand, as part of the Australian team, to compete at the Oceanic World Championships. What made this win even more special was the fact my brother, Dale, was right there with me, to witness and share in the win and celebration. He was so proud of how far I had come in life. He was an awesome cheerleader and supporter of my mission to achieve that goal. It really did make my heart swell to see him there, experiencing it with me, and finding joy in watching me do something I loved.

7 days out from the Oceanic Championships – weighing in at 76.8kg.

Two weeks later, I would compete on stage against the best of the Oceanic countries in New Zealand. Our team was made up of males and females and one person I was very happy for was my training partner, who had won the middle height class—Daryl Gill. I was over the moon happy that he won first in his division and in his class as well. It was a proud moment for both of us—for us and for each other. We had overcome many disappointments and battled to get there, but we did it.

I walked off that stage excited and thinking of my children and how proud they would be of me when I showed them my first place trophy. I had done it! I couldn't have been happier sitting backstage. It wasn't long after that all the winners were asked to take the stage again for the announcement and presentation of the overall champion for the competition.

Stage pose after taking out the overall winner of the Oceanic championships.

Never in my wildest dream did I expect I would have a chance against the big guys. After all, I was 76 kg and some of them stood on stage at a whopping 90 kg to 110 kg. The difference seemed to me to be out of my reach. As we stood on stage in the final line up, the head judge called the shots. Front pose, side pose, rear pose and then he asked us to turn in a clockwise direction in four stages.

When it was all over, it was time to stand on the white line in the middle of the stage in front of the 1000-plus-strong crowd. My heart raced. I was excited even to be in the line-up and to have gotten as far as I had.

I looked out into a room of lights and listened to the noise coming from the crowd, I felt the most amazing rush of blood hit me. I had finally found the feeling I always got in the service and, in particular, every time I had achieved or passed a test in my training to be an instructor. The moment was so overwhelming I never even heard the announcement. The guy standing next to me shook my shoulder and said they were calling my name.

Dazed, I cleared my head in time to hear him say "Would you please put your hands together for the 1991 Oceanic World Champion, Daryl Te'Nadii." My jaw dropped, as I walked to the front of the stage to collect my championship trophy. "Wow!" I thought. "My children are going to have a field day—each holding a trophy!" After I was crowned, each competitor came up to congratulate me. It meant so much to hear them say I deserved the win and after a while, even I believed it. It really was something special.

It was a significant moment among the many sporting highlights I would have in my life. Achievements that were my own and that no one could take away from me—I had earned them, regardless of how little or much I had, and they were mine forever. It meant a great deal to me knowing I had pushed the barriers in life, to prove a point to no one other than myself: that I was someone—not trash, not unwanted, not a slave, not an outcast—someone. I felt as if I finally belonged and was worthy of what I had been recognised for, regardless of the odds that had been stacked up against me.

That same week, I was offered a contract to train for the NABBA World Championship, to be held in 1992. I spoke to my kids about the training I would have to do and told them that I might have to train in another town for a while, to be able to be a chance on a world stage. They were super-excited and encouraged me further, to have a go at what we all knew was a once-in-a-lifetime chance. With a lot of tears, I packed the car with all I could fit into it and headed to North Queensland for World Championship training!

The next twelve months were spent training and competing, when asked to do so by my sponsor. I won a further three major shows that year, before suffering a terrible injury which forced me to back off my training and competing for two years. I was devastated. I tore my calf muscle completely in two and was on crutches for over three months. The pain alone was enough to send me into another world, but the swelling was so bad it looked as if I had a football attached to my leg. There was no way I could make it to the world stage—I had to accept that my time as a competitor was over, for a long time.

I packed up and returned to Victoria, where I was to undergo rehabilitation, to correct the damage and to be with my kids again. Being home with the kids was awesome—they kept my spirits up and helped me to stay focused too. I still had a little left in me and so I set myself an even harder task: to compete in twelve months, not the twenty-four months the doctor had predicted.

I worked hard at my rehabilitation and ended up competing a further three more times, before deciding to retire from competitive bodybuilding to move on to become a fitness coach in rugby, basketball, gymnastics, and swimming and a judge, in body building and body show events around Australia. In this way, I felt connected to the sports I loved and had spent many years enjoying.

Over the years I had spent bodybuilding, I had come into contact with many incredible people and competed in a total of 29 shows in many towns and cities in Australia, including:

- Geelong
- Ballarat
- Bendigo
- Melbourne
- Gold Coast
- Townsville
- Cairns
- Mackay
- Rockhampton
- Brisbane

I had even had the opportunity to compete in New Zealand. They were wonderful times, which I will always remember and be proud of.

I also won an armload of events including:

- One International event—Oceanic World Championships, placing first in the short class at the first event, then placing first in the short class and winning the overall in the same event the next year

- Two national titles, winning the short classes in both

- Four state titles, winning my classes in the under 70 kg twice, and the under 80 kg class twice

- Twenty-two regional events, winning twenty in mixed classes from novice and under 70 kg / 80 kg class groups and two second-placed titles

- Six Best Presentation awards

In addition to those, I also won awards and comps in two ironman events; individually and in a team, as well as countless awards in rugby, athletics, swimming, gymnastics and cross-country events, spanning thirty-plus years.

For all I have done, achieved and enjoyed, my most memorable moment will always be helping others reach their dreams. I had hung my belt up and I moved on, with no regrets.

CHAPTER 63

My Father

Thirty-five years

I had never met my biological father and he had never been a part of my life. He had never contacted me, or my brothers, or my sister. My brother, Brian, was five years old and I was a new-born when our father divorced our mother and we were left to the plight of strangers in the Salvation Army.

I was thirty-three years old and still competing in bodybuilding, when my brother, Dale, tracked our father down to an address in Auckland in New Zealand. It turned out our father had remarried and had had another three children who were living with him.

Dale asked me to return to NZ to meet our father. I debated whether or not to make the trip, as he had never taken the time to find us, so why would he want contact now? Why would I? In some ways, I wanted to punish him by ignoring him. It was really hard for us as kids, going through what we did, without any family protection or support, so in the back of my mind, I questioned why I should give this total stranger the privilege of being in my life.

I guess curiosity got the better of me and I began contemplating it all. I wanted to know about that side of my family, and my heritage, and I also loved the idea of having a father—a good father. It would be a dream come true and would mean so much to me. But lurking along with those thoughts were serious concerns and fear… what if he was completely disappointing like my mother had been? I was still undecided, when I found out that the Australian Body Building team, of which I had been selected as a member, would be flying to NZ a few months later to compete. It seemed that meeting him was destined to be, so I let my father know, through Dale, that I would be coming over to NZ and would like to meet him.

Three months had passed between when Dale asked me and my flight to NZ —in a heartbeat it seemed. As D-day arrived—the day I would stand face to face with my blood relative, the man known as my father, I began feeling anxious and a range of different feelings swelled up inside of me. This moment wasn't lost on me. The years and years of longing for a father had arrived at an end. All my life I had wondered what it would be like to have a father.

I saw kids and their dads almost every day, growing up, and wondered what the feeling of looking up into the eyes of a strong protector, your greatest hero would feel like. How would being scooped up in his big arms feel? What was it like; knowing you had that one person who knew everything about anything? How did a father's hand feel, tousling your hair in mateship? This among a thousand other things.

After finishing my competition, I drove to the address Dale had given me—my father's home. As I pulled up to a house that looked to have been built in the 20s, I wondered how a man and wife and children could live in such a small place. However, I would later learn that his kids had all married and that his wife had moved out, which left him alone in the house.

I walked up the path and a slimly built, frail man was standing there waiting. He greeted me with opens arms which felt so awkward, I was not even sure how to accept his welcome, but I embraced him all the same.

With my Father on Christmas day. This would be our first and only Christmas together. He died 6 months after this photo was taken.

All my personal visions of this man—my mother had painted a horrible, even frightening picture of him over the years—disappeared, as I looked at this elderly man before me. In fact, her physical account was so far removed from the truth that I felt ill in my gut and my heart that everything she had said about him was wrong. You could feel it.

All my beliefs, all thirty-five years of them came to a crashing end in a matter of just two minutes with this man—my father.

For years I had hated him….and never wanted to meet him. Now here I was, looking at him for the first time in my life and seeing a mirror image of my beautiful brothers, Brian and Dale .They were standing before me, in the shape of this stranger that I had detested for so long—it was confusing. All the years of past emotions; of hate and anger towards this man all came at me at once, together with an overwhelming familiarity, a connection and a yearning to know this man. Sorrow and shame were etched into every line on his face. I instantly felt sorry for him.

I just stood there in shock with my feet planted on the ground like lead weights, bewildered by the range of unexpected feelings coming at me as he talked. It was so hard to understand why, but as soon as he uttered his first words to me, it was as if my whole world opened up—I felt comfortable in a way I couldn't explain right away. The lost years, anger, and disappointment—everything just disintegrated in the blink of an eye.

He asked me to come inside and we entered the first room, a small sunset-facing room with rooms off to each side. As he escorted me into the next room, I could see it was like our homes in Australia, with a kitchen, dining room and lounge all as one room. Inside, the house was much bigger than it looked from the outside. I sat in an upright timber seat he pulled out from the kitchen table. He asked if I would like a drink. Straight from my competition, I said thank you, I would love water.

The room seemed old-fashioned in many ways, with furniture that seemed to date back in time. There were paintings on the walls of gardens and flowers and on the wall in the lounge I could see pictures of people whom I assumed to be his kids from his second marriage. Not wanting to be rude, I didn't ask, or bring up his new family.

In the weeks leading up to meeting him, I'd wondered how I would break the ice— do I ask the questions? Do I let him start the conversation? I just didn't know what to do, but I needn't have worried. Conversation with my father flowed easily and faultlessly.

I had a long list of questions I wanted to ask him, and I had a lot to say, as did he, but he let me speak first. Needing answers, I explained how for years we—his sons and daughter—had been told of the many moments in his life when he would leave for days, and how he hit our mother and turned his back on us. I figured those three statements would surely open up a conversation and bring the clarity I dearly wanted.

They did, and his explanation was plausible, as he relayed his account of what happened, especially knowing my mother. I asked why he had never tried to find us or at least to contact us. He told me that he had promised my mother never to look for us, or interfere in our lives. He told me he did not place us (Brian, Dale, Teena and me) in the orphanage and that he returned home from work to find the house empty one day and my mother and we kids gone.

He said he tried for days to find us and it wasn't until the police arrived that he learned of the actions my mother had taken along with a court summons to prevent him from having any contact with us.

We stopped at times and took in the moments we were sharing, before I asked my final question; did you love us? It was at that point that I saw a grown man kneel in front of me with tears streaming down his face and his voice shaking. He told me he had always loved us and, to that day, has never stopped loving us.

I was so taken by his declaration, my own tears flowed as I held the man— my father's—trembling hands. I could feel the warmth coming from his hands before I took him into my arms and held him close. How or why we formed this unique and solid bond, in such a short time, was beyond my understanding at the time. All I knew was that, on the day and in that room, I felt the need to have and hold my father for the first time.

After many hours of sitting and talking, listening, and asking a hundred more questions, the truth of my life was spread out before me like a blanket. It was so painful and unbelievable, reading through the documents my father had kept—including the court orders stopping him from seeing or contacting us—and hearing the answers to my questions left me breathless at times.

Over six hours had passed before he asked why I had come to NZ, after so many years. I told my father I had travelled there as a member of the Australian Body Building team, to compete in an international event. He asked me when was I competing, and I told him I just had, and that I had won my class and was also awarded over-all champion of the event.

I took the medal which had been presented to me, out of my sports bag and handed it to him. To my surprise, he started to cry. Reaching out he hugged me and told me he was so proud of me. Oh, those words! My feeling on hearing them was indescribable.

As we talked I learnt that I had two more half-brothers and another half-sister who were living in NZ. I didn't mention that I already knew this, through Dale. I wanted to hear his story from him and said I would like to meet them someday.

As we sat and spoke, my father suddenly broke down in tears. After some time, he finally looked up and said, "I am sorry, Son, I am so sorry for all that has happened to you, your brothers and sister; the hurt, pain and suffering" he sobbed sincerely.

I could see a lot of good in my father, but I saw a lot of pain too. When I spoke about my mother, he closed the conversation down. I could see he was uncomfortable with me raising her name—clearly, the damage she had done still bore a painful dagger through his heart. All he would divulge was that he was sick of her going out and partying with her friends, spending time with other men and leaving three kids at home alone. When she fell pregnant with me, things got worse and he couldn't stay any longer.

My father stood up and went to a box on top of a set of drawers in the lounge. The many words we shared helped me to realise he was not the bad person my mother had portrayed. He took out a photo album and showed me photos of him in his younger days, when he had been a champion boxer and had held his Second Dan black belt in karate. It seemed as if my father was a top competitive athlete also; I didn't know that about him.

He took a picture out and asked if I would look after it and remember him by it. I have that picture in a safe place today, still, along with many more treasured things, but that day we shared tears, and more tears as I listened to his stories, and he listened to mine. Each of our stories deeply affected both of us as they cut to the core. So many years, thoughts, feelings, dreams, and even nightmares had led up to this point. To have my father in my life was special, but also very sad. I found it hard to know what to do or how to be around him, it being so late in his life, but for the most part, however, it was comfortable.

What came next, after all this time was just cruel.

My elation at connecting with my father came to a grinding halt, as he handed me one last document to read. It was a medical diagnosis—my father was dying. More tears welled up in my eyes as I asked him how long he had. After half a lifetime, and a journey across the ocean to meet him, I would have just six to twelve months with him, before he would leave my life my life again, but this time forever.

I sat stunned and wordless for a while, I'll admit. Hearing it was destroying. He stood up again, this time to retrieve a little box from the top of his personal drawers in a table he used as a desk. Turning he handed me a chain and told me that it was his father's, and his father before that. It was over 150 years old and he wanted me to take care of it and pass it on down to our next generation. Such an honour and to this day I have it placed away to pass on to one of my children, one day. The chain carries the nineteen knots of life.

He did explain it to me, but at the time, and with so much going on and having to all of a sudden process the fact he was dying, I had trouble remembering the full story behind the nineteen knots of life. I did find a fragment …

> *When you meet a setback in life, a knot is formed.*
> *Your rope of life will not seem so perfect anymore,*
> *but built on understanding.*
> *Don't let it become a weakness,*
> *but more something to remind you,*
> *of how determination can overcome any default moment.*

We talked some more, and I told him that I really wanted to bring him to Australia to meet the remaining family. This would be our one gift we could bestow upon him—an opportunity to meet his other children and grandchildren. A smile spread across his face as he asked, "Is it even possible? Would they accept me and take me into their hearts?" That I could not answer, but "knowing my family I am sure they will" I told him.

Five months later, it became a reality. We flew my father over to Australia and he spent his first and last Christmas with us; Dale and Robin, Teena and Bob, myself and his nine grandchildren, before he passed away some months later on his return to New Zealand. Watching him sit amongst family, showing so much love was more than we could have ever hoped for, as children and grandchildren. My father got to spend a moment in time with us, knowing it would be his last.

It was a sad time in my life, but I'm very thankful I got the chance to meet him, to know him, and am able to move on with enough questions about him answered that it helped me understand and heal in many ways.

Yes, my father did fail me in many ways, and he acknowledged this, before he passed away, with tears of regret streaming from his eyes. However, what he told me only reinforced the many stories other family members had told me, over the years—that he didn't have a choice in some of it. I will always respect and hold him strongly within my memory as a man who did his best.

I never saw any of the documents or paperwork that he had as evidence, again. I am guessing they were destroyed on his passing. Knowing what I had found about my father, upon meeting him, it is still hard for me to deal with—if only I could have the time over so I could get to know him for who he was much earlier.

I was bitterly disgusted in myself for believing my mother's lies. I can only assume she never wanted me, or any member of the family, to know the truth so she defamed him to save face and to keep us away from him and the truth.

I had to forget the past, though, to move on from it, and more importantly to hold a space with the memories we had with our father and I continue to do that.

"Dad, I'm keeping in my mind the many things you told me, and the love we briefly shared. I wished you could have stayed forever—I will never forget you. You are gone now but never forgotten and you will always remain in my heart. I found a special smile, a special face, and a special father I can't replace. I love you, and I always will. You filled a space that no one else could have filled, and I thank you for that."

CHAPTER 64

The Protector

Thirty-six years

Having an older brother is something that I am sure is every boy or girl's dream.

Separated from birth and not re-connecting until I was five years of age meant that I not only didn't know him, but I initially didn't understand "brotherhood" either. However, our blood relationship quickly developed and soon became unbreakable.

Being in an orphanage where you lived in fear of daily abuse, having an older brother got me and Dale through the tough times and kept us safer than the boys without older siblings. We formed our own family and bonded forever. Brian protected Dale and me from the Salvation Army Officers on numerous occasions and acted as a buffer for us—something we really weren't aware of until later in life. Even though Brian was only five years older than me he was committed to his role of big brother.

As he grew older, stronger, and more powerful, he became a threat they didn't want to mess with so they left him alone, and navigated onto younger, more vulnerable boys who wouldn't fight them back. His stature as an adult was formidable—he was tall, with big, broad shoulders and he carried himself like an athlete. He had the physical makeup of a champion; a legacy from our golden-glove father.

He would walk around Hodderville with his head held high, knowing he was bigger and stronger than most of the staff; but, in saying this, he never used his size to intimidate the boys or other staff. He only stepped into that when O1 and O2 posed a threat. He was highly respectful and a very caring man; a commendable trait that I admired in him throughout his life.

Brian had a crack at rugby but wasn't as passionate about it as I was. For him, it was trampolining that caught his attention and excited him. He would spend hours during his senior years working on moves and improving his skills to become better than all others. He joined the gymnastics team where he developed his tumble and aerial moves, and went on to become an elite performer for the squad.

As a young boy, I remember going to the senior gym on two occasions to watch him. Those moments were memorable and inspired me to strive to be the best, if not equal to others, as he was. Like our father, and unbeknown to all of us, he (along with Dale and I) also ventured into boxing. Not only was our father a champion boxer, both our uncles— we were told—also ventured into the ring. Brian did well in the sports he had a crack at and enjoyed them, but his focus was normally short-lived as he would be distracted by his passion and love for music.

Talented in many areas, it was music that was the thing in which he truly excelled. Brian was able to listen to and play a song from any artist in the world by ear—he was amazing. I loved hearing him play the many incredible songs he wrote. He began on six-string guitars, and then moved to the bass, which he loved for its deep, rhythmic soul sound. Music was his life, and in the years following Hodderville, he became a member of several bands.

The years passed and with this came the opportunities Brian had dreamed of and waited for. At the age of sixteen boys were allowed to move out of the orphanage and take up positions working on farms in the local area. Not wanting to spend another day at Hodderville, Brian jumped at the chance to take on the role of rural training with a local farmer. He spent two years at the farm, before deciding to pursue his dream and passion to make a career in music. Brian enrolled in music classes, in a bid to extend his knowledge and skills in music, before writing his own songs, setting up a band, and travelling the world playing music.

With three other guys—Darrell the rhythm guitarist, Geoff the keyboard player and another guy whom I never got the chance to meet—the four of them were more on the road than off, and sometimes years would pass without any word or any idea of where he was or what he was doing.

It had been a while since I had seen him, actually, it was a long while—I hadn't seen him since moving to Australia—when Brian turned up at the front door along with two of his band members, out of the blue and while I was staying with my sister in Lara, Victoria. Teena and I stood there in shock, but relief at knowing he was still alive!

We spent the remainder of the day just sitting, talking, and asking a thousand questions; back and forth, catching up on lost time. I explained how after my move to Australia I was left to live on the streets which greatly upset him when he heard it. I told him Dale was traveling around Australia and no one knew where he was.

Teena told him about her life, her marriage, and her girls, as it had been many years since they had seen each other as well. Neil, Teena's husband, arrived home so along with the big dinner which Teena was well known for, we clocked up more hours chatting away and narrating our stories.

Teena's home was massive with five bedrooms, so after Neil's invitation, Brian, Darrell, and Geoff decided to stay awhile. Neil was a leading hand at Fords, and got the guys a job on the afternoon shift, which was wonderful as we were able to spend even more time together over the following days.

Brian talked about his band, and his partner, whom he married later in life. Life was good, or so he thought. Arriving home off the back of a two-week tour with his band, his world fell completely apart after he opened his front door to find his house completely empty and all of his personal items missing. After weeks of searching for his wife and answers, he learned she had left him for another man and had sold all of his possessions to finance her move and her new life.

All his musical equipment and the songs, which he had spent years writing, were gone along with any personal items he owned—she had sold the lot. In the years to follow, he learnt she had turned to drugs and lived day-to-day and in and out of rehab.

I could see he was carrying the pain of being abandoned, but I had no answers to help him—I just listened as he poured his heart out and hope that helped him. Brian told us he would only be staying for a month, as the guys from the band wanted to head to Europe, to connect with friends and to tour some more. I think he was keen to get back on the road and in a big hurry to escape and start over.

A month passed, and the guys from the band moved on, whereas Brian packed his van up and decided to head to Queensland first. Immediately I knew why. He wanted to see our mother. I realised I had to tell him the truth—she was not what he expected. I told him to be careful and not to say too much about his past. I felt he was about to walk into a minefield of exploding lies and warning him was the only way I could protect him from more hurt.

He called from the Gold Coast two days later to tell me he had arrived safely and that he had enjoyed the journey up to Queensland. Then, he went nomad again and I didn't see him for another few years. I had always seen Brian as a wanderer of the land.

He did meet up with our mother, and as predicted, she had managed to stick a knife into his heart and twist it, inflicting pain as only she knew how to. All he had hoped for was to meet, connect, and develop the mother-son relationship he had dreamt of all of his life—sadly that wasn't to be. Within no time of being with her, she went on about her own life, how she felt betrayed and hurt and had had to walk away from her second marriage because of the physical and mental abuse. She couldn't care less about him.

It was in 1992, some sixteen years after we reconnected in Lara, Victoria, I was training, and somehow Brian was able to get Dale's home phone number. Dale gave Brian my mobile number and he called to tell me he was sick, chronically sick. He had been diagnosed with asbestosis, a chronic disease that scarred the lungs, leading to breathing issues. He had worked in the building trade and for years and had been subjected to asbestos building products.

My body went into a kind of shock—it was devastating to hear him say the doctors had given him only one to two years to live, at best. He said he needed to see me, and that he needed a friend, and he asked me to fly up to the Gold Coast. I took his number down and told him I would call him back later that night.

After I stopped training and left the gym, I called Dale and asked him to come to Queensland with me, saying that our brother needed us. Unfortunately, Dale could not get time off work, which left me to fly up alone. I called Brian to let him know I would be up the next day. Flying up to Queensland, so many thoughts entered my mind but above all, I just wanted him to be OK.

On my arrival at Coolangatta Airport on the Gold Coast, I phoned Brian and a woman's voice answered. I was a little taken aback, but then thought to myself, Daryl it's been sixteen years, he probably has a girlfriend.

I hired a car and arranged to meet Brian at a local hotel for lunch in Cavil Avenue on the Gold Coast. This was the only place I really knew how to get to. He got there first and he was waiting as I walked into the hotel. Wow… sixteen years really had passed. He was older and his hair was grey in places, but besides that, he looked healthy and fit—it was a relief, even though I knew of his fate. We hugged and he said to me, "Holy shit Bro, look at the size of you! You look like Arnold what's his name the bodybuilder!"

I laughed and told him about some of the training I'd been doing over the years. As we sat, having lunch and talking about the old days and how everything was just so wrong, tears began streaming down his face. I had a feeling he had asked me to come up for more than just support and it looked as if I was about to find out what it was.

As he looked at me he said "Mate, I need to tell you something. Something I have never told another person. I can't live, knowing I have hidden this, and I don't want to die knowing I never told anyone". That's when he purged the past horrors he too had endured at the boys home— terrible stories of his being victimised at the hands of the Salvation Army officers. I looked at him in shock. I felt sick and deeply hurt for him, thinking of the pain he had suffered, just like so many other boys. It cut me to the core, just knowing that he had carried the weight of that pain and torment all those years before confiding. It hurt like hell.

He said he had been sexually assaulted many times by officers of the Salvation Army, prior to my arrival at Hodderville. Over thirty years of pain tore from deep inside him as he spoke of living with, and hiding, those memories without help from anyone. He went on to tell me of the assaults and rapes he witnessed on some of the other boys and he recalled the terrible beatings he received as a young child after his arrival at the home.

Brian spoke about one slimy Salvation Army Officer, in particular, who knew how much music meant to him and who forced Brian to be his sex slave so he could attend music studies. God, it was painful to hear my older brother tell it. I had had no idea, although I should have had; what could I have expected? With no older brother there to protect him, he was on his own, surviving in a hell like no other. That's why he kept an eye on me and protected me wherever and whenever he could, so I didn't suffer the same fate.

I was lost for words. He stood strong with his head held high during my time there—I would never have guessed he had endured what he had. Knowing Brian had also been abused made me even more determined to bring the despicable bastards to justice at some point in my life.

I was thankful Brian had opened up to me, as hard as it was to hear it and I was grateful for the time I got to spend with him during my stay in Queensland. I learned that he had married again and had a beautiful wife and children. He had found his feet with his new love, who had become his rock. They had settled in Nerang, a town on the western outskirts of the Gold Coast.

During his remaining two years, I visited him and spent as much time with him as I could, every time meeting away from his home. I never met his wife. I didn't understand why he kept our times together private, but the truth came out later and, as in the past, my mother had had a hand in it.

As the months passed and he grew more ill, our mother began interfering in his family's life. Abigale, Brian's wife and my mother did not get on at all, in fact, they hated each other. I guess my mother abandoning us, and her selfish and greedy characteristics were as unforgivable to Abigale as they were to Brian and me. Right up until the time Brian died my mother tried to stir the pot and to cause as much trouble as she could. That woman knew no bounds.

The cancer took over and spread through Brian's body, as I held on to him for dear life. I watched him deteriorate and wither away before me. It pained me just looking at him, knowing he was being consumed by the disease. It was so cruel and there was nothing I could do about it other than to hold on to my beloved brother.

Our mother could not even give him peace as he lay in his bed, at around 38 kilos, in his final precious moments with his wife, son, and daughter. She turned up and had Graham pull Abigale aside, so she could go inside and play the mother act. It was the final nail in his coffin, but she could not see that. She ranted and raved about his wife, disrespecting and hurting Brian even more, as he lay there without the strength to tell her to go away or protect his wife and kids.

It was not hard to see why she will forever be hated by so many. That was a day they— his wife and kids—will never forget, and one which was painful enough without the drama our mother created. My older brother passed away, and on that day I lost the person to whom I looked up to; a brother who protected me so many times, and who had a smile wider than life.

Brian's two amazing friends come over to pay their respects, Jeff, from England, and Darrell, from New Zealand. The three had travelled the world together, playing their music and doing what they loved and for years, prior to Brian's passing. I am glad he had that in his life and that I was given the chance to watch them play, as well as to smile and laugh together.

I still hear his music and his stories of how he would be a star one day. He never really had a chance to fulfil that dream, as he seemed to spend too much time with people who lived for the moment and not enough time with people who had the same vision. Ultimately he had self-sabotaged his own dreams of success.

I found out years later—in fact, twelve years later—that my mother had told Abigale that I "BLAMED" her for Brian's sickness and his death. She dealt her final blow to Abigale and the kids by telling them that I hated them for taking my brother, and never wanted to see them again.

After I learnt this, I contacted Abigale, telling her how sorry I was for the lies my mother had told her, and said that I had never blamed anyone for my brother's death. He was sick and what made me proud was having her be there for him.

I caught up with her, in 2010, some sixteen years after Brian's passing, which was wonderful. The kids had grown up, and Abigale was still working and supporting her children as she did back then. Brian would be so proud of his wife and children today, and also of knowing that we are still friends.

My oldest brother Brian.

I sat with you many times, Brian, as you fell asleep. You said you'd be back and promised that we would be together again one day. I sat in the park around the corner, asking you to come back to me many times; don't leave me alone in this world. You're my friend forever, I don't know what to do, and I don't want to be alone.

My beautiful brother, you passed away. I said goodbye. Your face brightened my day, your voice was music to me, your smile, love, and kindness are forever with me. I remember asking why? Time passes but the memories will never fade away,

I'll find a way to keep you alive, and I'll hope forever someday you'll come home to us.

You are my brother; you are my friend. I'll always watch out for you and I know you watch out for me, no matter where you are…

Kaua rawa e warewarehia i nga wa katoa

Never to be forgotten, loved always.

CHAPTER 65

Love

Thirty-seven—Forty-three years

Back on base, I threw myself into work, to distract myself as much as possible from the loss of my brother. Every rec leave, I headed back to Geelong to visit my family and friends, which seemed every more important than ever since Brian's passing.

On my R&R I'd also stop in at my regular barber's to get my hair cut in the standard short back and sides' style. My usual hairdresser was Sarina, and had been for some time; however, on this day¨, she said she was booked up that day and couldn't fit me in. She asked if I wouldn't mind having the apprentice look after me.

I preferred to stay with the same barber, but as I was heading back out to camp the next morning, I didn't have a real choice, since by the time I came back it would be way too long, so I agreed. I waited in the foyer and took in the shop with its original barber's chairs, long mirrors that covered the wall, and typical barber's shop floor of black and white tiles. Finally, a pretty young girl came to get me and seated me in a barber's chair. She shyly placed a wrap around my shoulders and proceeded to cut my hair.

I'll be honest, I was a bit nervous and so was she. I was nervous because I wasn't used to someone else cutting my hair and she was probably nervous because she had to cut her senior's client's hair! We didn't talk that much; she was fully focused on doing a good job, which she did to my delight. After the tidy up, I thanked her, paid, and left the shop with an impression of her that stuck and my mind kept wandering back thinking of her.

Even after I had posted and had to visit the local barber, my thoughts drifted off thinking of her. I couldn't even tell you the one thing that seemed to have captivated me about her, but she definitely had.

As fate would have it, years later, after I had moved back to Geelong, I was asked to accompany my nieces—Rena, who was eighteen, and Rebecca, who was twenty-one—to their birthday party. The girls were both born on the same day, but three years apart and had arranged a party to celebrate.

Fairlie had hired a venue at a hotel, so Rebecca and Rena could have a private function with family and friends. At the time I was doing some private security for a number of clubs in town to save money and I called in a few of the boys I knew to help out at the door and to keep out people who weren't invited.

During the night, I had girls lingering around and draping themselves over me, as hotel security guards often do. I was completely uninterested, having just come out of a relationship, so I tried to give the girls, who were friends of my nieces, the message that I was off the market, so to speak, as kindly as possible but they kept persisting.

After the party wound up, I went to another club downtown with some friends and had only been there a short time when the same girls from my nieces' party came up to me and began hassling me again. Trying to avoid any conflict and not wanting to insult them, I planned my escape and made a break for it. I headed upstairs to the second level of the club, where there was a dimly lit bar and dance floor, where I could just have a peaceful drink and catch up with a couple of mates.

Unbelievably, just moments later, the girls had followed me, not getting the hint and began to drape themselves over me once more. I probably should have gone home as they just wouldn't take no for an answer, but the night was still young, and I was keen to enjoy it, so I sought another way to free myself from them. I walked into the bar and went up to a woman who was a stranger and asked her if she would like to come onto the floor for a dance with me.

In the low light, I didn't see the girl clearly and in truth, I wasn't interested in another girl, I just wanted to get rid of the two who were all over me like flies, without being disrespectful.

The woman looked at me and asked, "Do you remember me?"

I stopped looking over my shoulder and looked at the woman clearly for the first time and said "No, I am sorry, but I do not". That's when she smiled the most brilliant smile and it hit me like a ton of bricks! She was the pretty young barber! But she was not the shy, nervous girl anymore; she had grown up, and was confident and stunning!

I was thinking "WOW!" when she said, "I'm Janet, I was your barber years ago". My jaw was literally on the floor. She was even more beautiful, standing there before me. I could not believe my eyes. After all those years I had run into her again—what are the chances?

She was standing inches away from me and she took my hand and led me to the dance floor. I felt my blood rush through my body, pooling and boiling hot in my face as she swayed to the music. It was fantastic to see her again. I felt so at ease with her, holding her in my arms. Everything felt right, and I hoped she felt the same. It definitely felt like fate. We sealed the night with a kiss and fewer than six months later we were living together on the Sunshine Coast in Queensland.

I knew I had found that special person, the one person I felt right about–a true love. It sounded so crazy: from meeting this shy girl, in a random walk-in to have my hair cut, to re-connecting with her years later and then moving to Queensland.

A year later, in 1998, I drove home, walked inside our home and in a not so romantic way, I asked Janet if she would marry me. We have just celebrated twenty-one years together and over that time we have had an amazing journey together; and added to our family with the birth of our beautiful daughter, Baila Rae Te'Nadii.

To this day, I am still amazed she said YES to me all those years ago! I am one lucky guy. This woman—my wife— brought so much joy back into my life.

On the day of our wedding ceremony. Happily husband and wife.

It is incredulous that a fifteen-minute haircut, and years of not crossing paths, had not only led to another chance meeting but also to marriage and a daughter. It just goes to show you true love is patient, and Janet has it in bucket loads. I have dragged this woman to hell and back, as I have tried to rid myself of all my terrible memories, yet she still stands by my side, in full support.

We have shared a wonderful friendship, have travelled the planet, renovated two homes, built three new homes and about to build a fourth and final home, opened three hairdressing shops, two health clubs, and a whole lot more. She truly is my best friend and I dread the thought of not having her with me every day.

The happiness I have found, with Janet by my side all these years, is immeasurable. I feel so proud and fulfilled.

We have had twenty-two years of adventures that have kept our bond strong. Janet became my riding partner, getting her first bike— a 1000cc Harley Davidson Sporty—and would later trade up to a 2010 Harley Davidson custom 1100cc Sporter, a bike she loved. We have travelled the road together for thousands of kilometres.

Janet had always been an athlete in her own right, but in 2000, just two years after opening our first health club on the Sunshine Coast, she asked me to train her in body sculpting. At first, I took it as a bit of a joke, thinking she was just looking for more training options, since my kind of training was full-on and she knew it.

I soon realised she was deadly serious, so I sat with her and talked her through the sacrifices she would need to make for the sport, such as the eating arrangements, lack of sleep and the on-going and brutal early morning training schedule that would break even the most passionate gym junkie. Undeterred, she was still eager to begin and said "Bring it on!"

What followed were hours, days, weeks, and months of a crucifying six-month commitment to the sport's physical demands. As Janet grew in confidence, her training intensified beyond my expectations and her natural ability was at a level I'd not seen in other athletes I had trained. Half a year later, I could see she was completely committed and we began looking around for beginner comps for her to enter.

I will admit, in some ways I was jealous as she threw every moment into her training, with and without me, but I had had my time and now it was hers. I was more proud than anything else.

The time came for her to show in her first competition and I could see she was excited and ready! Janet is an absolute dynamo and a high achiever, and she took to the stage after fourteen months of hell, under my training, and shone like a diamond up there. Her presence and the way she handled her composition dominated, and I couldn't have been prouder when she was announced the winner of the competition.

Janet competed another eleven times, over the next five years, before retiring from competition life. In that time she was awarded with:

- Two regional first places in the Figure short class ANB
- Second place in the Queensland country under 50 kg IFBB
- Two Queensland state championships

- First place in the figure short class ANB
- First place in the Queensland state championships women's figure masters' class
- Second place in the Australian championships figure short class
- First place in the Australian masters figure short class
- Second place in the Australian masters
- Queensland women's figure over-all champion

Janet also qualified for two international events, as part of the Australian team. Unfortunately, due to international tensions, her first trip was cancelled and the show was moved to the following year. When she received the second invitation, she decided to pass the opportunity to the girl who came second to her—who went on to win the World Championship two weeks later.

I was and am so proud of my beautiful wife. Never once did she falter or slack off with any excuses. She just put in 100% commitment and dedication, much as she does in our marriage. She is one in a million, and took on the impossible, something many women younger than her would not have dreamt of having a go at, let alone competing in, at the highest level.

Janet after winning the Australasian Championships – Women's Figure open class, masters, and overall champion.

Janet not only taught me *how* to love but also to trust in it, relax in it and to enjoy it. She taught me it was all-encompassing—friendship, sexual attraction, intellectual compatibility, and of course, love.

I think I made it through the last two decades of my life because of her. She has been my soul mate as well as the amazing mum to our daughter. I am forever grateful to her in immeasurable ways.

CHAPTER 66

My Hero

The loss of my older brother Dale was a moment in my life I wanted to forget, a time I wanted to remove from my life, and never to talk about it ever again after his death and the cremation. If I had to talk about this man the way I believe he deserved, I would be here forever.

I was closest to Dale out of all my siblings. I still remember his smile; it was one of those smiling grins you could not mistake. His crazy way, dance steps, passion for singing, and his enjoyment of a beer were Dale through and through. The love he had for his wife and children was so strong that even in death it will go on forever.

Like everyone, he had his good and bad days. When he struggled, he called me and asked me to come over, needing a friend to talk to—but more so a brother who would and could listen. The boys' home did irreparable damage to all of us. Some days, even getting through an hour was bloody hard and, in one such moment, he asked me how I got through it. I replied, "Friends mate, friends".

Dale was like me in many ways. Behind the big, tough, macho exterior was a man who was hurting. He was bashed, abused, and hurt so many times at Hodderville that he was broken to the point where life just wasn't an option anymore. Like me, he had considered suicide at a very young age, to escape a life that was too hard to live.

As tight as we were, we still had our ups and downs growing up, as all siblings do, and there were times when we just didn't see eye to eye. But, thankfully, they were few and far between. I remember a couple of occasions in particular that we crossed swords, one of which left me with the best black eye I had ever worn.

It was a sunny day and we had just eaten lunch and were enjoying playtime. Always on an adventure of some kind, we decided our next destination would be the park across the road. It wasn't big, but still large enough to kick a ball around and run wild. On this particular day, we three brothers (Dale, Darren and I) decided to challenge each other on the swings.

One by one we took turns—each of us had to have twenty full swings, to see who could get the highest or to the swing bar level at the top. Darren cheated and took an extra four swings which made me lose my cool—even back then I was competitive! I grabbed him and pulled him off the swing. He fell to the ground and I jumped back on the swing and began swinging back and forth.

Dale picked Darren up and walked over to me. Without warning, he let fly with an almighty punch that connected with me on my left eye as I swung past him sending me flying into no man's land. Thinking back, I recall it was a beauty and took a fair bit of time for me to get back up. It was a good lesson learnt from my big brother; no matter what we face in life, the only person revenge really hurts is yourself.

The other altercation I had with Dale was when we were kids in our lounge. I was watching Gigantor, a cartoon show on TV—Dale knew I loved this show, it was one of those shows where the big and powerful people win all the time. On this day, for whatever reason (probably because he was older and just could), Dale walked in and turned the knob to another channel.

I lost it and jumped up and threw a right hook out of nowhere. My connection was good, but even better was the return punch he got me with, which sent me cascading to the floor. I got up and grabbed him in a rugby tackle thinking "I've got this" but as always, I was wrong. A silly act, but one I did without thinking, as he pushed me back.

After I stood up, I picked up a coffee cup from the table and I threw it at him, only to watch it sail across the lounge and straight through the window. We both stopped, looked at each other, and thought "Crap! We'd better come up with a good explanation for this!" We managed to put a stupid story together and escaped what would have been the flogging of all floggings, for sure.

I can clearly remember the many times I would sit and look at Dale. He really was such a humble man, who wanted nothing more than to help and give. In many ways, both would bite him on the ass, but he always picked himself up and moved on to the next adventure, right or wrong.

At night we would talk for hours at times. Even though I was the younger one, I did most of the listening and gave advice if and when I could. Dale confided in me, telling me about his crush on a girl up the street, or asking me about my training for rugby, and even how I was able to save money from nothing—just thoughts about life he felt comfortable asking no one other than me.

He would tell me about the times at the boys' home, before my arrival, and how often he was bashed by the officers just like the other kids. How he was always having to watch his back with the Edwards brothers, who seemed to have had a fixation on Dale and were always ganging up on him.

But, I think the hardest moment with Dale was when he would ask me why our mother had never loved us, like other kid's mothers did. How do you answer so many questions so often and more importantly that question about your own mother? To help, I would say my piece, which upset him, but knowing the truth was what kept me going.

I would always tell him, don't trust them; my mother or Gerald. They are filled with nasty ways and we are just another pay packet to them. Dale being Dale would always say to me, Daryl you need to let it go. I don't know how many times he said that to me over the years but it was a lot.

I felt so hurt and sorry for him, but also mad. No brother wants to find out the many secrets their older brother hides from family and friends. Dale knows he hurt some special people in his life, and did things he regretted, as many of us do, but he never denied it or walked away from taking responsibility for his actions, and that made me so proud of him.

As simple as they may sound, there are so many times that connect to memories I have of my brother that I will never forget. When I needed someone to talk to, Dale was there; when I felt hurt and lost, Dale was there for me, and when I needed to get away and get through hard times, Dale's door was always open for me along with a great feed cooked by Robin

I owe him so much in so many ways. If wishes were an option, I would wish for one day back with him, just so I can tell him how much I appreciated him, how much I thought of him, and how much I miss and love him.

I felt as if I lost my soul mate. I said goodbye to a man who was one of the few people who really knew me; a person who stood by my side through hell and back at the boys' home. I would have never survived the torment and suffering there if it wasn't for Dale and Brian.

I remember Dale almost dying, protecting me one day. The memory of him as he lay motionless and bleeding is still as clear as if it was just yesterday. He had intervened in a fight at the home, between me and the two Edwards brothers. Well, to put it in prospective they were smashing me! I had just been selected for the junior national rugby team that they had expected to be a part of as well, but they didn't make the cut. They took their frustration and anger out on me, by belting the hell out of me.

Dale walked around the corner and without any hesitation stepped in giving the two brothers a few jabs and don't argues. They were backing up, when their older brother showed up. Dale turned around and yelled out to me to run, which I did. He also ran and led the way towards the dorm.

Sprinting towards the closed door, he made a grab for the handle but misjudged it in his speed and his hand went straight through the panelled window and blood spurted out from his wrist, going all over the place—it was like a hose had been turned on. I later learnt that he had nicked a main vein in his wrist. The scar never healed, and it became a reminder of what he did for me on that day, every time I saw him.

He had a sense of fearlessness and determination that was evident even at a young age—nothing was too big, too high, or too hard for Dale. He was a real go-getter. He was my champion.

Even though he loved sports, it didn't go well for him. He tried bloody hard but never really grasped the main points with sports. Regardless, he'd have a red-hot crack at it, as with everything he did—you could take nothing away from his try-hard attitude.

Wanting to fit in with the other boys, Dale would come to the weekend sports, be it rugby, swimming or athletics. He would always do his best and never gave up or cracked the shits. Even when I often took control of the game, or sport in question, he never got jealous; I could do what he couldn't—Dale was there for me, helping and talking to me, the way he would have wanted it to be for him.

He became my off-field coach in many of the sports I played or the competitions I competed in. He always had the time to ask me about my sports and to ask how things were going. He was a coach, my brother, and a soul mate.

Smack bang in the middle of Brian and me, he was a bit of a rogue and Brian was always telling him to stop doing silly things, and to grow up, or just "no". He had to put up with the thousands of requests from me for help, advice, or to please play. He managed to get through all of it with a smile on his face.

Like all brothers, our ups and downs followed us through many years, and it came to fists a couple of times; but after the dust settled, we looked at each other and always said sorry.

His life's journey was similar to Brian's and, in many ways, he lost his way there for a bit, but it didn't take him long to get back on track and to set about making new friends; living in new locations, and tripping around Australia, learning more about the country he fell in love with. Mind you he wore his Kiwi heritage proudly too and was the one person in our family who wore his nationality and birth country proudly on his chest and in his heart.

Through fate, Dale also joined the army and was soon keen to do something for his new country, so he went on a tour of duty overseas, which landed him in hot water. One day he decided to take shore leave and have a few drinks with the boys. After a wild night and waking up in the brig, he quickly discovered he had decided to get a few tattoos. Not just one, two, or three. The crazy bugger let the artist do eight tattoos from his ankles up to his back, on his arms and—of all places—one on his manhood. He was the lovable wild child of the family.

Dale took discharge to start a new life. His absence was not too hard, as he was living close to the army base he had once proudly been a part of, so I could see him. After a period of time, he decided to move back to Geelong. This was where he met his new wife, years later, he founded a family of three amazing kids—two boys and one girl. He enjoyed spending hours sharing and teaching them the NZ culture, sharing his love of music and his passion for fishing.

For a short time, he moved to Melbourne to live, but for whatever reason, he moved back to Geelong and bought a home, where he spent his last days.

When we caught up, Dale would talk for hours about his kids. Even when I tried to change the subject, somehow, it always came back to the kids. He adored them and for good reason, they were awesome kids!

Adam his firstborn was like his father in many ways. He enjoyed many of the things in life that Dale did, from "Aussie Rules" to fishing, and gardening. He has a quiet strength that has been the backbone of their family, and he is a great support to his mother—I am sure Dale would be incredibly proud of the man, husband, and father he is today.

Jarrod, his younger son was lost for a while. Closest to his father in character, I recall Dale being concerned that he would grow up and make the same mistakes he had as Jarrod had that rebellious nature as well. Much to his credit, Jarrod worked hard to correct the mistakes he made and managed to get control of his wild nature and has 360-degree turn back to his family. I am proud of both of them, particularly in that they have never forgotten their father or the things he taught them. I know Dale would be watching over them thinking the same too.

Loz, Dale's only daughter also struggled for a while; mostly, I believe, because she blamed herself for or was angry about, losing her father, the one person who loved her more than life itself. Dale had a soft spot for Loz—as parents do but don't admit,—she was the star in his sky at night, and he would break out into his amazing smile every time she was around. What he saw in her was nothing short of the most incredible love, and devotion to the point where he would have given his own life without question.

Dale's wife spent countless years loving, supporting, and sharing many moments with him as they built their life together. She was his everything, even though Dale failed to show it on many occasions. He was Dale and the many years of abuse meant he also struggled to show affection, but when he did…OMG lookout. They were an awesome team those two.

When he found out that he had cancer, Dale was in a great place, and with the best of people. He called me and said 'Daryl, do you know much about cancer"? My heart sank, and I felt a deep sickening heaviness in my gut. I didn't know much about cancer, but I do know that I broke down and cried, after he told me he had been diagnosed with cancerous tumours—it was devastating.

Just six weeks after that call he had surgery—the tumours so big that much of his neck had to be removed. The surgeon was confident he had got it all. Dale healed well, and we all felt lucky to still have him, even though he had been left badly scarred from the operation

Sadly, it wouldn't be for long. Only two years later they found a lump behind his knee that would not stop bleeding. Some tests later, and it turned out it was yet another tumour and he had to have more surgery, this time they removed his leg just above the knee. Still, the cancer spread quickly and it wasn't long before Dale went back under the knife—this time for the removal of the remaining part of his leg, up to his groin which they hoped would get ahead of the disease spreading through his body .

I had seen a lot of hurt in Dale's life but none more than what his mother would do before the last operation. On learning Dale was to go back under the knife she decided to be a mother and fly down to Geelong to support Dale. All swords were put away, to give Dale the time he had left to feel the love he had always hoped for. Robin and the kids kept the peace, along with me.

On the day of the operation, we were all there; Robin, Dale, the kids and I. Waiting for our mother to arrive seemed to take forever. With the time drawing closer she arrived. I walked outside to stay clear, knowing I would start an argument and it was one Dale did not need.

After a short time, she walked out allowing me to go back in. Dale told me he was about to go under the knife and that our mother was going to come back the following day after the operation. I left so he could have his final prep and told him I would see him in the morning. On my return the next day Dale was still a little groggy but awake. It was a matter of waiting for the biopsy results to come back, which would take a few days.

Robin and the kids were with him, which gave him so much strength. We waited for our mother to return, but the time was getting away and still, she was a no show. I decided to go downstairs and call Fairlie, with whom she had been staying. This was when another wave of lies came out. Fairlie told me our mother not felt welcomed and her being there only upset her. I asked where they were, to be told they were at the pub playing the pokies. I just could not believe she would do this to her son, who had just had his leg removed and was awaiting the possibility that the operation could be a failure.

All my anger escalated as I told Fairlie to tell her never to come back into his life, never call Robin or the kids, and to stay away from her remaining family, who wanted nothing to do with her from that day onward.

Fairlie asked me to wait and the next minute my mother was on the phone yelling and carrying on as if we had dishonoured her in the cruellest way. When I asked her how we had done this, she replied you walked out of the room when I arrived and Robin and the kids ignored me.

I told her then and there that her son might die, and his only hope was that they got all of the cancer and that all he had wanted was her, this one time in his life. I told her she could not even give him that. I told her that my feelings and the feelings of the other family members should not have come between Dale's happiness and hers, and that she was a self-centred person who had never had any compassion, love or care for her children.

I think that was the final straw for her, as she hung up. I returned to the room to tell Robin that she was not coming back. Dale heard, and I could see in his eyes how sad he was.

The results came back and the test wasn't good. We soon learned the cancer had travelled through his leg, and up into his hip, and that no amount of medication, treatment, or surgery would stop the spread. Knowing this, I had to accept that my brother was slipping away from us.

Knowing that he had a certain time left to live never got him down. Instead, he used the few years he had to enjoy the time he had with his family, me, Teena, and even our father, before he passed just a year later.

I never asked him how it felt not to have two legs anymore. Instead, I avoided the issue and just treated him as if he were my two-legged mate, as he'd always been. I could see the lack of mobility frustrated him at times but I never stood up to a thing for him, but asked if I could help. Dale was independent in so many ways and over so many incredible years, if I had learned just one thing from him it was not to take control unless asked.

The dreaded call from Robin came. I was living in Queensland at the time so I made arrangements to fly down. I soon found myself flying into Melbourne Airport and then in a hire car headed to Geelong. I arrived at the Grace Mackellar Hospital/nursing home and was shown to Ward 13, to look into the eyes of my beautiful, full of life brother who had been transformed into a frail and dying man.

He had lost all hope and his once-fighting spirit had been taken away. Sitting and talking with him was a one-way conversation with no reply other than an exhausted squeeze of my hand to let me know he knew I was there. I felt so broken, but knew he just wanted to go to sleep. He was tired from the fight. Knowing his last breath was soon to come, I felt pierced deeper than I could imagine or feel.

It was so hard trying to hold back the tears, knowing he was dying, yet having to be strong for his wife and children who were by his side all the time. I found it impossibly hard to comfort them as my own world was literally falling apart. As he lay there, a husband, a father, brother, and friend—taking his last breaths, I asked the kids to say goodbye to their father. Each of the kids stood by his bed in tears one by one and held his hand.

Their words of love to a father and best friend completely ripped out the last of my energy to stay in that room. Watching, listening, and feeling their pain was so much more than I had prepared for. As they walked out of the room, I felt pain beyond anything imaginable. I had to watch my family, Dale's children, turn for the last time to look at their father, in tears while screaming in so much hurt. As I held onto Robin and Dale's hand, I stood in silence knowing my time to say goodbye was yet to come.

I walked to the door as the kids left the room, seeing them in agony as they walked down the hall in tears. They knew it would be the last time they would see, talk to, hold and tell their father they loved him more than anything in life ... ... all I wanted to do was yell and scream and ask "WHY?!!!!!"

The time had come and Robin was suffering in silence, to stay strong for the kids. Needing time, she left the room for a few minutes, these minutes would be my last moments in-breath, with you, as I spoke to you for the last time as only a brother can.

Mate I love you, never forget that, and a tear ran down his face. I felt his gentle squeeze on my hand, as I took him in my arms to hold so that he would now he was not alone.

As I kissed him, I felt a feeling of freedom. My brother's pain had left him never to harm him again, as he took his last breath relaxing in my arms. I walked outside to let Robin know Dale had passed away. I had nothing in me left to say how sorry I was for her loss, as I held her.

That night was one of many nights I have had to get through. With family support from Robin's side, we managed to pick up the pieces needed. Robin and the kids and I planted a single rose tree in memory of a husband, father, friend and brother.

"DALE"

Holding you then at that time in my life I will never let go of.
I cried tears of pain and anger but also felt happiness for you.
It was over, you fought through many years and always
with a smile

You passed away the 5th day of December 2002
Just 32 days short of your 46th Birthday
We laid you to rest on Monday the 9th day of December 2002
"REST IN PEACE MY BEAUTIFUL BROTHER"

It was unbearable to watch as he slipped away our hearts ripped at the seams. Loz was particularly hurt, and the pain of the moment cut so deep as their connection was severed. Why take so much love from others? As he lay in my arms, I made a promise to my older brother to watch over his family and Loz in particular.

I worried she would never recover from losing her dad. Over the years I stayed as close to the kids as I could. In many ways, I may have stepped over the boundaries, but my promise to Dale was my world when it came to the kids.

Loz was strong and also stubborn, just like her father, and I pushed her a bit too much, almost completely fracturing our relationship, I hate to say. I knew she missed her dad immensely, and I wanted to be close and to look out for her, but I had to give her room to breathe and to make her own way.

She had mentioned she would like to do hairdressing which I was thrilled about so I arranged an interview with a close friend who had her own hairdressing shop in Geelong. Loz went for her interview and was hired as an apprentice. As she was nearing the end of her apprenticeship, I discovered my friend was selling the business, which I saw as an incredible opportunity for Loz and talked with her about buying the business, but she wanted to head off and do some travelling.

She was strong-willed and had a mind of her own. She stuck to her guns, when I tried to persuade her to build a base for her future first, and I became overbearing and stepped too heavily. She put me in my place, which I have to say hurt me. I thought my intentions were admirable and that they came from a place of love for her, but in her eyes, I had interfered. Truth was, I did, because I didn't want to see her hurt or to fail in my promise to Dale about looking after her.

Loz ended up finishing work and went overseas to explore the world, as I held my breath and kept my fingers crossed that she would be ok. I accepted that she had grown up and, if she was anything like her father, which was something I had always seen in her, she would land on her feet and be perfectly fine.

It was a year before she came back into our lives, and I missed her greatly in that space of time. I didn't encroach on her freedom; instead, I sent her special wishes on her birthday, and at Easter, Christmas, and the New Year.

Today Loz is an incredible woman, whom I treasure greatly and she is a big part of my life. I love her immensely and enjoy walks down memory lane, revisiting her and my times with her amazing father. Today, she is married to the most amazing man and had two beautiful kids. Loz is a tremendous wife and mother and Dale would be so proud of his princess.

My connection with all three kids is still strong, and I love when we catch up. Robin, Dale's wife ended up moving on and I'll admit it hurt initially, but I also remembered what Dale told me—he wanted her to move on and to find a new life with someone else so she could enjoy the rest of her life. The only thing he hoped for was that he was not forgotten, and I know that he hasn't been.

Even though many years have passed by, I still think of Dale and miss him so very much. He has a special place in my home and in my heart.

Never forgotten

I keep remembering I had to face the day, when my mornings will not have you with me, when I'll wake up and feel like something is missing and nothing is there. Every day I feared that time was getting closer.

Dale, I fell asleep for years, I slept in hopes of dreaming that everything would be like it was before, but I will ever get that chance.

I will always have to confess one thing, at the time nothing scared me more than losing you—I have always had you by my side.

At night I felt so alone and lost without you for years, I know I can't have these hopes forever, but I will always feel in my heart and in my soul that you belong with me.

No matter the distance, no matter the place, no matter the time you will always be my brother. My mornings get cold, my nights getting restless, but I will never stop thinking about the day I had to say goodbye. As that day came closer, I wished it hadn't, the day of your departure I watch helplessly as you closed your eyes. A part of me died that day when I said I will let you go to sleep brother.

Missed deeply

No te mea kua aroha tonu taku tuakana mo te wa katoa Daz

Kaore i pau i a Adam Lauren raua ko Jarrod au tamariki

CHAPTER 67

Lost

One of the many things I attempted to do, over the years following my teens, was to get help to rid me of my past memories and heal.

Just prior to entering the service had reached out to a counsellor, to help me change some patterns I had brought into adulthood from my childhood, which didn't serve me well. I spoke to my rugby coach at the time, who knew someone who could help only and who was a few kilometres away from where we lived.

The coach dropped me off after training and I spent the next hour or so talking with the counsellor, often not getting out until 8:30—9:00pm. I found the sessions difficult and frustrating, and they ended up lasting just three visits, as I felt my life had been turned upside down with all the questions—it was too much for me to cope with. In many ways, the issues we dealt with were more about how I felt at the time, which seemed to over-shadow the reasons I wanted the help in the first place. I quit, and didn't get counselling again, until after I had after separated from my first wife.

Back then, I talked to a friend and decided to take his advice and discuss the issues I had carried since childhood. Since separating from Debbie, I had felt that my life had been taking a turn for the worst in many ways. Finding a way to cope each day while hiding the guilt, shame, and pain was draining me, and I realised it was not healthy. I tried training, running, and bike riding to clear my head, but the many memories kept coming back.

I saw a counsellor in Cairns. In the first consultation I think I went in with all guns blazing and downloaded every emotional problem I had, from my entire life, as she sat there and listened to me. She asked some questions to get me to open up even more, and after an hour, she asked me if she could arrange three visits over the next two weeks. She said that because of the history of my childhood she would apply for an exception through the government for funding to pay for the cost of up to ten consultations. She explained this was a normal practice for those who showed signs of suffering, after the abuse they experienced, as children, at the hands of their carers.

I agreed and booked the next three private consultations with her. During the first visit, we went back in time, talking about the effects of growing up as an orphaned child, and talked how I managed to escape the day-to-day abuse. She took notes and asked more questions about how I felt personally and how seeing the other children suffer affected me.

The second visit consisted more of my middle aged years, after arriving in Australia, and she asked about how I was accepted in society and how I managed with a new family. Along with the questions, she asked me if I felt any hate towards people, to which I replied, "My story tells it all". It is the reason I have so much bitterness towards people such as my biological mother and her husband, Gerald. From the answers I gave, I could see she was building a pattern of relationships about which she could talk with me in more depth later.

The third visit was interesting and in ways had me back paddling. Her manner was different from the first and second meetings, giving me not so much time to talk or answer but focussing more on the points that maybe I needed to let go of a little. Going over the same ground rattled me, as I had explained that I found it hard, if not impossible, to open up to other people, and even more so with my friends.

Like the past, I felt the consultation was missing the point. I didn't want to be told to let go and move on as I had so many times before. I wanted to have an open discussion about what was really happening to me, and what had transpired over the years to continually haunt me. However, it didn't unfold like that and it frustrated me to the point where I didn't go back.

I gave in and decided to run away from the truth, and away from the help I needed. All I really wanted was a friend, a soul mate to love me, to listen to me, and to understand my past pain. I felt that having this would help pull my walls of protection down, piece by piece over time, rather than in a single moment and thought that I would heal myself. But I kept searching, none the less.

I befriended another person from Geelong, who worked in the dive industry, and who became a very close friend in later years (Buzza). I think he could see I had many issues that raised their heads at times, and even though I never spoke of the abuse at the boy's home, I was still able to talk to him a little bit and it helped get me through some of the more challenging times.

I went to a card reader—one who specialised in Tarot cards—to try to find some answers. Not knowing too much, I asked others about the impact and relationships tarot cards had with people. I was seeing a girl at the time, who along with others, others suggested I take the time to have a reading done. She also felt I was distant at times, so with her encouragement I made an appointment to see the reader.

At the card reader's address, I was met by a mature woman with a powerful presence that was only softened by her gentle, calm, voice as she introduced herself. She asked me not to speak unless I asked a question and to remove any jewellery I may be wearing before coming into the room.

In the lounge area she asked me to sit at the table and relax. In front of me a black cloth lay on the table covering something. The reader sat and welcomed me, while explaining her responsibilities. She removed the black cloth, which covered a pack of cards. These cards had colours and images which were larger than the regular cards I had used in the past for card games.

She cut and separated the pack several times before placing it down in front of me. The room had a crazy set up with crystals hanging all around. The aromatic breeze floating through the window made me feel instantly at ease and comfortable. The reader started to turn over the cards and to place them down, one by one, as she began.

I was sceptical about this to be honest, I've seen those movies where people ask leading questions and are told virtually everything they need to hear. I didn't want to offend her, but at the same time I let her do the talking so I didn't direct her.

She mentioned the year 1969 and said "You have had a tough life with many atrocities far beyond what any child should have face". I said nothing and just listened. She laid another card down to reveal a picture which seemed to represent a person and she said "You lost your father, never having had the opportunity to get to know him."

I said 'True'.

Her third card seemed to have an image of travel. She looked up from it and said quietly, "You need to go back". She continued to tell me that I was taken away from loved ones at a young age and that they were still waiting my return. I tried to hold my emotions in check as she continued on and turned over another card. As quick as she had laid it down side ways and looked at it, she picked it up and turned it face down again and said "Daryl, I am sorry, but I cannot go on".

I sat looking at her, confused. She said that my "aura" was more powerful than hers and as such she couldn't read anything further and covered the cards back up with the black cloth.

I said, "Oh well, so much for that then!" and stood up to go, but she stopped me and said "Can't you feel it, Daryl?" I truly had no idea what she was talking about, so I went to hand her the $65 fee and head to the door, but she said she couldn't accept my money She asked would I mind if she had my cards read by a friend who was her teacher and mentor.

I had no reason to say no, so I said "Sure". She said she would get back to me. A few days went by and I received a call from her asking if I could come to her place the next day. When I arrived, she greeted me at the front door s on the previous visit and welcomed inside, to where a gentleman was standing in the front room. He must have been around fifty years or more and was well-dressed. He introduced himself as a reader of cards, and said he had been asked to come and see me.

As in the previous appointment, I sat at the same black cloth-covered table. The man sat down and said a few words that were unknown to me and then he looked at me and said "Let's begin".

Once the cloth was removed, I noticed the cards were a different colour, but the size and arrangement on the table were the same as at the last reading. The reading started similarly, with a few questions between each card.

One, two, three, and then four cards lay in front of me. As he took another card, he looked at me and then laid it down across the last card on the table.

He paused, looking from the cards to me with a questioning look on his face. He said, "Your journey in life has just begun; the tragic moments you hold deep within you have to be released for you to move on". His second comment of "You have been hurt so many times the scars from these atrocities had weighed you down" made me sit up and pay attention. Maybe this wasn't going to be a waste of my time.

He went on to say, "In 1969 you were taken from the ones you loved. You were reunited with your father, who later passed away before you had the chance to know him." I didn't learn a whole lot more from the man that day, but he did part with the comment "Daryl, you are a warrior, and you need to learn to be that person. It's your calling, and your people are waiting for you." Strange as it was, it encouraged me.

I relocated back to Geelong to be closer to my kids and took up a position as manager in a health club in Geelong. For whatever reason, I needed to speak with the owners who where making final arrangements to go to Spain on holidays. When I arrived at Joe and Anna Lopez's home, I saw two familiar faces; Geno, who became a friend through the gym and Gary Toskanoff, a champion bodybuilder from Perth.

I went inside to talk with Joe and he introduced me to a friend of his family. The gentleman was from Spain and spoke little, if any, English. After a few words with his family friend, Joe and I got onto talking business and he and I sat and went over work-related points and things I saw as a requirement to build the business. After a time, they agreed to give me the go-ahead.

As we sat, Joe asked me if I would like to have my signature read. I wasn't totally sure what he meant and asked him to clarify it. He explained that the family friend I had met from Spain could read signatures. I figured it would be something like the cards and didn't see any harm to it, so said sure.

Joe said he would act as an interpreter between his friend from Spain and me. He instructed me, "print your name on this paper, Daryl", which I did and then he placed it in an envelope. He handed me another piece of paper, on which he asked me to write down my date of birth and this also went into an envelope. The last thing he had me do was to sign my name and place the paper in another envelope.

Joe then asked me to follow him into another room where the Spanish gentleman was sitting, and he handed him the envelopes. He opened the first one, and then looked at me and said something to Joe in Spanish. Joe said "Daryl please sit down". The man rattled on in Spanish; I had no idea what he was saying.

After a while, the man said something else which prompted Joe to say "He says you need to let go, or that you will never honestly know who you are in the journey of life."

Ok, first envelope down, he picked up the second, opened it and looked at it thoughtfully before talking to Joe, who then conveyed the message to me "They have never blamed you for leaving them alone in 1969" he said. I could feel the hairs on my neck rising, but I tried not to show any emotion.

The third envelope sat burning a hole into the table, so it seemed to me. What would it reveal? I wondered if I should just stop right there and leave, but of course I was far too curious and so I waited until he delivered his next message, which he gave to Joe first.

Joe looked at me and asked me why I had never told anyone about my father and more importantly, why I refused to accept my position as the selected tribal leader? Joe said "Daryl, he says you are a lost warrior, and they are waiting for you."

I sat in silence. Joe was walking the room as he always did when he was confused or when he had something on his mind, and the Spanish gentleman had left the room. I just could not grasp what had taken place. This was what I had been told many years before, by another woman who read stones and my birth dates in Cairns. I'd been looking for answers, anywhere I could, for years.

I walked out of the room and Geno and Gary looked at me. "What?" is all I said and kept thinking it was some kind of set up or something. However, they told me they saw a light and next to me a big and mighty warrior was trying to hand me what seemed to be a wooden pole or some kind of stick.

I left and drove back to the gym, all the while thinking about what had happened and about all the readings over the past years. In truth it was all a bit much for me. I closed it off and never wanted to talk or think about it again. I just didn't need the distraction.

Life moved on for me and along with it many moments of sadness, disappointment, and years of frustration. I tried reaching out to people, here and there, to help me but they only let me down and took advantage of me or stabbed me in the back. It was tough enough, with the weight I carried, so I often stayed alone, protecting myself, until I met Janet and moved to Queensland with her.

Over the years we built a stable life and businesses. In 2005, after selling my health club on the Sunshine Coast in Queensland, I took up wellness support and therapy in the form of remedial massage treatments. I started by working part-time for a health and wellness facility in Fortitude Valley, Brisbane.

After a month or so, the owner asked if she could talk to me. My first thought was, "Oh no, my treatments for her clients are not needed anymore". But no, it wasn't that, she asked me if she could do my reading. She said she felt a heavy burden in me and wanted to help. I really didn't want to go down that track again, but being as she was boss, and I didn't want to decline and offend, I braced myself for it.

Surprisingly, her interpretations were different and were done in her therapy room which looked like a scene out of Chariots of Fire. The room's walls had wallpaper images that were straight out of a scene from the Roman days—strong and victorious gladiators. The room's lights were dimmed and she had an oversized table in the middle of the room that was constructed of marble. It had cut-out grooves around the side where she had placed candles that gave off a soft flickering glow. It was charming and deeply relaxing.

She asked me to lie down on her therapy table and she covered my eyes, as soft music began to play in the room. I had never heard music like it. It filled my mind as she placed her hands on my shoulders, then my waist, knees and feet followed by a gentle hand on my head. I felt at ease and balanced in a way I hadn't felt for a long time. This went on for over thirty minutes or even longer I guessed, and at times I heard her soft voice talking to someone in the background.

I figured another person had entered the room, but it didn't concern me because I was drifting in and out of awareness in a meditative kind of state I'd never felt before. Strange scenes and over-whelming feelings came to me, as I felt myself drift between an unknown place and the room, where I could still hear the soft background music playing.

Like all fantastic rest periods, the end came sooner than I wanted it to. Then she said she had something to share with me. The music softened, and the room's lights were brought up to an ambient level, as she took the cover off my eyes.

Looking at me, she asked "Daryl, why haven't you moved on and taken up the role for your people? They are waiting for you to lead them into life through the writings of words. Daryl, do you understand you are the chosen warrior of your people—the protector, and the only one who can give them peace?" I thought, are you kidding me, here we go again. I didn't know how to respond to this and thanked her for the therapy session she so generously given me.

It was another three years down the track, when I was handed some paperwork from my mother. She had been given some documents that I needed to process, so I made the trip to the Gold Coast to collect them. The paperwork was the living remains of my past family, the Tumori tribe in New Zealand, and the ownership of shares in a property which my great grandfather and his tribe owned and which had been handed down through generations.

I am not sure if this is what all the readings were about, but after many years of searching, requesting documents, and investigation, which started in 2008, I finally completed the necessary work to have the land title handed over to me. I made arrangements to travel to New Zealand in 2020, with my family, to complete the required paperwork and to sign it over into my name. Unfortunately, as I write this in the last couple of months of 2020, Covid-19 restrictions have prevented me from finalising that last step. I am hopeful, however, that all of the past revelations will finally lead me to complete what I feel they were directing me to do.

Only time will tell, but I am sure I am doing the right thing for them, my father, my grandfather and past generations of the Tumori tribe that I represent.

I believe the telling of my story, through this book, is the other part of my destiny that they may have been guiding me to complete. In undertaking this mammoth undertaking, I hope all the tortured, vilified souls of my orphan brothers can rest in peace, vindicated by the truth.

CHAPTER 68

My Angel

I can always remember daydreaming of having a mother. My vision was of someone who looked at me in a loving, kind way—who understood just what I needed, guided me, nurtured me, and who was my greatest cheerleader and my safest space to be. Someone who would never give up on me, and never let me down; protecting me like a lioness protects her cubs.

Over the years, in those times when I found myself scared, unsure and in a hole, I would feel the loss of not having the kind of mother that I dreamt of in my life. But, it was also in these moments I was truly grateful for having a sister like Teena Lynette Te'Nadii, who was like a mum in many ways and also my saviour; watching out for me.

Teena was born on the September 30th, 1955 the second child to my father and mother Wally & Mavis Te'Nadii. She was only four years old when our mother decided she couldn't be bothered to be a mother any longer and sent my older brother Brian to Hodderville Boys' Home, and Teena, Dale and myself to The Nest.

I felt incredibly lucky to have such a supportive and caring sister in my life. As I mentioned earlier in the book, the orphaned girls from the Grange, who had brothers at Hodderville Boys Home, would travel by bus to visit them once a year, and it was a truly special day. Teena would also bring all of the letters that she had written to us over many months. As I didn't have a skill for reading, the matron would take me aside at night and read the letters to me and I then I placed them in my treasure box, under my bed, so I could take them out when I needed a reminder that someone out there cared about me. Her letters where short, normally a page but, at times she would write a little more on a second page and draw a picture filled with trees, flowers and animals under a sunny sky.

I kept my life savings which were very small and everything that was important to me n that special box under my bed at the boys' home. I was so sad when I was not able to take them over to Australia with me. How I wish I had them now. But the memories and love will live on in my memory today, and forever.

Teena watched my back when I arrived in Australia, as Brian and Dale did. She had an incredible personality. It was as if she floated freely day by day; a hippie soul with a carefree nature that attracted many friendships along her life's path.

Her complexion was golden with a soft tan that all Polynesians were gifted with, and her hair was frizzy and she would always try to steam it straight. Finely built, she was very feminine and naturally beautiful not that she ever felt that way. She was also lucky that, out of all of the siblings, no medical issues were passed down through to her the generations.

Like me, Teena clashed with our mother which resulted in massive fights. This was the main reason she decided to move out of the house as soon as she could.

A talented girl she was blessed with a sweet voice, which she would share in the mornings singing or humming songs. She also had a special natural talent, which was her handwriting. Teena could write words down in such a way that they resembled the writing of the gods. Each word flowed into the next in fonts that were so creative and beautiful. Like all girls, she loved bright colours.

Because she had been put down by our mother on many occasions, Teena had also built a wall of self-protection around her. However I, and many others, saw the amazing person and the beauty of who she was every day. She was a special someone, my sister, and everyone who met her loved her within minutes. She was charismatic and drew people into her life with her vibrancy and zest for life.

I spent a brief time living with her and her husband, Neil, after when they moved to a small property in Lara, which is on the north side of Geelong in Victoria. We spent some amazing times together. It was awesome seeing her go about her day-to-day life as a mum to two beautiful nieces, whom I got the opportunity to get to know and grow close to.

As my brothers and I did, Teena battled her own demons, from a childhood spent in orphanages. In 1976, I found out that she too had been abused and tormented while at the Grange Orphanage for girls. She didn't tell me much, but shared little moments when we visited memory lane. During those times she would cry and feel lost. It hurt to know she had had to endure abuse as well.

She fell off the rails in life, here and there, as she struggled to overcome what abused children do in their adult lives. It always haunts you, no matter how hard you try to forget, ignore or not see or be reminded of it—it's always there and picks away at you like a woodpecker at a tree, opening the wound again and again.

We talked about things, not only while in New Zealand but also when we lived together in Geelong. I tried to get an insight into what had happened to her and what pain she still carried, but it was difficult. Teena preferred to shut it down after relaying some of her stories. I felt connected to her days and abuse in the orphanage though, and could easily read between the lines.

I also felt that there were more painful moments, when she surrendered to not knowing right from wrong and those were when we were under the same roof as our mother and Gerald. I did mention to her, once, how I felt about the way Gerald held her while dancing or how I would see him fondling her at times.

On the nights we talked, Teena drank, to numb her pain and she would end up in a drunken mess, her eyes glazed over; staring out at memories only she could see of the painful moments she never shared.

Then she would pick up the pieces and get back on the straight and narrow for a while before succumbing to her darkness over and over again. This went on until this and her alcohol-induced temper explosions eroded her marriage, one night.

The evening was supposed to be a night of celebration at her work Christmas party. Things got out of hand with a gate crasher and in the midst of things, Teena got punched. Tragically, the punch was from her husband who was trying to defend her, however in the state she was in and in the chaos of all that had occurred, she accused Neil of wife bashing.

I spoke to Neil and others, and tried to tell her it was a horrible but honest accident. Nothing I could say or do could change her mind though, and every time I tried to explain the events she would call me a liar and shout at me to stop trying to protect Neil. It was too much for Neil and was the end of what was once a beautiful marriage.

That night was her turning point in all of the worst ways and sent her on a path of terrible self-destruction. With nowhere to go, Teena bounced from one man to another, until she met and married another wonderful man, called Bob. They had two more children over the next four years. Between Teena and Bob (who also had a child from a previous relationship), their gorgeous family grew to three girls and two boys. Bob was an amazingly supportive man, however even he wasn't a match for her alcohol addiction, which eventually destroyed her marriage to him as well.

Teena moved to Queensland with her girls, and built a pretty turbulent lifestyle for herself and her kids. She just couldn't get into balance, fighting her demons, and was up and down like a yoyo, often seeking community support. The kids were still young so this disturbed me deeply. I visited as often as I could, to try to help her and the kids, but she pushed me out telling me to mind my own business. No matter what way I tried she could not see what she was doing. At some point she had re-connected with our mother which brought even more problems.

It wasn't too long before my big sister started having serious medical issues caused by her excessive drinking. Her liver ultimately gave out and a return to good health became impossible—the damage she had done was just too extensive to be repaired.

Even then, my mother continued to give Teena money for cigarettes and alcohol, enflaming the situation even more. It was so hard to watch such an amazing woman slowly dying in front of my eyes. I couldn't keep watching it happen and I couldn't keep supporting her when she spent all I gave her on her addictions. They were slowly killing my angel, whom I loved so much.

Over her last few years, when I visited, Teena was never home. Instead, I would track her down at the local RSL, wasting her pension. I could not find a way to get her out of the state she was in and knowing she was slowly dying made the efforts so much harder.

I wanted so much for her to see the damage and to live her years out under the love of her entire family, but it wasn't to be. On my last visit to her, in 2005, I desperately pleaded with her to stop, but her will to live had gone, and all I could see was death approaching fast. She told me to let her die in peace. Hearing it was hard, and walking out of her door for the last time was even harder still. I lost all hope just as she had done. Driving home from the Gold Coast to the Sunshine Coast was a journey from hell. Every minute on the road my mind drifted, remembering our days as children and teenagers and I began to grieve for my angel, who I knew wouldn't be here much longer.

I was at home with Janet on the day that I was told my beautiful sister had passed away from liver and kidney failure. It was Monday the 15th of May 2006. Even though I had already grieved her, I still felt crippled by the news I knew was coming. I sat in tears; so sad that she had gone. It was hard. I remember thinking I was the only one left—all of my brothers and sister had now passed. In some way, I felt guilty not doing more, but at the same time I knew I had done all I could to help her, in the fifteen years she tormented her already bruised soul.

The day of her funeral was devastating. Burying the last of my siblings felt like a knife was being plunged into my heart. Surely, I had been through enough? I asked life "Why was it so cruel it had to take the people I loved from me, too?" Standing there with her children, other family members, and friends I tried desperately to be strong, but I couldn't; it absolutely broke me down.

My mother was her typical self-centred self, judging and ridiculing everyone and making the day unbearable. I just couldn't cope with her doing that as well. I felt so helpless, as I had nothing left in me to shut her down, as I listened to her go on to others and complete strangers, about her losses over the many years.

As always, I felt she used the saddest of days to get sympathy, no matter the cost and insult to others. To see her sitting in the church, mourning my sister, who had lived the way she lived because of the abuse she had suffered at my mother's hands, was the epitome of disgraceful for me. Even outside, after the service, she raved on—it made me feel sick to my stomach.

My mother had spent some time with Teena in the last two years of her life and as she had provided her and the girls with support, she felt she was entitled and had the right to be control Teena's affairs and everyone and everything attached to her life. We knew that she only fed Teena's habits as a way of manipulating her and keeping her attached to her.

What hurt me even more was, while paying my respects to Teen's kids at the venue, I was approached by a gentleman who told me that my mother had arranged the wake, anticipating that the cost would be covered by Teena's boyfriend, only to find out he had no money to do so.

I spoke to the kids and discovered they were in no position to pay either. When I abruptly told my mother she had no right to arrange a gathering without asking them or advising them of costs, she just turned and said…"Don't you think I have done enough already?"

I was disgusted in her and angrily said "Yes, you have. You have done far too much!" The aftermath and pain in our lives was a direct result of her actions and I was not letting my sister pass over this way. I had my say and along with, Bob, her estranged husband, I paid the bill and said my goodbyes to my nephew and nieces, before leaving. I couldn't stay in the same place as my mother for a second longer.

Today, her girls live in Queensland and have children of their own. They have worked hard and even though I don't see them, I keep in contact with them from time to time and am very proud of them, as their mum—my beautiful sister—would be too.

Teena, what you mean to me is more than I can express. I had no sister when I was little, to call on when I needed help, and then you came into my life out of the blue with your smiles, hugs and love—all of which I'd never experienced before.

To share life with you I will never forget. I never could have imagined what a sister's love was, until I met you, and then I really found out that this love is a circle that cannot be broken.

A sister's love is unconditional; it's a love that has no end.

A sister's love wants the best for their brothers or sister, it's a love that will always defend, and you showed that to me.

Sometimes we got mad with each other, or began to fight over little things, but that's the fun part about having a sister. We both think we're always right! I'm so glad I had a sister like you.

Rest in peace big sister, Teena Lynette Te'Nadii, away from the pain - love always Daz.

Whakarongoa i te mamae o toku tuahine toku aroha ora i nga wa katoa Daz

Missed deeply by Heidi, Tammy, Tamika, Mathew, and Robbie

Kua ngaro a Heidi, Tammy, Tamika, Mathew, me Robbie

CHAPTER 69

Facing Facts

After the loss of Teena, and spending time with her children on the day of her funeral, I began reflecting on my life; our life. I found myself thinking more and more about the years we'd spent, and the way we had grown up—Teena at her orphanage, and me and my brothers at ours.

It seemed important to me that her life, my brothers' lives, and my life had some sense and some kind of justice. I had come to a point where my personal life was in a good place, but I still had a deep sense of unfinished business with my past that needed to be righted somehow.

I felt I was still here for a bloody good reason and maybe it was my purpose to bring to light the life we had been forced into and to expose the abuse many of us endured.

My brothers and sister had been wronged, I had been wronged. All the children that passed through those Salvation Army orphanage doors had been wronged. It was time their voices were heard, and justice was done.

I'd spent years trying to forget, in a bid to heal, but I realised I didn't need to forget, I needed to remember and to look back on what I had done over the years. I needed to document them, to process it not suppress it, to bring the abuse and stories from the dark to the light to be heard, and to begin to move forward myself.

I had written down some thoughts here and there over the years at trying times, mostly just to document them and to reflect on, in other challenging times, about how I dug myself out of them. Every time I read through them, I found it helpful in some way to read over my notes and claw my way out of the hole.

I also attempted to find some meaning and a way to accept what had been my life. Through returning to where it had all begun, and unpacking my hundreds of memory boxes, I hoped to discover the meaning of my life and to vindicate those no longer here. I hoped it would work, because— to date—I felt as if I had failed at trying to forget it all.

I decided to return to the place it all started; to seek answers, to visit the past and to take steps to bring those who were responsible to account. There was no time left in my life for settling for what had occurred. I wanted answers—the truth—and those in my life, who could not seek them or speak out and be heard, deserved those rights as well.

I realised that it might take years, but knowing what I needed to do I became determined and fully focused on seeing it through to the end. For far too long I hadn't done anything about it—I had been paralysed and crippled by the pain of the past, I guess, but not anymore. That was over, and I was ready. My time was now and my time was going to remain until it was done, whatever it took and however long it took.

CHAPTER 70

Baila Rae

Fifty years

My writing took a backseat for a number of years as I poured myself into my marriage. Janet and I worked hard and were rewarded with friends, many overseas holidays; and toys, such as motorcycles, and boats. We built our dream home close to the ocean and had a flourishing hairdressing salon that Janet ran, while I took on a position working out in the mines. This meant we were separated for weeks at a time, which we found hard after having so much time together, but we saw it as our way of getting ahead, establishing ourselves, and achieving our dreams.

I had more than I could have asked for; a stunning wife and two beautiful children. Together we had built many happy memories, but I felt empty, unsettled, and incomplete in some way. I tried to find an answer to it, but it eluded me. I would sit back in my crib, while away at the mines, looking for that lost piece in my life but could not find it.

Home on a seven-day break from the mines, I did what I had done many times; woke up and cooked breakfast for Janet and me, cleaned the house after seeing Janet off to work and followed it up by a great ride on my Harley. I returned home after a few hours, washed the bike, had a swim and a scotch and then waited for my bride to come home. For some reason, on this day, while I waited, I sat and reflected not on the day but the past, my life as it was, and on my future.

What came with this reflection was the dull ache of loneliness, which I'd felt a million time, but on this day, finally—I realised why. It had always been there right in front of me, but I had never seen it. I had a beautiful wife, a lovely home, a great job and the material things to keep my mind occupied, but I didn't have my son Damien and my daughter Casie J, who had grown up and had her own life, to share these times with. I realised I felt grief; for not having them around, and for not seeing them each day—it left a hole in my heart.

With time on my side and a few scotches for support, I waited until Janet got home from work and after talking about the day, I told her of my revelation and of what I really wanted to fill it. A long silence followed as Janet contemplated what I had told her… I wanted us to have a baby.

I think the air could have been parted just like Moses parted the sea. Her look of shock was followed by words that brought me down to earth. Janet looked at me and said, "Have you given this a lot of thought?" She raised some valid points, which brought me crashing back from the lofty heights of daydreaming to reality. She said…

- We have just started out

- We are trying to build a future

- Think of the cost of raising a child

- She would have to give up work

- She would have to sell the business

- What about our freedom?

So many points with good reasons, but I couldn't deny how I felt. She enjoyed our freedom and having a child was the last thing on her mind. I loved her deeply and understood her thoughts on it. Disappointed, I got it and had to move on. It wasn't to be.

I returned to the mines to complete a further six weeks FIFO (fly-in/fly-out) stint. As often happens in the mines, there are always one or two workers who can't return to camp for some reason, and I was asked to stay back for another two weeks to cover one of them. I called Janet to let her know I would be staying on at the mines a further two weeks and, as always, she understood that work and a job was important.

After seven weeks, she called me at the same time we normally called each other and stunned the hell out of me by announcing she was pregnant! I was so shocked and overjoyed. I asked her how she felt, given that she had said on my last visit home that she wasn't ready to have a baby.

Janet said that after our talk, she thought well she'd try, and if she fell pregnant it was meant to be. I was going to be a fifty-year-old dad! Janet was eleven years my junior and at thirty-nine, she was fit, healthy and happy about becoming a mum for the first time. We went over the points she had raised previously and worked everything out. We had a plan and we looked forward to a different adventure together—parenthood.

I made a promise that I would not get too excited or begin celebrating until after the twelve-week mark, but all I wanted to do was get home, hold Janet and say thank you! In the nine months of pregnancy, we put our plan into place together, selling our business, and building a home on a block of land we had earlier purchased in Bonnells Bay in NSW, to be closer to Janet's mum who had been diagnosed with cancer. I resigned from the mines.

The months played out like any pregnancy and soon reality set in as we found ourselves heading to hospital in readiness for the birth. The hospital was new and had only opened that day, so our child would be the first baby born there and Janet the first patient.

Our child—a gorgeous girl—was born on October 17th 2008, with the incredible support of the hospital staff. She was the mirror image of her beautiful mum, Janet, with some of my genes, such as her chin, ears, jawline and eyes.

When I picked her up I was in awe just like the times Damien and Casie J were born. I just had to hold her, as I looked down at Janet with the biggest smile. Nothing could be more perfect than that moment, as I gazed into the face of my newborn daughter.

We named her, Baila Rae ... meaning,
Baila after a Spanish dancer, and
Rea after the light of life.

I was so proud of Janet and thankful for the most beautiful gift any woman or wife could give to their husband. As the days passed, we settled in and were excited to get home to our new house and to begin life together as a family with all of the wonderful things to come.

Janet's mum and dad were so supportive, and just adored their newborn grandie. Living only 700 meters from their front door meant they could visit any time and Austin, Baila Rae's grandie, would walk down daily just to see her and to read her a book, even though she was only days old. He believed every child should have had 5000 books read to them by the age of five, and he read at least that number before, sadly, he passed away from cancer just before Baila Rae turned three. Janet's mum, Hazel, had a heart of gold and was amazing looking after her daughter and grand-daughter and became a much-appreciated part of our life.

I just could not get enough time with her during the day, walks, runs, cuddling, playing, rolling around and wrestling, it never seemed enough. I would lie next to her bed at night until she fell asleep, with her holding my pointer finger just to get more moments with her.

Baila Rae grew faster than we expected over the first two years, which lead us to have her medical profile assessed. It was brought to our attention that she could grow to a height of around 5'10 to 5'11 which would be much taller than her mother and me. She must have got her height from my father who was over six-foot tall!

As Baila grew older, we contemplated her future. Bonnells Bay had a population of around 6000, of which 60% were over the age of sixty years, so we decided to pack up and move back to the Sunshine Coast so she could do her schooling there. It was sad leaving Bonnells Bay, after being so close to Hazel, but we felt Baila would have greater opportunities back in Queensland.

Baila Rae's twelve now and has fantastic friends, and is going amazingly well in school. She is savvy beyond her years. She has been blessed with a mix of her mother's beauty and smarts along with my strengths and personality. As we were both sporty, we thought she would naturally be drawn in that direction too, but she's taken after Casie J, with a passion for art and creativity; for now—who knows what will attract her in the years to come.

Janet, me and Baila Rae.

Like me, she is fussy about things and one in particular is food. As a baby and infant she loved every part of eating and vegetables, but as the years have passed her tastes have changed. I am sure that, like her sister, it is only going to be short-lived, given her upbringing.

Janet is an incredible mother, and dotes on her as I so; bathing, cooking, and cleaning up after her and playing crazy girl games that have brought many smiles over the years and that I will always remember. I adore the bond they have which only gets stronger as Baila grows.

How things change in a man's life, when there are so many special events. I experienced those times with Damien, my firstborn, when he was a child and in his teenage years I experienced them again with my oldest daughter Casie J, my oldest princess, and now I had Baila Rae.

I worried from time to time, thinking I could be an embarrassment for Baila Rae as she grows up. After all, … OMG when she is sixteen, I will be sixty-six years of age! What will her friends say? "Why is your Dad so old?" I can only hope that, when she hits her teenage years, she remembers the immense love I have for her and it's a positive rather than a negative.

Today we still live on the Sunshine Coast, and are soon to move into yet another new home that we're in the midst of building which is closer to the beach. We share a blessed life and an abundance of adventures.

Having Baila Rae filled the hole in my life—I love this girl with more than words. I have been blessed to have her in my life, and I never take that for granted. I will protect her to my last breath, and support her and guide her. Above all, I will love her. She is my world, along with my son, Damien, and daughter, Casie J.

CHAPTER 71

Damien Travis Te'Nadii

May 1st, 1980—5th Nov 2010
Fifty-one years

Having to sit and write the story of my son, Damien, and his life is the hardest of all the things I have penned to date in this autobiography. Even at sixty-two years of age, the pain and hurt of his passing is still so excruciating, even though I write this eleven years down the track.

In many ways, I could sit and write thousands and thousands of words and hundreds of pages on this beautiful boy—my sweet son, whom I watched from a busy, happy toddler, to a teen and finally to the young man and adult that he became.

I was…. AM so proud of him.

This is hard, only a few lines into writing this chapter and I have to tell you I am struggling. I have already had to stop countless times as the loss of him cripples me with each word and thought—it's so hard to go on, but I will for him. I owe it to him even if it takes me a year to write it, I will.

I have dreaded the writing I am about to undertake for so long, knowing its contents, and the feelings that I have, will break me apart with each word typed. Many memories are still so raw that I have to work hard to suppress them, so they don't take my last breath.

I guess only a parent who has lost a child knows that, regardless of the time passed, the pain is still so intense the memory catches in your gut,

Damien.

in your heart, and your mind. Your body braces for the impact of it as it hits you, often unexpectedly. That I know it's coming is even worse in some ways.

'Dams' as he was known was born Thursday the 1st day of May 1980, my firstborn, and the first to call me Dad. Damien was more than I could have imagined, with his olive skin the same as mine, and his long black hair, handed down through the generations of Te'Nadii past. He had the biggest eyes, which filled the room—his eyes were the first thing I saw and—to this day—I remember them as if I had only seen them just minutes ago.

I scooped him up to hold him and bent my head to kiss and draw in his beautiful baby smell. His first three days were spent in the Women's Hospital in Brisbane. Like all babies, Damien slept a lot. In fact, far more than the other newborns in his nursery, which the nurses were happy about. He seemed to have an incredible appetite from the day he was born and which would endure throughout his years.

The day came to bring him home, and I felt excited but also an immense responsibility that I now had to protect him and keep him safe. We were not allowed to carry Damien out of the hospital on our own, in fact, the nurses back then carried your child to the car and ensured they had been strapped in safely. I think those days are long gone, but it was nice to know the care provided went that far.

Even driving home, I felt nervous and worried; not about my driving, but about everyone else on the road. I hoped they would all drive safely, so I could get my son home safely too. It's a feeling I know most new parents have experienced. My eyes swung left and right, back and front looking here and looking there, slowing down and changing lanes with great care.

His arrival home was a special day knowing we finally had him in our care and under our own roof, which made me feel a lot more at ease because I could keep him safe with us.

As with many kids, born into a service family, Damien got used to the many moves we had over the years to follow. After just two years of living in Queensland, we were soon making our first move to take up a role I had at the Command and Staff College, which was followed by a promotional posting to Puckapunyal in Victoria.

He happily lived his infant years in a provided service home in the town of Seymour, until another posting took us to the army apprentice school located in Bonegilla, Victoria, where I did another two years as an instructor in my field before we headed to Townsville in Queensland, where I received a promotion to sergeant.

During my posting to Townsville, Damien made many friends both at school and in his sports club, but he could be a loner at times, and was happy staying at home, hanging out with his little sister, and playing. He lived for the time I came home, so he could go outside with me and kick a ball, play on the swings or just help me out in the yard.

Occasionally he was disruptive at school and I'd have to go down and pull him into line. Mostly, however, it was him reacting to being teased for having dark skin. Other children would hit him and he would strike back with no mercy, which in most cases left the other child crying. I had to take the blame for this in many ways, since I had taught him to defend himself early on, showing him how to throw a left-right – left jab followed by a powerful uppercut combination. It works every time you know, but when I found out he was using it at school more often than I was aware, I realised I needed to sit down and explain to him that there was a time and a place. Like all kids, he had bikes, skateboards and balls, which took up a lot of his time after school and on weekends and he'd spend hours playing with them.

What surprised me was that Damien was never a kid for collecting many toys—he had his favourite one, but that was it. He was just a happy, well-adjusted, and well-mannered child. After the split from my first wife, I remember holding him one last time in my arms, at the airport, before he and Casie J flew out to Victoria with my ex-wife and to begin a new life without me. God, that day, reflecting and remembering it still cuts me to the core. Saying goodbye to him and Casie J and telling them I would see them soon was so hard.

At that time, I thought that day was the hardest of my days, how wrong I was.

Damien spent the next twenty-two years living in Victoria, under a shared custody agreement. Like most kids, he grew up having fun, playing sports, and hanging out with his friends, until he journeyed into the grey places, as I called them, in his later years. He began hanging out with an unsavoury group of people who did nothing but party, take drugs, get into mischief and commit minor street misdemeanours. I felt they were distracting him from his true path.

I'm not going to lie or brush over it. It's bloody hard to come to terms with the truth about a person you love with everything you have, who is blood, and who is your son, let alone write about it. Especially if it's not positive.

My son was so lucky in many ways. He grew up privileged with many natural talents and skills which he inherited from his forefathers. He was an incredibly talented and passionate rugby player, which kept him busy for most of the season and prevented him from straying into the grey places and towards the people who tried to coax and draw him further into that world.

Like all teenagers, he went through a period where his attitude stunk. He said and did some hurtful things, and went around convinced he was right and entitled to do what he wanted. I fully understood it, as most parents do, but I definitely didn't like it. Being estranged made it hard for me to keep him focused and on the straight and narrow. I tried to keep him busy in sports or fitness, so he didn't have time for all that other stuff. But regardless of my efforts, Damien gravitated toward the distractors; dabbling in recreational drugs, enjoying a few too many drinks, and he had a string of girlfriends as well. In amongst all of that, he didn't lose the value of respect—respect for his parents, family, and friends. This is something he maintained throughout his years with us and the love he showed us was undeniably incredible.

Generous, he was quick to share what he had, and trusted others without question. His caring nature and lover-of-life attitude made him popular among everyone who knew him, including me. His mother who would do anything for him and his little sister looked up to him and absolutely adored him. Damien and Casie J's relationship was tight. Not having a father at home full-time, she looked to him for male guidance and support throughout her teens and Damien stood up to the plate and became her go-to father figure whenever she needed him. He loved and protected her, and would do whatever it took to see her safe and happy.

Sadly, and it pains me to say it, he didn't have that same go-to person for himself. The stress of life, his responsibilities at such a young age and his not having me living in the vicinity to call upon every day, took its toll on him. He looked to medication to numb the pressure and to give him the freedom and release he sought, which started what was to become his ultimate downfall.

All that I had struggled with, through my younger years, and said no to, Damien succumbed to and said yes to—and it cost him his life.

I will never forget the week prior to that heartbreaking day—the one that would be forever scorched into my memory and which would continue to burn deeper into my soul as each day passed. I had been down to visit Damien and Casie J and spent time with him, delighting in seeing him with his own child.

Some months earlier, Damien and his partner (Amanda) had a gorgeous baby girl. I had gone down for the first time to meet his daughter and see my beautiful son as a dad. Damien held his little girl in the same way I had held him at birth. It was bliss watching him do that—euphoric. He fell in love and became a father that day, and his mum, Casie J, and I were overjoyed to be a part of his happiness. We were even more elated to see him morph into the amazing father he was.

I was aware of the issues Damien had faced over the years. He had battled with his emotions, relying on antidepressants which presented their own set of problems and issues as well as the judgement that comes with it. The one thing I learnt, growing up, was that there are many ignorant people in the world who will try to hurt you with nasty words, insults, or abuse, because of their own lack of education or understanding. This was something that I didn't put up with, after being kicked out from Gerald's after my mother left, and I had told Damien not to tolerate it either.

This advice got Damien into a lot of trouble. I know that in many ways I am responsible for the anger Damien had inside of him, and I fully accept the responsibility of my advice putting a target on his back. There are many things I would counsel him differently about now, after receiving the gifts of hindsight, maturity, education, wisdom, and healing.

I had some issues with Damien's partner—I felt that she was a gold digger who purposely fell pregnant to prevent him from leaving her and to force him into caring for her and another child she had from another man. I knew that over the year leading up to his death he had spent thousands of dollars of his hard-earned money on buying her a car because she could not afford one. He paid all of the rent and expenses because she was always broke, and helped her out every week, so that she didn't go without—all the time working away in the mines to support and help her to the best of his ability.

I took Damien aside and talked to him about it after I found out that she had had an affair while he was working away. On the last day of our visit and before heading back to Queensland, I told him—do not trust her! His good, caring heart wouldn't hear about it, and he told me I was wrong.

Sadly, I was right, and one day not long afterwards, Damien came home from work to find the house he shared with her was empty, most of his personal belongings were gone, and his daughter and partner were missing.

It totally destroyed my son, who was already under immense pressure and weighed down with his own personal battles. The following months—spent fighting the system to find and gain access to his daughter—proved too much.

I was sitting in the lounge with Janet, watching TV, when my mobile rang and I heard my daughter ripping apart with pain as she told me my son had passed away.

It is still too hard and painful to remember, let alone write about. I spent the next minutes, hours, days and weeks in a terrible nightmare, the kind where you wish like hell you could wake up, as you slip in and out of a painful blur. The hurt was so great it permanently scarred me for life.

Being told my son had passed and that I would never see, speak to, or hug him again was too much. Having to make arrangements to fly down was even harder, knowing the journey I was about to undertake would be to say goodbye to my only son.

It was excruciating to have to view my child in a church, as he lay silent and lonely and it took all of my strength. Rage seeped in and hate I had been able to hide from after the many years of abuse in the orphanage all came back to me and swelled to a frightening size. I was angry that had I accepted that he was OK and 'big enough to look after himself, as he had told me. In hindsight, I shouldn't have. I was angry about knowing I was with him, and yet I didn't see the real signs of his struggles. I was angry about learning—from a private journal—that he blamed the very person for his demise whom he trusted and the same woman I had warned him about. I should have been more firm about her with him.

After we arrived in Geelong, I dropped Janet and Baila Rae off with friends, so that I could be alone with my older daughter, Casie J. There was a lot I needed to know about the events leading up to Damien's death. As we sat talking, I had to stop many times to comfort Casie J. The ordeal had stabbed her in the heart and she was struggling to communicate.

I felt so deeply sorry for her. The connection she had with Damien was like mine with Dale—they were soul mates and shared a bond that couldn't be broken by anything, other than death. As strong as she was, it was tough for her, with three small children and a husband to look after, while she sat with me, making arrangements for my son, her brother's funeral— a moment I will never forget.

Damien's mother was at her wits ends about what had happened and having to watch her go through this hurt me also. No matter our past or present relationship, we both still supported our children and loved them equally.

Janet and Baila Rae was a tower of strength for me as I sat for days writing the eulogy. Some days I sat in silence at night writing line by line between the thousand tears that came; sometimes I couldn't write a word. How do you write about your son in a way that covers every day of his life? How could I express my grief in words, knowing the pain he would have been feeling at the time of his passing, after losing his loved ones?

Hour upon hour and day after day I struggled knowing that we, the family, had to return to his home to pack up his belongings and store them. When I walked into his home and saw his many personal things, I was truly reminded of his life. His motorbike was sitting in the garage, and his car was in the drive, along with his clothing and personal items. It tore me apart. I had to face the moment when I stood in the spot he was found asleep. It was made even harder thinking that the cruel woman, who pretended to love him, and who had given birth to his only child, had done this to him. Rage welled up inside of me.

The funeral day arrived as we where comfited by other family members and friends waiting for us. As we walked in to view his open coffin, pride welled up inside of me to see those who had become a big part of his life, paying their respects. After entering the viewing room, I gave his mother time to say goodbye. I shared a moment with Casie J, as Debbie said goodbye. This was her time and I gave her the time she needed. Accepting that they would never stand together; sit and share stories; hug, play, and share each other's life journeys together, ever again, was so beyond hard. My heart and soul wept.

I held his hand, as I stood alone. At that moment I wanted to hold him close to my body. I wanted to feel and smell his very existence, as I had when he was a baby, and the tears overcame me. My son felt so cold and alone—and there was nothing I could do for him, to keep him warm and tell him he was wanted.

Looking down I smiled through my soaked eyes, thinking about our incredible times and the times we will always have and I told him to remember my words!

Ko koe taku tama a Damien Travis Te'Nadii
Ka rite ki te taangata e tu ana au ki konei ko te wahi e noho ai
taku tama tama.
Ko te titiro ki raro inaianei kua pakeke ia.
Kua kite ahau ia koe he tangata nui ake, he tangata kaha hoki
Engari i moemoea ahau ka taea e koe.
Kei te mohio ahau ma te titiro ki a koe i tenei ra, kua
manaakitia ahau e te Atua
Ko nga huarahi i tera tau kaore au e whakapono.
He pakeke koe inaianei, ko tenei ka mahara tonu ahau ki a koe,
engari kei roto i toku ngakau me toku wairua i nga wa katoa
E taku tama iti.
Kei te aroha ahau ki a koe, ka pai hoki taku tama

In English my words mean

You are my son Damien Travis Te'Nadii
As a man I stand here now where my baby boy used to be,
Looking down now he is all grown up.
I have watched you become a wiser and stronger man
than I ever dreamed you could be.
I know by looking at you today, God has blessed me in
ways that years ago I never would have believed.
You are now an adult in this would and that is how I will
always remember you,
but in my heart and soul you will always be
My little boy.
I love you and will for always my son.

It tore me apart watching Casie J say goodbye to her everything in life, as we laid Damien to rest that day. I couldn't even start to imagine the hurt she was feeling as she tried to stay balanced. I knew how I was feeling and the pain ripped and etched itself into my heart, with each memory and mention of him. Casie J had to grieve and cope with losing her best mate, while being there and supporting her three children through the loss of their amazing uncle, and she had to be strong for her mother.

As you will know yourself, the loss of anyone is unbearable, and losing so many of my loved ones, in such short spaces of time, was something I found difficult to express. Words just seemed empty for the feeling I carried.

I had written and read my eulogy for my son, over and over, so I was sure it evidenced the man he truly was; the son his mum and I were so proud of, and the brother his sisters loved. However, I froze, reading it on the day—not because I could not read it, but because these words would be the last to go with him; the last I would say to him before he would be cremated.

As my son lay amongst family and friends, I held his hand and said my final words to him with wounded tears. I kissed him for the last time with a longing love.

Damien Travis Te'Nadii

I never thought the day would come, a day when I would cry, cry in a way
I never knew possible. But losing so much, and feeling such hurt, those
thoughts still live and follow me through every day.

Broken down and left to see that moment in every way. The day had come,
my thoughts were deep. A painful moment, I wish would sleep.

I enter a room, with heads held low, and see loss in every tear. I have to say
goodbye, but I don't know how. You lay there quiet, no words—no sound.
Just an open box, of a man who makes me proud.

If I could share just one more moment, it would be with you my son, don't
fear, I would say and hold your hand and make it clear your world—your
life, I will take care. We will live a life, others will never share, I'll hold on
tight and take good care.

You are my son, my pain is deep, my loss for you, I hold you so dear.
My love and more will bond us tight, I will never let you slip away. Know
that the days will never pass, as I stand in thought and wonder why.

Why is this world so cruel in ways? I miss you son in many ways. Son as you
sleep, await my time—the day will come, once more your life will shine in
mine.

I love you Damien

I still find it hard on days to realise you are resting.

You had so much to live for, and even more to give, and that's what makes
your loss so hard.

There was so much more I wanted to experience with you Damien. I will
never let go, you are my son and part of my life forever.

I WILL PROTECT YOU FROM ANY FUTHER HARM MY SON
SLEEP UNTIL WE ARE TOGETHER ONCE MORE.

Ka arai ahau ia koe mai i tetahi whanau matua i taku tamaiti
KAUPAPA KI TE WHAKANGA ANAKE

My love for you was not about how many days, months or years we lived
together

It will always be how much love I have for you EVERY DAY

E pouri ana taku tamaiti - Aroha tonu a Papa

469

Father and son. Our last photo together.

I said it might take a year to write this one chapter; I was wrong; it took two years. Having to face so much—so many memories and so much loss—seemed to make what I wanted to say impossible. Every time I was blinded by tears which blurred my words, but never my love.

PART 5

In Search of the Truth

CHAPTER 72

Back to Hell

Fifty-one years (2010)

Back in 2008, I decided to put all work on my book aside to spend a couple of years with my daughter Baila Rae. I enjoyed sharing the home duties with Janet and being more involved in raising Baila Rae. It was a positive experience for me and for my marriage.

It wasn't until Baila Rea was about two years old that I began to feel the urge to continue with my book. I had spent many hours thinking about it over the years and knew it was time to sink myself into it again, but it was tough. There were many gaps and I needed to find answers, to complete my book. I spoke to my wife about the frustration of not having the answers I needed on hand, and decided the best thing I could do was to return to the place it had all started. I was anxious about what I would find, and scared to face the demons of my past, but I knew I had to do it.

I was removed from my homeland of New Zealand without a choice, but, as an adult, I now had a choice, but it wasn't an easy one. I had fought hard to become the man I wanted to be, for many years. Revisiting the past and the person I was—such a disadvantaged, abused, scared, and lonely little boy—made me feel sick to my stomach, but after 51 years I knew this was my time.

Maybe I would find some kind of peace with the truth? Once I had booked the tickets for myself, Janet and Baila Rae, I meticulously planned each day we would have away so I could leave NZ's shores with as many questions answered as possible. It also helped me get over the anxiousness of having to return.

The date of our departure for NZ arrived all too quickly. Our bags were packed and we left for the airport with a mix of excitement and nervousness. It was surreal in a way, sitting on the plane with my family, flying from Brisbane to Auckland. The unfolding of the years in between flying out and flying back seemed to condense as I thought about my journey to retrace my footsteps of the past.

Like all airports around the world, New Zealand's international terminal has undergone a major facelift from when I last saw it. It was cold on arrival, as winter had set in earlier than it had in Australia, and the Kiwi air hit my face with a cool breeze.

After we collected our bags and cleared customs, we picked up a rental car at the airport office and headed off to our first overnight stay—a little hotel south of the airport. I had made sure it had a hot tub—an essential luxury in NZ!

These tubs weren't like the ones you find in Australia, they had a distinct smell of the under-ground thermal energy that was abundant in New Zealand. As I filled it, the smell took me back to my childhood in seconds. After a soak and a delicious warm meal, it was time for a good night's sleep in preparation for a big day the next day.

In the morning, after getting our bearings, we headed towards Putaruru. The two-and-a-half-hour trip would take us five days, with leisurely stops for sightseeing along the way. Our travel itinerary had us visiting Hamilton, Rotorua and Lake Taupo. We immersed ourselves in the lovely, typical Kiwi lifestyle, pausing here and there to collect information or to watch the odd Rugby match.

I specifically made sure we were in NZ when the 2010 International Rugby Tournament was on. I was keen to go to as many matches as possible and to watch NZ play against the many deserving countries that would attend the prestigious international event.

We travelled in the North Island and the Bay of Islands and surrounding towns so I could show Janet and Baila Rae the many cultures passed on by the European settlers that were woven into New Zealand life. As she was a toddler, Baila Rae was a little too young to understand it, but like Janet and me, she was still excited to enjoy the adventures we went on, the different food, THE cultural events, and moments together.

I was thrilled for the opportunity to introduce my wife to my culture, as I had known and remembered it. Eating traditional Maori food, participating in Maori dancing, along with greetings and communication in the Maori tongue were a fabulous experience.

I was talked into doing the 'haka' by Janet. I found I was a little rusty—it had been more than TEN years since I last performed it. I stuffed up here and there to the delight of the crowd, who smiled and laughed at my errors, while my mind drifted back to being a young child performing it at school fetes and on the sideline at rugby with my mates.

We arrived in Rotorua where I was able to replace my Maori Tiki greenstone necklace, and my matau with a koru (fishhook) necklace—both of which I had left in New Zealand in 1969 when I was whizzed off to Australia. I wanted to continue my tradition with Baila Rae, so I purchased her a beautiful New Zealand greenstone Manaia Tiki necklace that she could keep and wear too.

With seven days of touring, the day arrived that I had set aside for our visit to Hodderville Boy's Home—my home from hell, all seven years of it. In many ways, I had been looking forward to this moment my whole life, and even more so, for the past twelve months. Now the time was here, the moment filled me with emotion and fear.

I was scared of not knowing what I would see, of what I would find out, and what would come back to me. Waves of panic ran through me. However, the many thoughts I had before our arrival seemed to fade away as the moment came closer, with every km we drove towards the orphanage.

As we traversed the winding roads, I talked to Janet about my days as a child driving these exact roads, speed talking in a bid to settle my nerves and to build the confidence I needed to face what was coming.

We arrived at the old entrance to the boy's home and I took a deep breath to steady myself. There was no turning back, now. What was once a grand driveway to the main administration building had long been closed. I remembered explaining how I felt upon my arrival to Janet and seeing the grand entrance to this building as a five-year-old. I felt those same emotions grip and grab hold of me, as I looked up the drive and saw it through my adult eyes.

Hodderville Boy's Home.

Rounding the bend in the road it was apparent that the second entrance, which originally led up to the rear of the main building of the home, had been moved further around. The original entrance was always a concern, being on the apex of the bend. I guess the change was to allow vehicles to pull up before turning into the drive. Originally, if any vehicle stopped to turn into the driveway leading up to the boy's home, any cars behind them would have to stop completely or drive onto the stony edge of the road which could be very dangerous. There had been a number of accidents during my time living there.

Getting to the top of the drive brought back so many memories. It was frustrating, looking from side to side and trying to take it all in. So much of the grand property had been destroyed by looters, and the tall pinecone trees that once ran all the way up the drive from the road had been removed.

As I pulled up, taking time to draw in every aspect of the remaining building that I could, I imagined the tiny boy I had been and ghosts of the past playing on many of the areas we made use of as children. Alongside the main building were the old laundry, woodshed, carpenters workshop, boiler room, and drying room.

Directly in front of us, where we parked, was the great hall that had provided us with many nights and days of entertainment, such as Easter and Christmas celebrations. As funny as it may sound, it felt as if I could smell the aroma of those occasions in the air, particularly the pinecones we collected and used for decorations.

Halfway up, the new driveway merged into the old drive and we pulled up at the main house, which once housed the brigadier and his family of the orphanage. On our arrival, we were greeted by a gentleman, who introduced himself as the caretaker of the property. After a short talk and our request for entry, we were on our way.

Through talking with the caretaker, I learned that we were lucky to have come when we did as the building was soon to be renovated, with much of the main building to be removed to make way for future developments. He said the boy's home had been sold to a group of investors who intended to use the property as a conference facility.

As we walked to the main building I explained the different areas and what we did there to Janet. I walked through the kitchen into the service area and then into the dining room before heading up to the Loft. Crossing the floor I pointed out my sleeping areas over the first two years, and the famous fire escape which held so many frozen memories.

We then continued through the remaining building and the rooms, which like the outside area, had been destroyed. It was a sad sight for me in many ways. Even though I once wanted to see the entire building burned to the ground, in amongst the worst memories there were so many great ones that came back to me as I stood and shivered, remembering what my life was like here and the hell that we endured behind its closed doors.

I felt as if my soul fractured, as I stood paralysed and haunted by a life gone by. I wondered and wished a friend would manifest from the past and come around the corner from the room next door to greet me.

Janet began noticing the little gulps in my sentences as they got shorter and I struggled to keep it together and she took our daughter back to the car, so I could continue to do what I needed to do. As I battled to get myself together, the tears I had been desperately fighting broke their banks and flowed down my face pooling around my feet on the old floor I had known every inch of as a young lad. Painful memories raced through my mind and I dropped my head and let the grief consume me.

Steadying myself, I sucked in some deep breaths and pressed on, walking into the area we called the room of pain. It didn't last more than a few seconds before I had to walk out. Bile rose in my throat and even now I am at a loss to explain how I felt looking into those rooms. Pictures of little boys being beaten, raped and shamed bruised my mental sanity. Some of them had been buried so deep down in my vault that it shocked and repulsed me as they were summoned forward.

I had come looking for answers and all I got were reminders of the atrocities I had once lived with, here. In a way, I had to accept this and embrace the moment so that I could return with some more clarity and information for my writing. It felt as of my brain was one big sponge, absorbing all I possibly could at the moment, to digest and process it later.

My walk through the ice block was as it was some fifty plus years ago; cold, lonely and draining. The shame I felt here was as brutal as the cold winds that swept through it. Disturbing memories engulfed me and I stood looking and thinking about the many nights they hurt us without any valid reason. If I felt as much pain, at any time in my life, as I did when I was a child at the orphanage, it was right then. Even though I had grown up to be strong in life, my promises not to weaken no matter what as I walked the building went straight out the door, as if flowing away in the breeze, never to return.

It broke me. I could not face the reality and furthermore, I felt I had failed myself and y vow to fight and never to let this place hurt me again. My fists clenched, my teeth clamped together and the blood pumping through my body left my ears ringing as I succumbed and cried. It was too much for me, as it had been many years before that day, and it chipped away at my soul.

I felt a shadow of children circling me, calling out to me to help them. I felt I needed to reach out and pull them away from the hell they were trapped in. How was it still possible to see pictures and images of my friends' suffering after all those years? I had no answers and no way to help them. I kept saying "sorry my friends, I am so sorry" over and over again.

I walked outside to a green paddock, where once I played ghost rugby, a place I would spend time with the other boys and, when needed, hide from those officers so that I wouldn't be the next victim. The pride of that field had been left to nature, but the overgrowth couldn't hide the memories or my tears from falling. Tears of pain turned to tears of happiness and I was grateful the other boys and I no longer lived here or endured its torment.

It had become very clear to me that my return to this place, which was once my life, was important. My memories of the many moments I had spent here and where I hadn't visited since then were the elements I needed to complete my writing. This day opened my eyes for the first time and I saw things as they were. I had needed to feel that pain and hurt once more, and now I knew it was the only way I could truly write my story and express the rawness of the bitter truth.

I stood at the top of the driveway and looked back at the place that I had once called home, knowing that my legacy of all those times would end here. I felt an urge to turn back the clock, so that I could start that journey again, but this time I would fight for what was right. The feeling was only lessened by remembering why I came here and what I needed to do now, and going forward.

I got back to the car and my family after settling myself and drying my tears. As I took one last look at the boy's home I realised it would be my last visit to the Palace of Pain as it was—I had escaped it physically, now I had set my sights on escaping it mentally and emotionally.

Driving the winding roads of NZ from Hodderville to Putaruru, the small town just fifteen minutes away from where my old school was, I did not speak much. Rather I tried to reflect more, so that I could soak up all I had learned. Seeing my old school Oraka Heights was like being in a time warp—it was still the same as the day I left it, except for a few more trees, plants, and a refurbishment to areas that must have perished over the years.

We parked and I readied myself to obtain as much information as possible from my time as a pupil here. If at all possible, I was hoping to collect some of the sporting memorabilia I had won in years gone by.

I had decided to do this leg alone and not to drag Janet and Baila Rae around with me. I ventured toward the sports field at my own pace, walking down memory lane. I went by the back gate, just to look across at the house Rebeca once lived in, and then I entered the main administration building, which had been relocated to the opposite end of the building.

Inside I spoke to the staff and told them I was a past student and asked if by chance any of the old class photos and documents had been kept.

I learned that the school was now a Maori cultural training school and that a new school had been built to accommodate the extra numbers of children just a few streets away. As for any records, these had been re-located to the new school with many of the old documents held in trust with the Education Department of New Zealand.

I realised I would have to make another journey, in the future, if I wanted to continue my search, as time had run out to retrieve them from the new school. After none days I would be returning to Australian with a mix of happy memories of spending time and sharing my story with my wife and daughter, and sad memories that I thought I had buried so deeply that they would never see daylight again.

The only regret I had was not visiting my fathers resting place. Ironically it turned out to be a good thing, since he wasn't buried where I thought he was. He had been laid to rest further north, in the town he had lived in with his second wife and three children.

To date, I have yet to meet his children of another era. I have never approached them and wonder if they know of my existence at all? I suppose this book, if it ever gets into their hands, might be the first they know about me and my father's previous family.

CHAPTER 73

My Land

After returning to Australia, in 2010, I was greeted with a letter from the New Zealand Maori Land Council. Prior to my historic journey to NZ, a family member had given me documents left to me, in trust, by my father.

The documents outlined the trust ownership of land and maps of not just one but nine parcels of land, which had been handed down through two generations. It was land that the NZ Government had given back to the rightful landholders. In my case the Tumori.

Through the grant, a percentage of land was handed down through the generations. The lands that were handed to my family had been divided into our family trust, in values of between 15%-33% - all depending on your birthright.

A rare smile as we waited for our photo to be taken. I was directly behind the boy in the bottom right corner.

The documents also explained that my father had shared the ownership between family members I had never met, or even knew existed. Trust ownership in New Zealand means land cannot be sold to any person outside the family, as outlined in the terms of the documents. The land is heritage-owned and can only be passed on through the family, who can build on it as they see fit. Any dwellings on the property may also never be sold outside of the family.

What seemed to be a simple exercise, in the beginning, ended up becoming a nine-year process with numerous emails and letters between me and the Maori Land Council, along with years of deed searches, submissions of land rights, and whatnot that lead up to what was to be the final hand over on May 28th 2020.

Arrangements had been made for me to attend the Maori Land Council, to finalise the application. I was to fly over and provide proof of identity before the council released the land titles to me. Unfortunately, those arrangements came to a grinding halt when COVID19 swept through the world and the country's borders were closed, planes grounded, and lockdowns and restrictions imposed.

A revised arrangement was made for it to be re-scheduled for September of the same year, however, the restrictions hadn't been lifted, so it was again rescheduled. At the time of writing, there are still some restrictions in place, but I plan to fly back over to NZ in 2022 and finalise the title transfers.

It was a lot of research and legwork to reach this point, and it's a wonderful windfall for this orphan boy. I can't tell you how thrilled I am. I feel a great deal of pride in being able to pass something of historical significance to my future generations.

CHAPTER 74

Lifting the lid

OMG, where do I start and how do I openly discuss events with those who have been the devils from hell in my life.

I recall a specific moment as a child, attending church on a Sunday, while at the boy's home. During the service, our leader in prayer referred to the devil as Satan, a person along with his demons who were banished from heaven. Before this time, it was said that they were people who were known as the personification of evil and the nemesis of good people everywhere.

When those words were spoken on that day, I felt my whole body shudder. I sat in that pew knowing what I was living with said people, and that the devil was alive and well at the orphanage. They were men, draped in the cloth of the Lord, only so they could use this as their personal licence to abuse children and destroy the very lives they should have been protecting.

On returning from NZ, and after many years of journaling my thoughts and memories in a bid to help me break free of the past, my decision to write my book was a way for me to pop the cork and let all the memories from the past come spurting out.

I first began a kind of a memoir of sorts, back in 2008, and got to around 14 chapters before I shelved it. Then I plucked up the courage to stand up and try again. With the new information and the research I had done, I was looking forward to putting my head down and tail up to get it done.

Heading down the rabbit's hole was like being on a rollercoaster. Some days, when I was working on a chapter that was hard to remember, let alone write about, it felt as if my soul was being hauled over a bed of nails. Other days, I just felt like throwing up, and yet other days the loss of my siblings and son felt as if I was taking the last breath of life as I knew it.

Late-night online searches to piece together some gaps, as well as visiting scouting forums, groups, people, and anything connecting me to my past almost became a part-time job in between my work as Truck Driver and Plant Operator.

Writing the chapter about my son, Damien, was one of the hardest and also took the longest. Regret plagued me. There was so much I wanted him to know and to tell him why I was sometimes a closed book. Above all, I was desperate to get the message to him wherever he might be in spirit, through my words, of just how much I loved him.

After many hours at the desk, researching into crazy hours of the night, my book came alive. With every chapter came a new meaning and reason to write more, to learn more and to seek answers.

I began in 2018 and I laid my pen down in 2021, after more than a decade of casually writing down my thoughts, memories and the events in my life; all of which were part of a burning desire I'd had for more than 50 years, somehow to avenge the ghosts of the past.

It wasn't easy coming out with the truth; it was anything but, digging deep when you want to turn and run the other way, in a bid to ignore your own truth, is bloody hard. I wanted to give up more times than I want to admit to you, but I had to be accountable for my part in all of this. My being accountable for things I'd done allowed me to hold those that were guilty accountable too, and thereby honour those who no longer lived or who couldn't seek justice themselves.

It wasn't until 2019, that I got enough courage up, finally to contact the Salvation Army office in Melbourne, Victoria. My aim at that time was to discuss what I had endured and witnessed and to seek answers to my questions; such as, "why I was abused as a child in their care?". I wanted them to own what they had done to me and the hundreds or thousands of other little kids. I wanted them to take responsibility and provide an official apology.

Sending that letter, I was hopeful. Receiving their reply enraged me.

Dear Daryl,

Although you have pointed out a number of events in your life, we must advise that your complaints related to the Salvation Army and any claimed abuse seemed to be reported as events within another country.

We can suggest you seek legal advice before continuing your complaints.

To me, it was yet another kick in the teeth from them, and another knot in the rope I intended to hang them from.

Seething, I sought legal guidance, which said that it was not within Australian jurisdiction and I would need to pursue it in NZ. I was disappointed and frustrated, but not deterred, and the set-back only spurred me on more. I spent even more time reading through the material I had gathered; searching and digging deep and compiling everything I needed to prove a strong and undeniable case.

I won't skirt around it. It was huge taking on such a giant as the Salvation Army and even more so in a different country. I asked myself "Is it even possible for me to win?" Would anyone really take my complaints seriously? Would they believe me? It had been 50 years. Had too much time passed?

It was tough, and for years I wasn't believed. When I was young I occasionally plucked up the courage to tell someone—and every time I was fobbed off or told I was lying and punished for it. It was unnerving dealing with those emotions and fears on top of preparing myself to fight this massive organisation.

I wanted that apology though, and I wanted justice for the boys who lived with the horrors they did, many of whom, sadly had not lived to tell the tale. Along with this, I worried that I could be seen as someone seeking attention and the thought of that made me cringe. Opening up my life—the good, bad and the in-between meant I was about to put my life and that of my families on show. I went over and over it in my mind, for years. Would it be worth it for the justice?

The past pain chipped away at me forcing my hand—regardless of the fears, my gut overwhelmingly propelled me forward.

I was mucked around for ages by the office staff at The Salvation Army. Trying to get clear answers was frustrating. One day I just had enough and thought bugger it, I'll go straight to the top of the whole organisation, and instead of requesting I will DEMAND the truth, accountability and an apology. I will reach deep into the Salvation Army's heart and rip out what I was looking for—what I wanted, and what I needed.

I was an ex-soldier with many years of experience battling incredible odds. For me, once I had decided and committed to something, there was no turning back. I had found my strength to fight on. I remember thinking that I would not stop until justice was served and I am given a full and personal apology—it in its entirety—from The Salvation Army for EVERYTHING I had gone through and suffered.

I didn't just want to send a letter, I wanted to send an account of my book to them, as well. It was in the early months of 2019 that I sat down and blocked out days over many, many weeks to get the story out of my head and into a manuscript, so I could direct and give my attention to the task ahead of me. It was also important for me to see when I would be working on the book, because I had to separate the hell I lived from the world I had now. I had to make sure that I could download the story, but not let the emotions spill over into my life with my wife and kids.

The computer filled up with files and notes as thousands of words poured out of me into a journal-style manuscript that would become the basis of my autobiography. It was liberating and I felt courageous.

At 2.30 am on Monday the 4th of February I sat down at the computer and charged forward, just like Napoleon, feeling the blood running through my fingers as I wrote my first words.

I started early, before my family woke up and I would spend an hour or two tapping away at it. Days morphed into weeks and then months. Not being a natural writer, it was tough some days, but in saying that I felt the story—the truth itself would tell it better than I could.

It wasn't all that long before I had written and completed the Hodderville chapters. I printed a copy for myself, as a reference, and an extra copy which I would forward to The Salvation Army in NZ. I searched the internet to find the most appropriate address to which to send my letter of complaint, along with a copy of the book I had written up until that moment.

I soon realised that in order to ensure that my words were heard I needed to send two copies. One to the Salvation Army head office and one to the senior church of the Salvation Army in NZ. I packaged it up and posted it. Now I would have to just wait and see what response I would receive, if I got one at all. I'd heard several stories where complaints had been swept under the rug, so there was a high chance that mine would also meet with the same fate.

The Church… any Church is powerful and I, Daryl Keith Te'Nadii, well I was only one man. Did I have any hope they would read my story? Time would tell.

It must have been around two weeks later when I checked my emails, and saw an email in my Inbox from the Salvation Army in New Zealand.

"OMG! Here we go" was the first thing I said. Not really expecting too much, I was still hopeful. I took a deep breath and opened the email. After reading it, I sat motionless as a tear ran down my face. It was a tear of happiness, knowing they had not just read my story but that, for the first time, they would be opening a full investigation as a result of it.

It was more than I'd ever received from them before and I was elated. It was hard to believe, initially. The months afterwards were spent replying to The Salvation Army's numerous questions, and also in continuing to write my book.

It was at that time that I had decided not only to write about Hodderville but also about my life before and after—the whole life of an orphaned soldier. I tried to pen it out at home, but it was difficult as the emotional aftermath of writing some of the really hard times spilled into my family life.

I spoke to Janet about it, and with her support, I headed to Thailand to stay in a hotel in a quiet village to finish my book. It was immeasurably harder than I had ever thought possible. For fourteen days I did nothing but write. I paused only to eat, sleep and call home to Janet and Baila Rae. Other than that I didn't stop until it was done.

After I finished writing the book, I must have spent at least 150 hours resetting it and adding a further 24 chapters! Day 15, my second-to-last day in Thailand saw me sitting by the pool of the hotel for the first time, reading and correcting chapters—page, by page, by page. It took another drawn-out night to make the changes to the book and it was ready…. or so I thought.

The next day I took my downloaded book to a printer in town and a few hours later I had my first full copy of my work in my hand—just in time to board the plane to head back home to my family, whom I had missed so much.

CHAPTER 75

Victorious

Not long after I returned home, I received another letter from The Salvation Army. A gentleman by the name of Mr. Murray Houston sent me a formal letter, advising me that he had been appointed as the officer in charge of my affairs and complaint.

He made it clear to me that he was not an 'appointed member' of The Salvation Army and did not wear the cloth. Instead, he was an independent officer, who received complaints, investigated them and acted within the laws of New Zealand, as required.

Over the next month, he and I communicated via email unpicking all the events I witnessed or was involved in at the boy's home. He would send questions to seek clarity, and I would answer them, sharing as much detail as possible with him and giving him an insight into what I had carried for far too long.

I conversed with him for ages, until I had a work accident and had to have surgery to correct the nerves in my hands. Typing and writing were out of the question until I had healed. It wasn't until January of 2020, and after yet another surgery on my hands, that I was able to resume proper communication with Mr. Murray Houston.

After more emails, it was agreed more investigation was needed. Murray arranged for a face-to-face meeting to be held in Brisbane, in the months to follow, which I was happy to do as long as I could record it. I wanted to ensure all records of my complaints were accounted for and held by me and were also stored within The Salvation Army records.

In the meeting, I made it clear that I was seeking a personal written apology saying the Salvo's accepted full accountability for what had happened to me. Mr Houston pointed out to me that The Salvation Army had recently made a national apology to all victims of its atrocities towards children by some of their officers, who were placed in positions of care, as part of their investigations,

I made it clear the national apology meant nothing to me at all. I wanted a letter addressed to me—Daryl Keith Te'Nadii. It needed to be personal and not generic. Mr. Houston indicated he would take my request to the head of the Salvation Army in New Zealand. All I could do now was to wait, once more and hope they finally had the decency to admit their wrong-doing and send the letter and apology.

Six weeks later, Mr Houston informed me that The Salvation Army in New Zealand had completed their investigation and had come to a decision. Here was the moment of truth. Forty-nine years of living with the pain, shame, and guilt—fighting for my rights and to honour those no were longer here came to a head.

Would justice be served? Would they finally admit and take responsibility for what had happened to us under their watch?

Their decision came first by email, and later by hard copy, in a signed formal letter addressed to me. As I opened it my whole body felt it was on tenterhooks. As I began to read the apology, I cried. I cried with happiness, I cried with relief. I cried because finally I was believed! I cried for those that were now in spirit and were probably sitting right by me as I read it, huddled together celebrating that justice had finally been done—albeit half a century later.

I cried because I was spent from the years and years I had fought and battled to bring those bastard officers to their knees in shame, just like they had done to us too many times. They ruined me, but didn't break me. I had led us all to a victory that was bittersweet.

In the letter of apology they said;

- My request to be recognised as a victim of atrocities, while under the care of the NZ Salvation Army, had been accepted,

- My complaints and records of evidence would be held for future records and as support for any other victim who might come forward,

- My request to have it known that I was only one child among many who suffered at the hands of a few Salvation Army officers, and finally

- I would be handed a personally signed apology with declaration to all that I suffered in the form of an officially written letter.

Today I cast my eyes over the apology letter, as I have on many days, since receiving it on the 28 February 2020, my mind drifts to those who will never get to see it in real life. I think of them with love and know that in some small way they ARE resting a lot more peacefully.

With our account of the happenings and the NZ Salvation Army' accepting responsibility, it now meant change could occur to ensure nothing like the abuse we endured at Hodderville would ever happen to another child in their care again.

Each time I spoke to Mr. Houston, I made it clear that my records and writing would be published one day in my autobiography, so that my family, loved ones, and the public could read about and learn from what happened.

I see the official letter of apology—the letter sits in my life cabinet in my office along with service memorabilia and trophies of excellence in sports, next to me to see every time I walk into the room. It makes me happy that I can hold my head up high now, after knowing that or years I was seen as a liar by many, including my own mother.

CHAPTER 77

Scars

Time heals they say, and for me, I guess I can say I'm as close to that as I've ever been to healing. Physically I am still branded with scars, visible reminders of what took place in another time and another country. Spiritually, the emotional scars rub at my psyche, often when I least expect it.

I know I will never truly be able to remove either the inside or outside scars. They'll fade and blur in time I guess, but for now, I choose to use them to remind me of all the good days and times I spent with my childhood friends.

Some of the most treasured times in my life were, and will always be, the friendships I made with other orphans at the boy's home. We are forever soul-bound, united in trust and mateship of moments shared that none of us will ever forget.

Today, I sadly bow my head in remembrance of the many of them who, tragically, took their own lives. Their faces are still in my mind, as clear as the day I met them, a ghostly and grim reminder of how tough it was to survive the abuse and of how hard it was—even together— to live beyond it. We lived for each other, hurt for each other, watched out for each other, shared what little we had, and helped each other as best we could, so that one day we could make it out of the horror of Hodderville and into the free world. Some of us made it, some of us didn't. I will forever hold all of those little boys close to my heart.

I found it hard to open up to anyone, after being conditioned for so long to be quiet and not to speak up or say anything. I've lived 62 years of my life and most people I know don't have a clue of what I went through— many of them are going to be shocked when they read this book, but all of my nearest and dearest friends will definitely understand why I didn't or couldn't talk to them about it.

I have learned to find my balance, just as I have learned to open up (a little more) and talk to those around me. I allow more people into my life than I did, those days, and for me, that's a huge step. Feeling they belong, and are wanted and loved is something all people want, regardless of their age. It took me almost half my life to feel that and not to question it.

My family and friends have helped me through the worst of days when the memories of the past came to haunt me, grabbing hold of me. On days I wanted to go to the ground and never get up, they held out a hand like the tree of life, grafting their hand to mine and I clung to it, refusing to let go.

In many ways, after I received the apology and completed my book, I felt I had finally released the demons within me. I had sent them home to another time and place, to disintegrate to ash on the lands from whence they had been birthed.

During all the moments, when I wanted to end my life or was beaten, frozen, abused, starved, broken, bloody, bruised, and cast aside or left to die on the streets, I had dreamed of peaceful days, hoping that I would see, feel and live them one day.

Fighting and proving my worth were all I had ever known—they were how I measured my self-worth. I could not have been more wrong or misguided. The demons still lie inside me, rumbling.

I have gone from being an orphaned soldier, surviving hell, to arriving at the point where I can tell my story; a silent soldier, ultimately fighting a battle I'll only win on the day I close my eyes forever.

I wanted to forgive my parents and the Salvation Army, but I cannot.

Ready to hit he road on my Harley Davidson "Fat Boy".

It is sad and makes me feel lonely, knowing I will take those words to my grave, but I will give it everything I have to focus only on the good times and envelope them in a blanket of love, valuing what I gained instead through my life with family and friends.

That will be my protection when the demons get restless, and all I'll need when my time comes to rest.

THANK YOU

I have been blessed in so many ways along the path, but none more so than by having my gorgeous wife, the loved memories of my beloved son, and of being gifted with my two beautiful daughters.

I could not be prouder of where I am in life, right now—living with my family in our own home. I have more than I need and am grateful for it.

Suicide is the hardest word to say, but that feeling of just wanting to be happy and free of the demons—well, it seemed as if it would be the easiest thing to do at times, to escape them. I was prevented from doing it once by a friend, and it crossed my mind a few more times since then. It wasn't until I met my wife, Janet, that the urge disappeared.

My jigsaw of a life that had been devoid of colour suddenly began to brighten and blossom with the colours of life, of love, of acceptance, of contentment, and of healing and happiness. Janet picked the very last pieces up off the floor and put them together.

She showed me how and helped me realise that yes, I have a right to live in this world! She showed me that I deserve all the good things. She came into my world and became it. I could not have lived my life without her and my beautiful daughters, whom I love with every cell of my being.

Daryl an Janet.

Janet, Baila and Casie J.

My circle of friends is small, but important to me. They have made building lifelong relationships with them easy, by giving me the unconditional love and acceptance that helped me to trust. They welcome me as me, nothing more, nothing less—just me, without judgment, and I value each of them immensely.

In saying this I would like to share a special word of thanks to them.

Over the years I have learned so much through the camaraderie of my friends—some of those friendships go back to my childhood days in the orphanage. Many are from my teenage years and still more I made throughout my adult years in and outside of the service.

I am so grateful to each of them, who were there for me many times, or who gave me guidance and a sense of direction without even knowing it. I took on much of what they said and lived my life by it. I'll treasure their care, love, and friendship more than they'll ever know.

I have not mentioned all of them here, not because I don't love and value them, but because I want to respect their privacy. In some instances, there are just too many; such as all of the fantastic people I've trained and spent hours and hours with over the years. I thank you all for the time, kind words, and support you gave me.

Without question, I have reasons to say thank you to them publicly in my book, but no last names have been used, out of respect.

Gary C.

Gary pulled me from the streets in what could have been the end of my life and saved me. He gave me courage when I was scared, direction when I was lost, and friendship when I was alone. His years of care and mentoring are the very reason why I never took my life. Gary took me home and befriended me, giving me all when I had nothing to give in return. Thank you for being that person, Gary. Thank you for being the best man at my first marriage, and for always being there without expecting accolades and humble as ever. I have treasured our friendship and will continue to do so until the end of my time.

Mick S.

After an initial case of mistaken identity, I forged a friendship with this guy I'd be proud to call my brother. I remember one day in particular Mick opened up to me, sharing something with me that made me even more proud to know him. I echoed his statement that day 'I am very proud to know you and be part of your life. Daryl, I wish you were my brother'. I will always remember that day fondly too, Mick.

Paul N.

If ever anything could be weird but amazing at the same time, then it was meeting Paul. Reflecting back, we were bound to meet, it was only a matter of time. Born on the same day, but a decade apart, we connected instantly and became firm friends just as quickly. Paul was my best man at my marriage to Janet and I am grateful for the mateship, trust, care, and respect he has shown me over the years I've known him. I will forever be thankful our paths crossed paths when they did.

Paul B.

In the same moment as I met Paul N, I also met Paul B. and we became the three musketeers' in a way. Some friends you know you're going to have forever and I knew that when I met these two lads. We were together almost every day, and we lived, enjoyed and shared so many memorable times— wonderful times. Paul's asking me to be his bestie at his wedding was such an honour and I'll continue to hold it close to my heart. Pauly, as I call him, is without question one incredible man, filled with everything that makes a man who he should be. He has such a beautiful nature. It makes me so very proud to hold you inside my circle of closest friends. Thank you so much for the times we have shared.

Chris. B.

Chris brought such meaning and understanding to my life—he showed me how to appreciate things. I never did this very well, as a lonely, abandoned child, but he showed me how, and immeasurably changed my world for the better because of it. I have watched Chris grow, embracing life as only he does, and fall in love and marry his wife. Standing beside you on your special day has and will ever be one of the many moments I will treasure. Your friendship throughout the years is every part of the greatness I appreciate in you, and I sincerely thank you for this my friend.

Rachael

We met at a time that would change the world in many ways for me. Bonded by an incredible friendship, we enjoyed so many fun and crazy times, along with memorable ones. I'll always remember being at your wedding party—a special memory I hold in my heart. Your path led you to a new life, but we didn't lose our friendship over the distance. When fate stepped in to re-connect us, it felt as if only a few hours had passed since we had last caught up. Rach has played an important role in my life, working with me every week for the past year—guiding me in my storytelling, laughing with me, crying with me, supporting and helping me structure and bring my story to life for you to read. For this and the many years of friendship, I thank you deeply, Rach.

Brad W.

At times, I questioned why a person 23 years younger would have anything to do with me, let alone build an undeniable and trustworthy friendship such as ours. Brad has become the fishing buddy, golfing partner, and treasured friend I'm supremely proud to have. Meeting this lad at 16 years of age I never expected a friendship to grow with him, as it has. It's been inspirational to watch him challenge himself through life, perfect a skill that took him to national and international competition and achieve the recognition in his chosen sport that he so deserves. It was an honour I am very proud of to have stood with Brad's family and friends, watching him marry his queen, and then become a father himself.

Johnny S.

It's funny how all at one time in our life we come across that one person who fills a missing gap within your circle of mates. Johnny entered my life through fate, and I'm forever glad he did. He's my go-to-person when I just want to sit, open up and talk and liven things up. I treasure our friendship, one that many never find in a lifetime and I love spending time with you and your beautiful family. Thank you for that, and the more to come.

My Clients

Such a starchy word so let's call them—my fitness family.

I want to thank them for putting their trust in me, over many years, to help them achieve their fitness goals—it's been a true pleasure. I have loved our chats and exercising together, while fulfilling my purpose as a fitness professional.

I know there have been times when you've hated me pushing you to the brink and I would expect nothing less and understand it as a coach. I'll admit it's given me a laugh on more than a few occasions and I appreciate that you still love me, even after I punish you ha ha ha!

It's been a privilege to watch my fitness family achieve incredible results in their personal health and fitness. Many of them have competed at the highest levels, and many have climbed the ladder in life as well, inspiring others to reap the rewards also. Things can't get better than that in any coaches eyes!

They say nothing of value comes easy, and I see this every day as a fitness coach. I also see blood, sweat, tears, passion, purpose, guts, determination, and pure heart every day. I'm very proud of my fitness family who continue to work hard for me. I am so proud to call you my friends, and for this, I thank you sincerely for the most amazing times in my life.

CHAPTER 77

Healing

It is hard to think that, after all the events in my life, I would, or could, even begin to think about healing, let alone reaching out to others to ask them to help me. I considered myself a beaten man. A man who was deeply detached from the real world and who— on a few occasions and for many reasons—felt that giving up was my only option.

In some ways, self-persecution was my weakness and one that I let control the way I lived my life for a long time. In all of this, I didn't think I had an excuse for allowing the emotion of what had happened to me take over the way it did. Looking for hope and a way out as a child was never going to be an easy task.

I don't know how or why I survived it all; purpose perhaps? The answer still hasn't made itself clear to me, even now. But, as the years have passed, I have surrendered less to the weakness that overcame me at times, causing me to lose my way and have hung on to any glimpse of personal power I saw, swinging wildly from its limb to propel myself towards another.

Disturbing thoughts, such as suicide, have worried me as much as the next man. Sometimes as a kid, I wondered why I had been born just to be sacrificed to a woman who couldn't care less about me, and who gave me up to people you couldn't even class as human, only to be snatched from their clutches and dumped backed into hers to be her common slave.

Hard words and words that many would think could only come from a demented person. I guess this was all I understood as a fairly uneducated, abused orphan—I didn't know any better, but somewhere within myself, I did expect better from others, and from myself.

Some may think that it is weak to think of these things. For me it wasn't so much the thought, it was as if I didn't have a choice. Gripping the limb of life, I managed to swing away from the dark thoughts, mostly with the help of a person who came into my life just at the right time and place.

I think back to 1991 and my return trip to New Zealand, to reconnect with my father. I remember explaining to him why my life had taken the direction it had. On that day, he told me so many things—uncovering a cache of lies that I'd been led to believe all of my life by my mother. The truth was hard to swallow, but it was an even bitter pill to swallow knowing know I'd believed it for all of my years.

My father handed me an item that day, which he had been given from his father, and something that had been handed down through the Te'Nadii generations. It was a little box. He retrieved it from the top of his drawers and handed it to me. Inside the box was a chain, which my father told me was over 150 years old. He said he wanted me to take care of it and to pass it down to the next generation of our family.

He explained that the chain had been handmade with 19 singular connected knots, and said that it carried many years of tribal strength. He called it the Chain of 19 Lives. Each knot represented a journey in life, passed down from generation to generation, to learn from. On returning to Australia I realised I had to search for hope and to find my place in life. I had to ensure the knot I would leave in my legacy was a worthwhile story to tell and one that my future generations would be proud to tell. I promised myself I would achieve this.

Healing was part of that promise and one that would give me a new purpose in life. Although I was challenged, I fell that I have won this battle—all bar the fight to forgive. The scars just run too deep for me ever to forgive those who inflicted them on me.

I've read so much about forgiving, and tried everything I could numerous times, but it still avoids me.

In 2008 I was faced with yet another opportunity and hopefully thought that I could forgive and ultimately heal in some way, by reconnecting with my mother. I was actually very happy, knowing I would share a special moment, the future birth of our child, with her and my wife. I stupidly looked forward to it, daydreaming of all the sadness, pain, and hurt vanishing. I thought about her embracing me lovingly, accepting me, and being remorseful for all she had done.

Having my wife by my side I was strengthened on the hopeful day—the day I desperately wanted to begin a new life with her, the one I'd dreamt of a thousand or more times. It is almost impossible to think of a day that could be any worse than that day was.

My mother was humiliating, disrespectful, insulting, selfish, and concerned for no one other than herself. She was excessively and exclusively all about herself—callously taking great pleasure in hurting me, embarrassing Janet and leaving me feeling even more shame than I had ever felt before.

I was angry at myself for thinking she could possibly be different and I felt sick I'd subjected my wife to her bullshit, as well. "Why do I continue wanting to let this woman back into my life?" I screamed in my head. I hadn't learned a thing and was livid with myself and my mother.

She was the truest epitome of a narcissistic psychopath—one who genuinely believed she was a nice person. It beggars belief quite honestly. I don't know why it took me so long to work out she would never change; she couldn't change. She had absolutely no emotional intelligence, whatsoever. It clicked and I accepted it. There was just one thing I got walking away from her that day, and that was the immense happiness and gratefulness that I was nothing like her. Thank God.

From that day on, any time I saw her I treated her exactly how she treated me— I felt like shit doing it, but there was just no other way—it had to be done, otherwise, you'd be left walking away in all sorts of agony. At least that way I had almost everything else intact.

For many, it must be impossible to comprehend the feeling of being damaged by someone so relentlessly, unless you've felt and lived it yourself. Along with my choice to do this, I also had to slowly drift away and never look back.

It still hurts my heart. As I write these words, tears still spill from my eyes, and I'm deeply sad, still grieving for a mother I never had, but there's just nothing I can do about it and nor can anyone else, for that matter.

CHAPTER 78

Reflection

I have sat behind a desk, looking intently at a screen for so long; my fingers gliding swiftly along the keyboards as words appear. However, I still reflect on the words in these pages that you will have read by now.

I sit and reflect on my life, uncovered here in black and white, and realise—for the first time—that this journey is about to come to an end. It feels so unreal. In some ways it feels as if I'm parting from my best friend, the one I've poured my whole world out to, and cried, laughed, hurt, and raged with. I have clung, bragged, and whispered to you, and joked with you. No longer will I sit and share in this way again, and I guess finding a way to do that and walk away from it, is yet another challenge.

Knowing that I lived with this book—the moments and memories—and knowing that it was all about to come to an end has brought unexpected feelings of loss. Knowing that I used this time and the writing of my book as a final bid to escape what was my life, truly made me feel lost once more. But it's had a purpose, and my purpose for doing it is done.

Me as a child.

Writing has been cathartic, and instrumental in helping me to heal more portions of my life. Sitting back in my chair and looking at these few pages I realise I can put it all to bed and close this book. Then, I will be freed of the weight it represented in my life.

I am renewed and feel lightness and a stirring of quiet excitement, thinking of how I can fill my thoughts more with my successes, now, and I will have the space to celebrate achievements, no matter the size.

As a child I branded myself an outcast and, through much of my life, I thought that would be my destination. I never realised dreams were actually possible, but at 63 years of age, I now know that I belong, I matter, I am loved, and I can achieve anything.

Me as an adult.

A smile spreads as I think and remember how;

I can

I will

And, if I am brave enough to start,

I will succeed.

That child became the boy, who then became a teenager and an adult, who lived to tell the tale.

Today, I hope I am remembered for my courage and for my heart, and that I am a true SURVIVOR.

Baila Rae and I.

BIBLIOGRAPHY

Training Video - https://www.youtube.com/watch?v=QSzPJcov2ak

All images provided by Daryl Tenadii – Friends – Archives

BIOGRAPHY

Daryl Te'Nadii lives on the Sunshine Coast with his wife, Janet, and daughter Baila-Rae.

You can contact Daryl at *daryltenadii11@gmail.com.*

www.ingramcontent.com/pod-product-compliance
Lightning Source LLC
Chambersburg PA
CBHW060017030426
42334CB00019B/2079